Man Mismanagement

Man Mismanagement

Second Edition

Alan Fox

Hutchinson

London Melbourne Sydney Auckland Johannesburg

Hutchinson Education
An imprint of Century Hutchinson Ltd
62-65 Chandos Place, London WC2N 4NW

Century Hutchinson Australia Pty Ltd
PO Box 496, 16-22 Church Street, Hawthorn, Victoria 3122, Australia

Century Hutchinson New Zealand Limited
PO Box 40-086, Glenfield, Auckland 10, New Zealand

Century Hutchinson South Africa (Pty) Limited
PO Box 337, Bergvlei 2012, South Africa

Brookfield Publishing Company, Inc.
Old Post Road, Brookfield, Vermont 05036 USA

First published 1985
Reprinted 1986

Printed and bound in Great Britain by
Anchor Brendon Ltd, Tiptree, Essex

British Library Cataloguing in Publication Data
Fox, Alan
  Man mismanagement. – 2nd ed.
  1. Industrial relations – Great Britain
  2. Industrial management – Great Britain
  I. Title
  658.3′15′0941   HD8391
Library of Congress Cataloguing in Publication Data

ISBN 0 09 159380 8

With thanks to Brenda

Contents

Preface   9

1 The managerial problem and its context – society and the
**   organization**   13
  Material and social technology   13
  Two perspectives on the nature of Western society   18
  A pluralist perspective on the business enterprise   26
  Motives for compliance: expediency and obligation   36

2 Coercion and its limits   45
  Problem-solving and win–lose situations   46
  What prevents rank and file identifying with management?   48
  Management and the search for legitimacy   51
  Control through coercion   55
  Conditions of effective coercion   59
  When does coercion fail?   61

3 Industrialization and the strategy of consent   66
  Control through consent   66
  Pre-industrial work relations   68
  An idealization of the past?   69
  The impact of industrialization   71
  Contract and master–servant relations   74
  The employee response   74
  Employer responses: industrial welfare   76
  Employer responses: scientific management   81

4 Consent and 'social' versus 'economic' man   86
  Social man and the human relations approach   87
  The fallacy of social man   90
  Employee perceptions and their determinants   93

Economic man and his significance for management   97
Organizational character   101

5 **Consent and participation in decision-making**   105

Prescribed and discretionary aspects of work   105
Decision-making and moral involvement   108
Participation through collective bargaining   111
Participative supervision   113
Participation through joint consultation   116
Participation through employee-directors   119
Participation through enriched job discretion   128

6 **Collective bargaining: its role and meaning**   139

Collective bargaining and management   143
Collective bargaining: a standard model   144
Divergence from the standard: management and the unitary
frame of reference   146
Divergence from the standard: the work group and the
radical frame of reference   149
The appeal to government and the political power
structure   150
The role of trade unionism and collective bargaining
in Britain   153

7 **Participation and the *status quo***   157

Managerial prerogative and its changing definition   157
Industrial and political issues   159
Thatcher governments and Labour politics   164
The debate on 'direct action'   166
The 'politicization' of industrial relations   169
Current aspirations and the future   176

8 **Participation, bargaining and the wider society**   182

Intended and unintended outcomes   182
Collective bargaining and the British problem   184
Reforming the system   188
Industrial relations and the New Right   195
Economic decline and the Labour Party   197
'Macho' management and shop-floor 'realism'   200
Economic failure and an old nightmare   202
The conditions for a new social partnership?   203

Index   220

Preface

When the first edition of this book was being written ten years ago in the early 1970s Britain and the rest of the world wore, in some important respects, a somewhat less ravaged face. Admittedly much that haunts us now haunted us then. The surreal logic of nuclear deterrence theory may since have become incomprehensible to all but a few senior wranglers but it was well advanced along that road even then. Arab–Israeli conflict and Arab–Arab conflict were always with us to create dangers in one of the world's major cockpits. The demand of growing numbers of people throughout the poorer parts of the world that their allotted span should yield them more than a slavish and anonymous preoccupation with survival was as assertive then as now – though their frustrations are currently magnified by world slump and have aggravated political instabilities. More parochially, the realization of Britain's relative economic decline (absolute decline being still to come) was already well established – her position in the growth league having begun to slip badly after the early 1960s. Contemplating this decline, an extra-terrestial visitor studying the media would have been encouraged to believe, then as now, that the only groups in Britain exerting latent or manifest power to further their interests and their restrictive self-protections 'at the nation's expense' were the trade unions.

Nevertheless in certain vital matters the scene has conspicuously darkened. The oil-price revolution and subsequent fluctuations; the dislocation of international trading patterns; the prolonged world slump; and massive debt structures have rendered the world financial system dangerously unstable. The effects of these events on Britain's weak and uncompetitive economy have been compounded by a draconian monetary policy which has achieved success in reducing inflation at a huge cost in terms of unemployment, bankruptcies, and lost production. The impact on the trade unions and the Labour Party has been dramatic. Ten years ago the unions were approaching the peak of their post-war powers, charged by their more extreme critics with tyrannizing over management at the workplace and virtually running the country in the wider political field. Even temperate observers were suggesting that the unions' political creation, the Labour Party, might now be becoming Britain's 'natural party of government'. Whatever party was in power still held to the post-war convention that national economic management must include the maintenance of full employment; that British 'public opinion' would never tolerate a return to the mass, long-term unemployment of the inter-war period. Conservative politicians maintained the practice, carefully cultivated by Stanley Baldwin and his successors, of treating labour leaders as persons of some consequence deserving of respect. The values and assumptions of the welfare state seemed almost to be entrenched items of the constitution, Conservative leaders believing for the most part, on the One Nation doctrine, that they would conserve best by remaining within hailing distance of Labour reformism.

In all these respects the situation has been in varying degrees transformed. The trade unions are industrially weakened by recession and politically bruised by exclusion from top counsels and consultation. The 1983 general election saw Labour's share of the vote slump to 27.6 per cent, its lowest since 1918. It is widely believed that mass unemployment will be with us for a long time, probably forever. Not since the 1919–1922 Coalition government have so many leading Conservative politicians exhibited such sustained public disparagement and hostility towards labour leaders. It is clear that the whole apparatus of the welfare state, along with public services and publicly-owned industry, is and will remain, so far as Thatcher administrations are concerned, 'under review'. With the poor getting poorer and the rich getting richer in terms of marketable wealth, the whole scene is perceived, not only by many on the left but even by some on the more traditional right, as the most unabashed intensification of the class war by a Conservative administration for sixty years.

Along with these changes, however, there have been many others which have been welcomed by those who, while by no means necessarily identifying with the more punitive expressions of Thatcherism (and perhaps even having strong sympathies with the unions), believed that 'reform' of the industrial relations system was desirable and possible. Many of these impulses towards reform embodied hopes of a speedier creation, particularly at the workplace, of orderly and systematic joint procedures for job regulation and grievance settlement, together with the promotion of more 'constructive' relationships from which all parties – management, employees, and the national economy – would be conscious of deriving benefit.

In the early 1970s it was felt that this process had a long way to go, but that advanced sectors were certainly showing the way. Shop steward representation was growing apace, but much of it was still at an early stage of organization and sophistication. So far as formal and systematic procedures of negotiation and grievance settlement were concerned there were still many blank spaces on the map. The notion that higher management and directorial boards must accept an active and creative involvement in labour relations was certainly abroad but little heeded. What was to become almost a torrent of legislation on trade unions and industrial relations was then only a modest flow.

The pace of change then markedly quickened. Many voluntary initiatives and much statutory intervention – some of it bearing benign intent towards the unions, some hostile – were brought to bear on the industrial relations system. Structural, institutional, and legal changes considerably modified the face of that system and present us with the need for appraisal. How far and in what ways are they affecting actual behaviour? Social institutions and structures do not activate and operate themselves; they have to be activated and operated by people. Neither do the purposes and hopes of those who support and perhaps initially shape these institutions and structures necessarily imprint themselves upon those who must subsequently do the activating and operating. Outcomes are the result of people working the system in the light of their own perceptions, frames of reference, and motivations, and may diverge significantly from what was intended and hoped. In trying to gauge the impact of institutional change at the workplace, therefore, we must seek insight into these perceptions and frames of reference. It is here that the dimension of history and tradition becomes crucial. Our physical bodies are the result of growth through time, and so are our social perceptions and dispositions, which often owe much to far older shaping experiences, especially if our society has not been subjected to such potentially disruptive discontinuities as revolution or subjugation by military defeat. This requires us to bear in mind the possible persistence of historically generated dispositions, attitudes, and traditions.

The major differences wrought in this second edition are therefore twofold. The nature and reasons for the changes of the past ten years are explored, along with the political background that has changed so significantly in ways which cannot help but continue to affect industrial relations. Many of these changes have been in directions favoured by those seeking to reform industrial relations behaviour. The need for judgements is apparent. Is evidence yet available of success or failure? How far can we expect behaviour to be affected by historical continuities? What has really changed, and what, if anything, can be expected to persist – and with what consequences? This revised edition tries to help the reader in making such judgements by identifying some of the principal social forces that have shaped British society in general and the industrial relations system in particular. (For a full-length analysis of these forces the reader is referred to the author's *History and Heritage: The Social Origins of Britain's Industrial Relations System, 1985.*)

This concern with the last ten years and with how far determined attempts to change Britain's pattern of industrial relations are likely to succeed has meant drastic revision, sometimes virtual rewriting of chapters 5, 7, and 8. The other chapters retain their basic shape but have also been revised, sometimes heavily, to take account of recent events and the sharp shifts in economic and political climates. I have seen no reason, however, to modify the analytical approach developed in the first edition, and have simply extended it to cover the very different circumstances now prevailing. That approach sought to explore the management problem of control and the array of strategies applied down the ages in the attempt to maintain or enhance it. Some are older than others, and all tend to fluctuate to varying degrees in usage and fashion according to the state of the labour market. But all are still currently in use somewhere, and all repay study by enhancing understanding. Perhaps the first lesson is the wide variability of method that can be found within a given society, though it is often possible to identify a predominant style created by national history and tradition.

In conclusion, I could wish, like many authors, that there were more gender words in the English language that cover both sexes; the reiteration of 'him or her' is clumsy and wearisome. My use of the male gender must be taken to refer to humanity at large and not the male sex.

Alan Fox

1 The managerial problem and its context – society and the organization

Material and social technology

A visitor to a factory or any other place of work is soon aware of what might be called the 'material' technology. He sees people operating machines, applying tools, manipulating data-processing devices, using typewriters. This is the technology that can be seen, touched and heard, and is susceptible to the confident control and prediction of scientists, technologists and engineers. But it would all remain inert and unused without the application of another and totally different kind of technology: the 'social' technology which seeks to order the behaviour and relationships of these people in systematic purposive ways through an elaborate structure of co-ordination, control, motivation, and reward systems. This social technology, or social organization, takes such forms as job definitions, pay structures, authority relations, communication and control systems, disciplinary codes and all the many other rules and decision-making procedures which seek to govern what work is done, how it is done, and the relationships which prevail between those doing it. How well this social organization serves the purposes of those who seek to impose it depends in the last resort upon conceptions in the minds of the men and women they recruit for these purposes. These conceptions may or may not include notions, clear-cut or vague, of obligation – of how they *ought* to behave with respect to these top management definitions of their duties, rights, and relationships with respect to the material technology, higher authority, and each other. They will certainly include notions, perhaps vivid and immediate, perhaps beneath the conscious level, of how they would be best advised in their own interests to behave, given the degree of effective power which confronts them and the structure of rewards and punishments within which they work.

At one extreme, the conceptions which rank and file bring to this management structure of rules and policies may lead them to work indifferently, regulate their own work behaviour in ways which obstruct management purposes, quietly subvert authority or openly challenge it, and totally withhold all spirit of loyalty to, or identification with, the company. At the other extreme, their responses may be such as to prompt them to work keenly and conscientiously, offer willing co-operation with management's leadership, submit readily to its command, and identify themselves loyally with the company. This combination of responses will be referred to throughout this book as 'moral involvement'. Between these two extremes lie many intermediate positions where rank-and-file employees offer a measure of passive compliance with orders but little more, demonstrating thereby neither a positive alienation from, nor a positive commitment to, the social technology which top management seeks to maintain for the pursuit of its purposes.

Employers and managements have always differed widely in terms of how high they pitched their hopes and requirements with respect to these conceptions which so shape the rank-and-file response to managerial rules and policies. They have, of course, been at one in demanding at least what they regarded as a minimum level of employee compliance with rules, orders and directives. But beyond this their behaviour has revealed diversity in the degree of their active concern to promote the more positive employee commitment and involvement just described. Some have devoted much effort to this end; others have allowed the issue to go by default.

We shall not concern ourselves in this book with the question of how far management in any given situation is well advised, in pursuing its objectives, to devote considerable resources to attempts at generating moral involvement among its employees. This is a complex issue too often oversimplified by advice manuals which take for granted that this kind of involvement is a universal necessity for managements in all types of industrial situation. In fact there are many variable factors to be taken into account in assessing how much of an effort in this direction is justified by *economic* values – factors which include technology and the type of productive system being used, the nature of the labour force, employee aspirations and attitudes, the state of the labour market and various others. The state of the labour market, for example, has over the years visibly affected the degree of interest manifested in new ways, or new versions of old ways, of 'motivating' employees. When labour scarcity tips the balance of power at the workplace towards the employees and management feels its disciplinary powers slipping, there is apt to be a quickening of managerial interest in methods of control which do not require the exercise of overt discipline or coercion. Strategies for 'winning consent', arousing 'employee co-operation' and 'stimulating commitment' become fashionable. When the situation reverses and labour becomes abundant, the balance of power tips back towards management. Employees become more biddable and some managements revert with relief to what they feel to be the tried and tested traditional method of relying on the more open assertion of power, abandoning fashionable fads recently peddled so enthusiastically by expensive consultants.

Any attempt to elucidate these complexities further, however, would be a distraction from our present task. This is to examine a range of strategies which management has applied to the problem of securing from rank-and-file employees whatever degree of compliance it deemed appropriate and, should its aspirations run that high, evoking also some desired level of moral involvement, identification and commitment. The strategies examined are all in use today, though their origins extend well back into our industrial history. They include coercive power, social conditioning, manipulative persuasion, unilateral attempts to gauge and satisfy employee 'needs' in so far as this serves management interests by evoking desirable employee attitudes, and, finally, bilateral consultation and negotiation between management and employee representatives designed to achieve mutually acceptable compromises, arrangements and understandings on a limited range of issues. We shall be asking not whether the adoption (or non-adoption) of these given strategies was sound managerial judgement or not (for this depends on specific context), but what the assumptions and aims of each strategy are, whether in general it has succeeded or failed – and why.

Here we find ourselves in a vastly more complex and subtle world than that of material technology, for it is the world of that most complex and subtle of all organisms, *homo sapiens*. As soon as we deal in the motivations and responses of human beings and the relationships between them we lose the predictive confidence enjoyed by the natural scientist. The conceptions which men form of how they ought, or would be best advised in their own interests, to behave; the expectations they form as to the behaviour of others; the forces which help to shape such conceptions and expectations – these are far less easily studied and controlled than the behaviour of inanimate matter in the research laboratory. A sense of this complexity causes many a manager to shy away from any serious attempt to understand such a tricky and uncertain field and to fall back on traditional beliefs, popular assumptions and easy clichés, especially with respect to what will be our predominant concern here: his relations with the rank-and-file labour force.

Those who do try to deepen their understanding may be tempted to reduce the problem by confining their attention to what goes on within the organization itself. They are encouraged in this by training texts and advice manuals which limit their discussion of management/worker relations to this context. Attention becomes focused on the organization alone, to the exclusion of the wider society in which it is embedded. This exclusion is fatal for a full understanding of the issues involved. As we shall see, our journey of exploration into past, present and possible future management strategies, and into the reasons for the changing emphases we shall observe, takes us to the heart of fundamental questions about how people live together in society, what work experience means for people at different levels of the social hierarchy, and what changes, if any, are coming to bear upon the way people view these questions.

Organizational issues, conflicts and values are inextricably bound up with those of society at large. This has major implications for our inquiry. Prominent among them is that people's attitudes and behaviour towards their managerially-defined work roles, rights and obligations, and towards the roles, rights, and obligations of others, are not formed only within the organization. They are formed also by the experiences, values, observations and aspirations which men acquire and construct for themselves in the wider society outside, and by the view they have thereby come to take of that society. Influential here are such factors as family, class, school, friends, locality, and the mass media of newspapers, radio and television. Thus the perspective they bring to bear upon the organization and their place in it, and therefore the way they respond to its rules, rewards and values, is shaped by what they make of this wider frame of reference as well as by the organization itself. There is, of course, nothing necessarily static about the perspective they hold. They may modify it as a consequence of their experience and observations either within the organization or outside it. In any case it is obviously inadequate to try to understand workplace behaviour without also trying to understand the wider social setting and how men interpret it for themselves.

In many respects these interpretations and perceptions differ sharply as between, and sometimes within, the social classes. Even as he takes up his first job, a 16 year old in an unskilled wage-earning family, for example, may have acquired from his school the assumption that he is destined to remain among the hewers of wood and drawers of water; from the experience of his parents and other relatives the conviction that work must be expected to be dull, frustrating and unrewarding except for the pay packet; from his 'subculture' the view that 'they' in authority must always be regarded with cynicism and distrust in their policies towards 'us'; and from all the communications and influences brought to bear upon him by the media an unsettling vision of a vast array of life-enhancing goods and services which he is exhorted to acquire but which have, of course, to be paid for. Others approach their work life with a very different set of expectations. A skilled manual worker may urge upon his children the importance of training, a sober adaptation to the world as it is, and expectations of comfortable home ownership. Even more different is likely to be the middle-class experience. The son of a professional man or manager, going on at 18 to university, may feel confident of becoming a manager or professional man himself, graduating up through an interesting, well-paid and high-status career in what he will see as an essentially benign society. He may well expect to be among those who control and make decisions for others, and to be able to share with relative ease in the modern cornucopia of material abundance. The fact that the middle-class young person may occasionally nowadays feel freer than ever before to drop out of what he deems a rat-race without feeling disgraced only demonstrates that the wider range of choice always enjoyed by the higher classes has widened even further. It need hardly be stressed, however, that there are many variant sets of attitudes besides these which people can bring with them into the organization, and it is not difficult to see that they can produce widely different perceptions and behaviour.

These social influences on attitudes to work and work organizations have many additional dimensions and all owe much to historical continuities. Our behaviour is not in the strictest sense determined by our history and traditions but it is powerfully shaped by them. Attitudes to authority, to the work organization, to the wider society, and to the state, all have a bearing on relations between management and employees and between governments and unions, and all have deep roots in the past. While not unchangeable they tend to persist. A chronic difficulty, therefore, for theorists and practitioners alike lies in deciding what behaviours might be judged unlikely to change except at a cost in coercion which few would be happy to pay. We can alert ourselves to these often stubborn dispositions by exploring international comparisons, which often bring to our attention traditional stances in our own society hitherto taken for granted. The perceptions, attitudes, and expectations to be found in a Birmingham factory are different from those of its equivalent in Stuttgart, Tokyo, or South Korea. They may even be different from those of a new micro-technology plant in the Thames valley.

The implications of all this can now be made explicit. In examining managerial strategies for promoting employee compliance and involvement, we shall be less liable to overlook important aspects of both managerial and employee behaviour if we never lose sight of the wider social setting within which they conduct their mutual relations. Some attention to the latter is therefore desirable before we begin exploring the former. But the picture which confronts us is not a simple one.

Two perspectives on the nature of Western society

The complexity evident in the make-up of *homo sapiens* is no less apparent in the societies he creates. This is one reason why observers disagree sharply even when they limit themselves to Western industrial societies and how they work. Even scholars who share the same personal feelings about these societies may select different facts for emphasis or interpret the same facts differently. And there is a further complication. Those who in general approve and those who in general disapprove of these societies are even more likely to stress different features or interpret a given feature differently. We thus find ourselves with sharply divergent perspectives often infused with correspondingly divergent personal attitudes towards what is being studied.

There would probably be agreement, however, that use of the phrase 'Western industrial societies' must not be allowed to obscure certain important differences between them. These differences do not, of course, extend across the board. Certain propositions would command agreement, such as that the economic systems of Western societies are mostly privately owned; that the minority public sector, too, is usually required to operate on commercial principles; that these economic systems are based on an extreme division of labour and are served by a 'free' labour market; and that welfare provisions help to relieve some of the casualties of the system. But historical differences in the social structures of these countries and in the texture of their social relations have resulted in capitalism and industrialism developing in significantly varying ways. Contrasts become even sharper when we compare industrialism in the West with its counterpart in the East. In Japan, the success of large companies in maintaining an authoritarian–paternalist structure of leadership, deference and 'company-consciousness' at all levels cannot be understood without reference to Japanese history, culture, and the way in which industrialists came to exploit national traditions that were helpful to them. But as already implied, we do not have to go to the further ends of the earth to discover industrial societies that have taken shapes notably different from our own. In Germany, for example, industrialization took place within a society long marked by authoritarian political regimes; by a glorification of the militaristic state which accorded it transcendent value over the individual; by conceptions of the business enterprise, imposed by employer upon employees with state encouragement, as a unified 'community' subject to absolutist paternalist control; and by widespread dispositions to accept strong leadership in the interests of some supposed higher good.

Leanings towards some of these characteristics could be found to a limited extent in Britain also, but for all practical purposes they were overlaid by very different traditions extending back for centuries. Here, landed aristocracy and gentry, determined to resist the establishment of an absolutist monarchy, had opted for a weak state, had played down militarism, and had evolved a strategy and legitimation of rule that relied less than elsewhere in Europe on arbitrary coercion, and more on the rule of law, an ideology of freedom, and circumspect concessions to claimant groups. The political doctrines and practices which came to predominate expressly elevated the individual and his rights and freedoms over those of any larger grouping such as the state. Individualism, at all social levels, already had a long and fierce history in Britain, expressed in her religious and legal as well as her economic and political structures. The concomitant has been that conceptions of 'community needs' or of a 'higher social good' have little power to move except in war. Eighteenth-century English political philosophy was only reflecting the realities of widespread English attitudes when it presented individual self-interest as 'clear and compelling', and the public or social interest as 'thin and insubstantial'.

The liberal doctrine of individual freedoms which this situation encouraged rendered it difficult to uphold indefinitely the idea of the business enterprise as an authoritarian structure of control in which the managed had no independent rights. Sections of the 'plebs' who had long shared in traditions of the 'free-born Englishman' were able to utilize this situation to assert spirited organizational independence against their masters in defence of their 'rights' – rights which, more than in other European countries, were often bound up with pre-capitalist restrictionism and exclusiveness. Those with the necessary strength and confidence found much to oppose. English individualism and a pre-industrial development of 'contract' were among the forces which led to a widespread view of labour as a simple 'commodity' to be bought and sold like any other, the employer accepting no responsibility for his workers outside the strict terms of the contract. A weak state with only limited coercive forces proved unable to prevent them combining to protect themselves – indeed was inhibited by its own ideology from trying very hard to do so. The collectivism to which they resorted for these purposes was not really at odds with English individualism. There was, of course, a dedicated minority of activists for whom the trade union was a near-sacred entity which might require and receive, on occasion, sacrifices quite unrelated to private interest. For most of the rank and file, however, it was no more than a device by which they might pursue personal objectives far more effectively than if they stood alone as isolated individuals. It was an 'instrumental' collectivism rather than one which invested the collective with transcendent value in its own right.

Totally without any ruling class inculcation of metaphysical notions of the state, and ruled by governments which hesitated to destroy their own legitimation by too forcible a repression, organized labour in Britain pursued its interests, industrial and political, predominantly in the same individualistic, piecemeal, empirical spirit as that which informed the behaviour of its masters. Given economic growth, the nineteenth century brought enough amelioration in the working lives of trade unionists to encourage them to continue with these relatively peaceful and constitutional methods rather than reach for the highly problematic benefits of violent social overthrow. Governments drawn from a pragmatically-minded ruling class saw the logic and, albeit slowly and grudgingly, conceded the unions legal protections, prudently denied employers help and encouragement in smashing them, and overruled the courts with legislation when they handed down judgements which seriously threatened union functions.

By contrast, the rigid, inflexible, and authoritarian structures and traditions of Germany proved incapable of this kind of adaptation.

In heavy industry, especially, trade unionism and collective bargaining were implacably resisted by the industrial barons, themselves powerfully supported by a militaristic and highly nationalist state and its police. In reaction to this, there developed a working class movement strongly flavoured by Marxist rhetoric, a development which intensified ruling-class denunciation of labour movements and socialism as subversive of the sacred national mission.

In Britain, meanwhile, an organized working class that doggedly maintained, where it could, a restrictive adversary stance at the workplace, predominantly refused to translate this into revolutionary doctrine at the political level. At the same time, like many other groups in society, it revealed its English–individualistic origins by continuing to see private interests as 'clear and compelling' and public or social interest as 'thin and insubstantial'.

Stanley Baldwin and similarly-minded associates did much, through the leadership and control they exercised over the Conservative Party and Conservative governments between the wars, to strengthen these trends. Ever ready to promote conciliatory procedures in politics and industry so far as was politically prudent *vis-à-vis* their supporters, they treated labour leaders with respect and sought to convince them of the value of the House of Commons by not exploiting Conservative majorities. Baldwin had no great respect for the employer interest and understood the trade union movement better than any other Conservative politician before or since – and better than many Labour politicians.

Out of this historical context, marked as it has been by a series of struggles for civic rights to the franchise, for industrial rights to a foothold in negotiating terms and conditions of employment, and for extension of the rule of law to the lower orders, there has emerged one view of British society as fully 'pluralist'. Here we come to the highly contentious issue of how British society is to be analysed and interpreted. The pluralist analysis is essentially benign in that it sees as broadly satisfactory the present pattern of opportunities for mobilizing power, influence, and justice enjoyed by the various interests and pressure groups. British society offers, it is believed, full and fair freedom for any legitimate body of opinion to organize, disseminate its views, press its interests, and try to persuade others, including relevant decision makers. The fact that these freedoms and opportunities are so readily available renders suspect, it is said, any group which seeks to exert power or pressure outside the legitimate recognized channels, for it indicates their underlying motivation to be malign and destructive of this admirable system.

It would be pointed out that, in the political sphere, the major sectional interests of society, business and organized labour receive institutional expression through the Conservative and Labour parties. In addition, we now have the SDP/Liberal Alliance, which claims to be free of domination by either and to be the voice for those not wishing to identify with the big battalions. All compete for the favour of the electorate through which they hope to gain access to the levers of power for governing the country.

In the economic system, as in the political, the liberal freedoms of speech and of combination ensure that democracy and a reasonable approximation to fairness prevail. Trade unionism enables labour to face the employers on something like equal terms – indeed, as many argued before Thatcher economic policies took effect, on superior terms, for were not the unions dangerously close to dominating both managements and governments?

Collective bargaining is seen, from this view, as giving organized employees a fully fair (sometimes more than fair) opportunity to negotiate with management on terms and conditions of employment. It is also, of course, one of the strategies through which many managements have hoped to strengthen employee compliance, but this aspect will be explored later. At the moment we are concerned only to register its significance for the pluralist – by which we mean here someone who believes not only that pluralistic dispersion of power among a variety of independent institutions in society is a good thing, but also that the desirable degree of dispersion already exists. For pluralists so defined, collective bargaining has ranked – until its post-war association with inflation and its manifest reinforcement, rather than mitigation, of social injustice – as one of the major institutions lending fairness and justification to our economic institutions and social system. For it has often been seen, though not by all pluralists, not only as levelling up employee power to an acceptable approximation with that of management, but also as reinforcing government social welfare and redistributive policies in gradually reducing class differences. As a consequence of these changes, manual worker affluence is regarded as rendering the old class conceptions out of date. For many Conservatives, especially, the language of 'rich' and 'poor' now seems sentimental and outdated. Social mobility and a supposed equality of opportunity are thought to add their weight to this great improvement in living standards to make an altogether more equal society. More and more it becomes possible for talent and hard work to reap their reward through an upward progress in what is sometimes called a meritocracy – a new aristocracy based on individual ability and effort instead of on birth and social rank.

The Thatcher government has gone out of its way to celebrate the principle of individualistic achievement, duly rewarded and honoured. Business is seen by many as having civilized itself: in place of the old ruthless search for profit maximization is the recognition of diverse social responsibilities to employees, consumers and the public interest. Subject to the wilder spirits in the trade unions learning the good sense, moderation and responsibility already acquired by their more sober fellows and co-operating with management and government to promote economic growth and control inflation, society can continue its gradual evolution towards ever-rising prosperity for all. Thatcher policies were designed to further this process by curbing the 'excesses' of trade union power at the workplace.

Perhaps relatively few hold these views in the form of a consciously-articulated and coherent structure of beliefs and values. Such a picture or some variant of it is, however, implicit in the attitudes and behaviour of many. We often have to draw inferences from men's behaviour as to what they believe. True motivations are apt to lie deep, and men may act and express themselves for reasons which they would find difficult to bring to the conscious surface. Because of this we often have to describe them as behaving 'as if' they held certain beliefs – in this case a set of beliefs about society and how it operates.

The set briefly sketched above is likely, for obvious reasons, to have special appeal for the more favoured and comfortably placed, since it offers a view of society as a reasonable and fair system of arrangements within which individuals and groups engage in healthy, regulated competition for the good things of life. Such a view reassures the successful that they deserve their luxuries and, if accepted by the unsuccessful, leads them too to legitimize the system and continue to accept it as right and proper.

On the other hand, this whole perspective on the way our kind of society operates has been subjected by some observers to severe and damaging criticism from which we can construct another and very different composite picture. This 'radical' alternative does not accept that the lower strata of society have been able to mobilize political and economic strength sufficient to achieve a fair approximation to that of the rich and powerful. Labour governments, it holds, are severely limited in their aspirations for social change by an awareness that most strategic decision-making power remains in the hands of those in industry, business, commerce and finance who are unsympathetic to their views and who could use a variety of covert methods to frustrate their designs. Similarly, argues the radical view, the power of trade unions to challenge management successfully on any really fundamental feature of our economic system is vastly exaggerated. The unions can cause managements and governments alike considerable difficulties on some issues, but these are relatively marginal to the total structure and conduct of business enterprise, which persists in much the shape that the owners and controllers of resources desire. Events since 1979 have revealed the hollowness of assertions that the unions run the country. The real centres of power, it would be pointed out, have, simply by their choices of fiscal and monetary policies, intensified the unemployment effects of world recession to a point where union effectiveness, both at the political level and at the workplace, has been greatly reduced.

Again, in propagating the gospel of 'social responsibility' business might be said to be making a virtue of necessity. It is not the salient values of business which have changed but the social environment within which it operates. Trade unions, 'public opinion', government, all now constrain business to be a little more accountable to other social interests. For business itself, financial success remains the touchstone whether the object is bigger dividends for shareholders, larger surpluses to finance growth, or higher status and reputation for managers. Trade unionism has made little impact upon the distribution of financial rewards as between the major interests of society. Collective bargaining has not substantially shifted the proportion of the national product going to wages and lower salaries, nor have welfare and other so-called redistributive policies had the equalizing effects imputed to them.

Such movement towards a less unequal society as was traceable in the 1940s has now been reversed. Poverty, bad housing and higher disease rates for the bottom strata have been 'rediscovered'. Opportunities for educational advancement are still heavily unequal as between middle-class and working-class children, who are disadvantaged in many ways now familiar to educationalists.

Thus, in place of a picture which presents society as moving steadily and inevitably towards a broadly egalitarian middle-class pattern within which men enjoy roughly comparable opportunities and advantages, there emerges a less optimistic interpretation. It sees a largely privately-owned economic system operating within a competitive, acquisitive society still marked by great inequalities of power, wealth, income, status and opportunity. These built-in structural inequalities ensure their own perpetuation, thereby creating the remarkably persistent patterns of poverty and deprivation which survive such good intentions as reforming governments bring to bear, and which private-enterprise capitalism tends constantly to generate rather than extinguish. Within this structure the wage-earner and lower salary-earner are still very much at a disadvantage. Society and its values, institutions and conventions still take forms which create severe and wounding divisions and afford the favoured groups ample facilities for defending their privileges. Against these defences, reforming governments, operating by the Queensberry self-restraints of parliamentary democracy, soon learn their own limitations. Reforms are indeed achieved, and important ones, but the essential character of the system remains.

Both the rhetoric and the policies of the 'new' Conservatism, as represented by the Thatcher administrations, dealt damaging blows at the 'progressive' egalitarian vision. Redistribution of income towards the better-off; overt hostility towards trade unionism and its leaders; transfer of public enterprise to the private profit-making arena; elevation of the market as the supreme harmonizing mechanism; a disparaging stance towards society's losers; all these constitute an unabashed assertion of values which have always been close to Conservative hearts but which previous Conservative governments have often considered it judicious to restrain. The new Conservatism has not captured the whole of the party and events may yet force it back into that second place in party dominance which it has until recently occupied. Already, however, its direct and indirect effects have helped to produce probably irreversible effects on Britain's politics and labour movement.

These effects do not yet include widespread popular rejection of our economic and social system. In the 1983 General Election, the Labour vote – for a left-wing programme – among trade unionists was only 7 per cent more than they gave the Conservatives. Yet it must be remembered that the so-called Thatcher landslide rested on the votes of only 30.8 per cent of the electorate.

Evidence seems to suggest that many people, perhaps most, have long viewed the system with a mixture of cynicism and acceptance, combined with scepticism about the chances – and benefits – of fundamental change. In this respect as in others, the well-placed groups derive an advantage from their command over resources and their greater prestige, education and articulateness. These make it likely that their own, more benign, pluralist view will effectively predominate, even to some extent among those strata who fare relatively ill within the system. There need be no surprise, declares the radical view, that so many of us pay more heed to the values, principles and ideas of wealthy, powerful, high-status groups, than to those of less well-off, relatively weak, low-status groups.

Such is the radical alternative to the pluralist perspective. But what is the relevance of this debate for our main theme? It is this – that the divergence of perspective on society as a whole is often expressed too in a comparable divergence of perspective on the social organization of the industrial enterprise. Just as the former debate alerts us to a less familiar analysis of the general shape and workings of the wider society, so the same approach turned upon the industrial organization confronts us with a comparably different interpretation and, of particular concern to us here, a different view of management's search for employee compliance and moral involvement.

A pluralist perspective on the business enterprise

The pluralistic interpretation of the industrial organization probably represents the received orthodoxy in many Western societies, even if it comes in a variety of versions. By this is meant not that it commands universal assent but that it is the view favoured, either explicitly or implicitly, by probably most persons of power, authority, status and influence who can be said to manifest a view at all.

Just as the pluralist perspective takes an essentially benign view of Western industrial society, so it takes a similar view of the work organization. It sees the organization as a coalition of interest groups presided over by a top management which serves the long-term needs of 'the organization as a whole' by paying due concern to all the interests affected – employees, shareholders, consumers, the community, the 'national interest'. This involves management in holding the 'right' balance between the sometimes divergent claims of these participant interests. The possibility exists, however, that management, under pressure, say, from market competition or from shareholders, might pay insufficient heed to the needs and claims of its employees if they were not able to bring those needs and claims forcefully to its attention. Through collective organization in trade unions, therefore, employees mobilize themselves to meet management on equal terms to negotiate the terms of their collaboration. The pluralist does not claim anything approaching perfection for this system. In some situations, imbalances of strength as between employers and unions or between management and particular work groups may be such that for one side or the other justice is distinctly rough. They are not seen as so numerous or severe, however, as generally to discredit the system either from the unions' point of view or from management's.

We come here upon an implication of considerable importance that will recur at several points in our analysis. This is that the system of employers and unions, or management and unionized work group, jointly negotiating terms and conditions of employment depends to some extent for its stability and health upon neither side feeling that it is being overly subjected to coercive dictation by the other. We can explain this by recalling a well-established proposition about power and promises. If someone extracts a promise from us by holding a pistol to our head, neither a legal nor a moral judgement regards that promise as binding in honour, and it is certain that we ourselves do not so regard it. As soon as the immediate threat is removed we feel justified in ignoring the promise, since it was extracted from us 'under duress'. Of course, were the threat to be maintained continuously – which might prove difficult and costly – we would continue to observe the required behaviour, but this observance would follow not from our recognition of a moral obligation but from expediency – from prudent calculation in the interests of avoiding punishment. Commitments and agreements which we feel to have been extracted from us under compulsion as a result of extreme weakness on our part do not evoke our sense of obligation so far as observance is concerned. What kinds of commitments and agreements *do* evoke such a sense of obligation? Only those in which we feel ourselves to have enjoyed adequate freedom in undertaking the commitment or concluding the agreement. And the sense of obligation is the greater the more nearly we approach a position of complete equality with the other party. When we accept the terms and conditions of an undertaking, not from any sense of being pressured or coerced, but from a sense of voluntarily agreeing to obligations whose nature and consequences we fully understand, we are conscious of a moral obligation bearing upon us. To be sure, we may sometimes be tempted to evade it, but when others appeal to us that the obligation exists – and seek to keep us to the line of duty by threatening penalties if we default – we do not consider the moral appeal to be irrelevant or the threatened penalties to be an offence against natural justice.

What is the relevance of all this to relationships between management and rank and file, and to the pluralist perspective on those relationships? First of all it casts light on those situations where rank-and-file employees are not collectively organized. Here the employee stands only in an individual contract relationship with his employer. The employer's superior economic power in this contract gives him, in many cases, correspondingly disproportionate ability to determine its terms. This was the predominant pattern during the earlier phases of industrialization and has by no means disappeared. Yet men of substance were apt to defend this system with the palpable fiction that it represented free contract between master and man bargaining as equals in the labour market, and as such called for full and honourable discharge by the employee of his obligations towards the master. Whether or not particular employees saw this situation as fair and as calling for scrupulous observance, the passage of time saw a growing number of outside observers who regarded this degree of power disparity as socially unjust, and of course the trade unions were propagating this message from the start. As they gained in strength the notion spread that, by mobilizing themselves collectively and presenting a united force, employees were gradually eliminating the acute imbalance of power between themselves and their employers. Collective bargaining developed through which both sides committed themselves to certain terms and conditions of employment, including procedures which defined the method of handling claims and grievances without resort to strikes, lockouts, or other forms of disruptive action.

The significance of our 'ethics' argument now emerges. To the extent that the terms and conditions of the employment contract are seen as being settled, not by the coercive power of the employer, but by free and equitable negotiation between parties of roughly comparable strength, employees can fairly be required to offer honourable observance of the agreements that result. Organized collective relations in industry have therefore developed to the accompaniment of the widely propagated assertion that both sides have a moral obligation to observe the agreements negotiated by their representative agencies. As we have already noted, this is not to say that a sense of moral obligation is, or need be, the only motive for observing agreements. Men may be punctilious in observance for reasons of expediency – or, in the phrase used earlier, prudent calculation. They may, for example, consider that it will serve their interests best in the long run ('Honesty is the best policy'); or that to default would expose them to penalties and give the other side a good excuse for defaulting also. But because these expediency motives rest on men's calculations of their own self-interest they are a somewhat uncertain basis for observance in a complex and constantly changing world, for men's views of where their self-interests lie may fluctuate during the span of an agreement, and in any case there may be differences between the perceived self-interests of a group of union members on the shop floor and the calculation made and negotiated on their behalf by union officers. A sense of being under a *moral* obligation to honour agreements can therefore help to sustain consent despite these fluctuations and differences – and if the outside observer sees the negotiation arrangements as fairly balanced he will be the readier to see employees penalized if they default.

We can illustrate this pluralist perspective by relating it to what was felt until comparatively recently to be one of the major issues in post-war industrial relations. British employers were bitter in their denunciations of the so-called 'unconstitutional' strike – the strike undertaken by a work group, with or without tacit support from union officers, in transgression of the official disputes procedure negotiated by union and employers. The written evidence submitted by the Confederation of British Industry to the Royal Commission on Trade Unions and Employers' Associations (1965–8) asserted that 'For many years employers have felt that the greatest single contribution which could be made to the better working of the industrial relations system would be better observance of agreements.' The attitudes taken by the pluralist on the moral issue here are clearly shaped by assumptions about the distribution of power in society and industry. The belief that the powers of employers' associations and trade unions, and of management and unionized work groups, are as fairly matched as can reasonably be hoped for in a complicated world, leads to the assertion that employees should always act 'responsibly' (that is, in accordance with their obligations) by observing the terms of the agreements negotiated on their behalf. Some of those making this assertion argue that where employees flout agreements 'society' would be justified in penalizing them in some way until they respect them. From this view, transgressors are seen either as lacking all sense of responsibility and obligation, or as having some psychological quirk which renders them anti-authority on principle, or as holding subversive political views which require them to render present institutions unworkable.

Most trade union leaders, when urging their members to observe agreements, base their case not on expediency but on obligation. Among those leaders who chanced to make this explicit in the post-war period was Jack Jones, sometime General Secretary of the Transport and General Workers Union. After drawing attention to the difficulties of guaranteeing absolute observance by the rank and file, he asserted that all 'a trade union leadership can do is bind itself in honour to try to observe the agreements it concludes with employers and this I believe in absolutely. In general the assurance we give to management is that we bind ourselves in honour – we will do our very best to see that the agreement is observed.' The Trades Union Congress, too, in its written evidence to the 1965–8 Royal Commission, declared that 'The General Council acknowledged, as would every responsible trade union leader, that procedure agreements embody promises and therefore should not be broken by any union representative.' The official union position therefore implies the stance that class relations at the workplace are sufficiently short of the extremes of domination to call for the observance by employees of honour and obligation.

The general picture of industrial relations that could be drawn from this pluralistic approach is one which, though far from free of conflict, contains mechanisms enabling the contending parties, not too unevenly matched, to negotiate their mutual accommodations in a manner appropriate to a society which aspires to industrial as well as political democracy. Within this framework, employees would be assumed to see management as simply discharging its necessary functions and receiving its rewards like any other group in the organization. In carrying out its job it tries to apply certain principles which appear to rank as inevitable facts of life – for example that those doing more responsible work must receive larger incomes than those doing less responsible work, that those wielding authority should earn more than those under their command, and that the managerial function is of self-evidently higher status than manual labour. In performing its co-ordinative, directive and innovatory functions for society, management has to control and contain the possibly divergent, possibly excessive aspirations of the various subordinate groups which make up the enterprise. These efforts inevitably involve it in friction and dispute. Yet these are not unhealthy conflicts which rock the fundamentals of the system (about which men are taken to be generally agreed), but understandable divergences of the sort only to be expected in a free society. Collective bargaining enables most of them to be resolved in a tolerable manner, though, to be sure, it creates problems, as in all industrial countries, still to be resolved.

It is some such picture as this that we derive from applying a pluralist perspective to the work organization. As already suggested, probably many of the more favoured members of our society find this perspective, or some variant of it, a convincing interpretation so far as political and social structures are concerned. Fewer of them relish its application to work organizations. Many employers and managers, especially, have for long deplored conceptions of the enterprise which acknowledge the legitimacy within it of organized interest groups that see their interests as divergent from those of top management and engage in conflict with management and sometimes with each other. Such conceptions, they feel, are bound to strengthen the legitimacy and public acceptance of the trade unions, thereby strengthening their collectivist challenge to managerial authority and threatening profits, economic progress, and the freedom of the individual worker. Better by far, in their opinion, to propagate a conception of the enterprise in which management is the only legitimate source of authority, control, and leadership. Thus would be encouraged a picture of the enterprise as a unified team pulling together for the common good. This approach, referred to in the literature as the 'unitary' frame of reference, is examined more closely for its implications in Chapter 6. Its use declined during the 1970s, when many employers and managers, faced with the manifest fact of a workforce composed of groups more militantly assertive of their separate 'rights' than ever before, were disposed to accept the pluralist conception and explicitly work to it in shaping their labour relations and personnel policy. With the return of mass unemployment and the weakening of shop floor power have come renewed hopes of welding a 'unified team' and this has renewed distaste in some quarters for the pluralists' insistence on the structural antagonisms and conflicts inherent in the work organization. This distaste has always been a specially marked feature of, for example, the Institute of Directors; it has reappeared in the Confederation of British Industry, whose Director of Social Affairs recently disparaged 'the concept of distinct and conflicting interest groups within a company' (*The Guardian*, 16 May 1984).

The unitary frame of reference is not the only alternative to the pluralistic version. Another is what has become known, somewhat unsatisfactorily, as the 'radical' perspective. Between them these three perspectives illustrate the sharply contrasting views men may hold of the social and industrial scene, and the way in which these views affect their interpretation of events and consequently their behaviour.

A radical perspective on the business enterprise

The starting point for examining the radical view relates to the distribution of power. Like the pluralist interpretation, it emphasizes the gross disparity of power between the employer and the individual employee. Lacking property or command over resources, the employee is totally dependent on being offered employment by owners or controllers – and a dependence relationship is a power relationship. From this position of weakness he has little ability to assert his needs and aspirations against those of the employer, who can therefore treat him not as an end in himself but as a means to the employer's own ends: as a commodity resource to be used for purposes about which he is not consulted and which he may not share. Unlike the pluralist, however, the radical does not see the collective organization of employees into trade unions as restoring a balance of power (or anything as yet approaching it) between the propertied and the propertyless. He may well agree that it mitigates the imbalance and thereby enables employees to challenge some kinds of management decision on issues of special and immediate importance for them. But a great imbalance remains, symptomized by the fact that there are many other types of management decision which employees might aspire to influence were they conscious of having the power to do so, but from which they are at present completely excluded.

The radical would agree, however, that appearances may sometimes suggest to the casual eye that, on the contrary, the imbalance is in the employees' favour – and certainly this was until recently a widespread and popular impression. Was not management, until unemployment reached the three million mark, often forced to its knees by a powerful union or organized work group? But, says the radical, examine the issues which are and are not at stake even in the most titanic-seeming clash. The former revolve around wages, who does what work and under what conditions, who should join what union, and other matters which, though of great significance for both sides, do not touch the basic fundamentals of the system. Trade unions strive to effect marginal improvements in the lot of their members and to defend them against arbitrary management action. They do not – and here we come to the crucial point of what issues are *not* at stake in management/worker relations – attack management on such basic principles of the social and industrial framework as private property, the hierarchical nature of the organization, the extreme division of labour, and the massive inequalities of financial reward, status, control and autonomy in work. Neither do they try to secure a foothold in the majority of decisions made within the organization on such issues as management objectives, markets, capital investment, and rate of expansion. Very rarely do they seriously challenge such principles as the treatment of labour as a commodity to be hired or discarded at management's convenience.

Why, asks the radical, do they not challenge management on all these issues which may clearly have major significance for the work experience, rewards and life destinies of their members? The answer he offers is twofold. First, employee collectives (unions and organized work groups) realize that while they can deploy enough economic power (that is the collective control of their own labour) and enjoy enough support from government and other sections of society to enable them to offer an effective challenge to management on a limited range of issues where their participation in decision making is seen as legitimate, they would need to mobilize far more power than is customary at present if they were to achieve significantly larger aspirations. For, faced with demands which in effect struck at the foundations of management power, privilege, values and objectives, management would draw not only upon its full reserves of strength but also upon the support of other managements, employers' associations and sympathetic sections of society (including government), which were concerned to defend the *status quo*. Such a basic clash would soon reveal where the latent reserves of real ultimate power lay, and the present capacity of the rank and file for a mass mobilization against the *status quo* would have to increase enormously for them to lie with the unions.

This leads into the second aspect of the radical's answer. A mobilization of power on this scale would require great resources of will, determination, confidence and aspiration. Why are these resources not presently available to the unions? Because their members, quite apart from being conscious of having something to lose from such a clash, are still too much under the influence of social conditioning to venture a bid of these dimensions. To some extent they accept as valid the principles on which the work organization is constructed and the conventions by which management operates it. If they doubt them at all it is certainly not with the universal unquestioning conviction that would be required for a successful onslaught against the full power of property and resource-control. But, says the radical, this acceptance, total or partial, of the principles and conventions of work organization cannot realistically be seen as a free and informed choosing situation in which employees rationally examine alternative possibilities and make an unforced choice. As we saw, the vast majority who are without resources must seek access to resources owned or controlled by the few, and such is their relative weakness and dependence that they are constrained, for the most part, to accept the essential nature of work organization as they find it. Power counts, too, in many indirect as well as direct ways. It was noted earlier that the values of wealth, position and status shape much of the content of public communication in newspapers, magazines, radio, television, advertising, public relations, education and training, all of which manifest either explicitly or implicitly these dominant ideas and assumptions and, equally important, define the terms and limits of current controversy and debate. Recognition of this does not require us to accept a conspiracy theory of history, simply to acknowledge that in a thousand different ways powerless men survive and possibly prosper by serving the interests, values and objectives of powerful men, and can usually find some method of salvaging their self-respect while doing so.

All this suggests that the approach of many rank-and-file employees probably consists of a low-key acceptance of the organization's essential characteristics. They are encouraged to see them not only as necessary and inevitable but also as legitimate and right, and while they may be keenly conscious of grievances these are not so overwhelming as to drive them to condemn the system *in toto*. Yet their subordinate and inferior position generally precludes them from participating in it with enthusiasm and commitment, for they cannot help but see it as having been imposed on them. Cynicism and distrust of 'them' may not be far below the surface, co-existing with a disposition to make the best of things, to reflect that they could be worse, and to conclude that since hierarchy, subordination and inequality are so universal and enduring they are probably in some mysterious way inevitable. If these ideas are changing it is only very slowly. Meanwhile they probably play an important part in maintaining the relative passivity which so many among the lower ranks extend to the major features of the system in which they find themselves.

When employees 'accept', therefore, as they almost invariably do, the basic structure, principles and conventions of the work organization, they do so not from free considered choice, but partly because they are aware of the superior power which supports that pattern of organization and makes it seem inevitable, and partly because their social environment induces them in any case to see it as 'natural', 'realistic', and 'only to be expected'. They limit their union and work group aspirations to influencing such managerial decisions as are immediately important to them and which experience has taught them are within reach through the medium of collective bargaining.

How do they themselves see this negotiating method? We have already noted one view of it as a process of joint regulation by parties who agree the terms of their collaboration and who acknowledge the imperative of moral obligation as well as of self-interested expediency in the observance of the resulting agreements. Employees with a radical perspective cannot hold this view. For them, collective bargaining is at worst a mere façade behind which the employer continues to dictate terms, at best a means by which organized employees can get marginally to grips with their masters on some issues although still leaving the latter with the real reserves of power. These reserves they rarely need to use because society and its institutions and values continue to retain the configuration necessary for their interests. For employees with this view of the social and industrial scene, the severe inequalities of power which subject rank-and-file employees to an inferior and subordinate position exempt them from moral obligation to observe organizational rules which run specially counter to their own needs and interests. This applies no less to those rules which have been jointly negotiated, for even in this process the employees are seen as being at a disadvantage.

As we have noted, the radical agrees that appearances may suggest the contrary. Do not wage and other settlements sometimes lie nearer the employees' preferred position than to that of the employer? The radical's reply would be that, quite apart from the fact that bargaining tactics and gamesmanship complicate, even for the participants, the issue of what their preferred positions are, the aspirations of employees are themselves shaped by their awareness of the employer's power and the need to be 'realistic'. Employees try to achieve what they feel they have some chance of achieving, given the prevailing power relations. Their claims take into account their awareness of the employer's superior position. Thus, says the radical, appearances are misleading and in no way contradict the proposition that employees, even when unionized, remain in a greatly inferior power situation. Similar arguments can be turned upon those negotiated procedures for settling individual or group claims and grievances – procedures which, by ruling out strikes, overtime bans or other forms of direct action, seek to guarantee to management that no disruption of work occurs. Through such procedures, management commits itself, in effect, to hearing appeals against its decisions. But to secure this concession, employee groups (and their unions) must forgo such tactical ability as their position may afford them to put pressure upon management during the process. In this matter too, then, says the radical, management's superior power is able to shape arrangements to its liking.

Thus, while employees may be able to secure from the employer certain marginal improvements in their relatively lowly position and its rewards, that position is essentially imposed upon them by these great structural inequalities of property ownership and economic power, officially sanctioned and supported by the coercive forces of the state, and by Labour as well as by Conservative governments. What moral obligation, asks the radically-minded employee, does he owe the employer to obey organizational rules, when even those that are 'jointly agreed' have been negotiated within what is in fact an unequal power relationship? Rather does he feel justified in pressing every minor advantage, manipulating every rule, exploiting every loophole, harrying every managerial weakness or leniency in his continuous struggle against those whom he sees as exploiting his economic weakness for purposes about which he is not consulted.

Motives for compliance: expediency and obligation

Whether the radically-minded employee (or work group) does or does not flout agreements and refuse to extend to the employer a spirit of give and take (the spirit which, in fact, to varying degrees characterizes most work situations) depends on his calculations of expediency. Our preceding argument suggests why he may feel no sense of obligation in his relations with the employer or management. But expediency may induce him to behave in much the same way as someone who does. Relevant factors here can include a calculation that this will serve his long-term interests best, an awareness that to maintain a permanent guerrilla campaign against management may goad it into a massive retaliation exercise which it feels it has to win, and knowledge that sharp practice on his part deprives him of effective argument against similar behaviour by management. Yet, as we know from experience and observation, work groups do not necessarily calculate that their net interests point in this direction. They may, for a variety of reasons, resort to very different behaviour.

In 1984 the majority of Britain's miners, exhibiting every sign of a deep and outraged frustration, followed the leadership of Arthur Scargill, who represents an extreme version of the radical position and was now applying it in his industrial policy. He is an avowed Communist who has evinced no commitment to any aspect of British society, least of all to the management of its publicly-owned coal industry.

In the 1984 dispute he asserted, in language vehement and immoderate by British union standards, a demand which did not permit of negotiated compromise – that there be complete cessation of pit closures. His strategy, and the day-to-day tactics apparently designed to provoke violent and bloody confrontations with the police, are susceptible of a political interpretation – as an exercise designed to raise 'class consciousness', heighten class tensions, and goad the Thatcher government into further public demonstrations of its hostility towards the union movement and its determination to break the power and spirit of one of its élite corps. Such exercises are rare in British industrial relations. They have increased in recent years as a consequence, it could be argued, of the style and tone of the Thatcher administrations, which have created the potentiality for this heightening of class tensions.

If Scargill's basic intent was to sharpen these tensions he clearly succeeded. On the one hand, most miners and many other citizens not necessarily of the left saw police as having been used in a dangerously obvious political role less familiar in Britain than elsewhere. They were nationally deployed through the Association of Chief Police Officers in a way always hitherto considered threatening for civil liberties. The tenuous control over the police by local authorities stood revealed, with a member of the Thatcher government, the Home Secretary, defining the miners' strike as having priority over local needs – as clear a case of national political intervention in police deployment as civil libertarians have always dreaded. On the other hand, many lined up behind the government, denouncing 'mob rule' and demanding the use of recent legislation against secondary picketing so that NUM funds could be legally attacked.

Such are the outcomes when a radical right evokes an extreme radical activist left whose leadership is accepted by a rank and file, much of whose frustration may have little to do with ideological political convictions. If Britain's social and constitutional fabric comes to bear permanent marks from this experience it will be because the trade unions face a Conservative government profoundly different in style and tone from that successfully insisted on by Baldwin after 1926.

Only rarely do British industrial relations touch this cosmic level, however, and our discussion must now be brought down to the more humdrum level of common experience in and out of season. We may resume by noting that the significance of a purely calculative or expediency approach to the procedures, disciplines and restraints associated with a stable collective bargaining situation is that, whereas an established and accepted moral obligation remains unvarying in what it admonishes us to do, the dictates of calculative expediency vary according to circumstances, mood, and who is making the assessment. An example can be offered which illustrates these differences. Let us suppose that a certain work group and the appropriate full-time district officer accept that the disputes procedure of the company concerned, having been, as they see it, fairly negotiated, deserves the fullest possible moral observance. While this conviction holds, the group's adherence to procedure can be expected to take a certain amount of strain. Some decisions emanating from the procedure may be unpopular and workers grumble, but the predominant opinion supports faithful observance of the agreement. But if their reading of the situation is that the disputes procedure in question, or the circumstances of its origins, are such that they cannot offer it their moral adhesion, their behaviour with respect to its provisions will be governed by expediency. They may, for example, observe them when in a weak position where they feel unable to do otherwise, and flout them when in a strong position where they are conscious of enjoying a temporary advantage over management on the issue in question. We would also expect the group's acceptance of the decisions or awards issuing from the procedure to be uncertain for, lacking moral adhesion to the system, their attitude is less likely to be able to take the strain of unfavourable outcomes. Finally, we must note the possibility that the work group and the full-time official may make different calculations of expediency. The latter may work to what he considers a higher-order expediency than that shaping the responses of the rank and file. He may look beyond their immediate personal interest to the union's long-term relationship with the company, perhaps with an employers' association, or to its institutional interests *vis-à-vis* rival unions. The possibilities of conflict are apparent, for the officer may find difficulty in convincing his members when they ask why his reading of the situation should prevail over theirs. One of the characteristics of an expediency approach is that any relevant participant can claim his assessment to be as valid as anyone else's. Divergences are equally sharp if rank-and-file members insist on an expediency approach while the full-time officer endorses the approach of the Trades Union Congress in its written evidence to the 1965–8 Royal Commission.

The threat presented to authority, control and leadership when rank and file react to rules, agreements and contracts only from an expediency calculation unsupported by any sense of obligation renders understandable not only that *management* should be found urging the moral sanctity of agreements and commitments 'freely and voluntarily' entered into, but also that trade union leaders too, in their concern for observance, should sometimes feel the need to reinforce expediency with the unequivocal ethical message that agreements embody promises which ought to be kept. In this they are all like rulers who seek to control their subjects' behaviour. We are, for example, threatened with detection and punishment if we rob banks. But if authority relied on this expediency argument alone the numbers of those who fancied their chances of evading detection would probably rise. We are taught, therefore, that it is also morally wrong to rob banks. With a combination of these two arguments authority hopes to keep us under control.

The reasons why trade union leaders have normally been concerned with their members' observance of negotiated agreements will be examined again later. Meanwhile we can remind ourselves that for anyone wishing to urge the moral sanctity of an agreement of any kind it is crucial, in most Western cultures at least, to be able to assert convincingly that the agreement in question was negotiated between parties of roughly comparable strength. For, as we have noted, to the extent that it is seen, or felt, to have been imposed by a markedly stronger party upon a weaker, the moral obligation bearing upon the latter will be felt to be that much the less. The significance for industrial relations of a belief that the negotiating parties are not so unequal in strength as to exempt the weaker from obligation is therefore apparent. It plays a useful supportive role for those concerned to promote stability and order in work relations. In so far as employees themselves accept the belief, their observance of agreements is reinforced by their sense of obligation. In so far as that vague and ill-defined entity, 'public opinion', accepts it, there may be political support for coercing employee defaulters into what is seen as their moral duty. With this kind of support within reach, those anxious to maintain stability are less dependent upon employees' calculations of personal expediency.

It is understandable, therefore, that interpretations of society based on the assumption of an approximate balance of power between the principal interest groups tend to be popular among those concerned to ensure that existing institutions work as smoothly as possible. Again, no conscious calculation need be postulated, only a tendency for men to be attracted by doctrines and interpretations which accord with, and support, the preferences, values and objectives they already hold. Conversely, those strongly critical of the prevailing social and economic order are likely to be found rejecting interpretations which appear to support a view of society as composed of balanced interest groups fairly negotiating the terms of their collaboration.

I have already indicated that I find the radical view, or some version of it, more convincing than the one with which it has been compared. As already made clear, whether, and how far, any particular individual or group holding the radical view chooses to shape practical policy and behaviour accordingly rests on expediency. Some union activists in industry holding radical–left views have, in their relations with management been models of pluralist give-and-take and 'good faith'. Analysis does not necessarily determine prescriptions. There may be a sincere judgement that to test relationships to destruction would run the risk of losing some good things that ought to be preserved.

Meanwhile it is important for the manager to resist the pressures of fashion, from whichever direction they come, and bring to the level of conscious inspection the views he holds himself, as well as gauge those of his workforce. Only when he realizes that his attitudes and behaviour implicitly contain assumptions about society and organization is he in a position to examine them and decide whether he finds them convincing. It can, of course, safely be repeated that only a tiny minority of us formulate our views in any conscious, articulated manner. Nevertheless, in our attitudes, responses and behaviour, we all express a general orientation the fuller implications of which we may be unaware. In this sense, some employee groups may display a general orientation carrying the implications labelled here as pluralist. But equally likely – and in the absence of reliable evidence this can be no more than an impression – is that many employee groups, unionized or not, consider themselves in a greatly inferior power position *vis-à-vis* their remote and impersonal top management, and that their observance of rules and agreements owes more to expediency than to any sense of obligation (though this does not imply that the latter is wholly absent).

What happens when such a group becomes especially frustrated or resentful while at the same time conscious of a modicum of strength is exemplified in those industries where management complains of unruly and disruptive behaviour in defiance of agreed procedures for the peaceful handling of issues in dispute. The groups in question are clearly, on those occasions, no longer defining expediency for themselves in terms of observing the formal procedures agreed by management and unions (designed as they are to restrain or delay the groups from using such strength as they can muster). While they may choose leaders with a clearly defined social philosophy based on rejection of the *status quo*, they themselves may be conscious only of resentment and frustration in a work situation which affords them little or no satisfaction apart from the pay packet; which subjects them to subordination, discipline and control for purposes they have not chosen and do not share; and which dominates them through decisions made remotely and impersonally on the assumption that they are instruments to be used and not ends in themselves.

Men with feelings like these often behave according to the implications of the radical view whether they consciously hold it or, as is more likely, not. Whether they act on these feelings in such ways as to cause difficulties for management depends on their aspirations, their job situation and how far it affords them scope for bringing pressure to bear, and on the extent to which they have the will to mobilize and exercise that pressure. The higher their score on these counts – which of course interact with each other – the greater the strain on any expediency calculation they may have made (or that has been made for them) to the effect that agreements should be punctiliously observed.

When men's adherence to constitutional procedure breaks under this strain they often come under moral condemnation for failing to honour the commitments signed in their name. A crucial question which such critics might well put to themselves here is whether the men concerned are capable of honouring *any* moral commitment. The simplest inquiry will usually reveal that in their other roles most of them are dutiful husbands, devoted fathers, loyal friends, steadfast workmates. Why, then, does this capacity for moral commitment sometimes appear to fail them in respect of their agreements with the company? The one answer which management seems determined to avoid is that, while other claims and other situations *can* command their moral adhesion, the company cannot. Yet the company does command the moral adhesion of many in the upper ranks of the hierarchy. Where it most demonstrably fails is in its appeal to the rank and file. Unless there is evidence that the rank and file are incapable of extending moral adhesion to anything, we must surely look for explanations of their defaulting behaviour in the very nature of their work situation as they experience and perceive it. We shall find ourselves driven back again and again in subsequent discussion to this widespread failure of the industrial enterprise to evoke the full moral involvement of the rank and file. We shall have occasion to note again, too, the overwhelming tendency among members of the favoured classes to explain this away by blaming the moral infirmity of manual wage-earners or lower salary-earners, rather than considering the possibility that the enterprise is so structured as to be largely incapable, in Western culture, of attracting strong rank-and-file commitment.

Meanwhile we conclude this chapter by noting that issues of profound significance have already emerged which will serve as the setting for our subsequent discussion. Having begun by raising the central theme, so crucial to employers and managements, of employee compliance and moral involvement, we then noted that attitudes and behaviour at work could not be fully understood without looking beyond the factory gates to the wider society. For the factory takes its structure, principles, beliefs and values from among those bred within, and in varying degrees nourished by, that wider society. But we then noted that these principles and beliefs do not constitute a homogeneous unity and consensus shared by everyone. Men diverge in how they interpret and evaluate social structures and institutions; they differ in their values and assumptions. Accordingly two contrasting perspectives, along with a third, the unitary view, were then presented, the pluralist and the radical, which demonstrated in what different terms men could perceive their society. It then became apparent that the same two perspectives could be turned upon the enterprise itself, resulting in very different consequences for how men see the organizational power structure and the whole pattern of relations between management and employees. This led us to examine certain crucial aspects of these relationships which bear especially upon our chosen theme – employee compliance with managerial rules, orders and directives. These aspects concern the two basic motives for obeying orders and observing rules – moral obligation and individual or group expediency. This discussion brought out the fact that the pluralist perspective on society and the enterprise must be seen not as socially neutral but as having great ideological significance. It presents an essentially benign view of society and the enterprise as deserving full legitimation by its members and thereby calling for their full moral adhesion on the basis of obligation rather than expediency. The alternative radical ideology disputes this interpretation and I have indicated that I find this challenge convincing.

My reasons for doing so will emerge cumulatively during succeeding chapters. For, having sketched the central theme and taken note of conflicting opinions about the social and organizational context within which it needs to be located, we must explore more fully the nature of the managerial problem we are concerned with here. Subsequently we shall discuss the various strategies employed by management to overcome it, the reasons for their relative success or failure, the explanations of the shifting emphasis observable over the years, and such possibilities as it seems sensible to visualize for the future.

Further reading

Association of Metropolitan Authorities, *Education and the World of Work* (London: AMA 1980).

Castles, F.G., Murray, D.J., Potter, D.C. (eds.), *Decisions, Organizations, and Society* (Penguin in association with the Open University Press 1971), Part 3.

Clegg, H.A., 'Pluralism in Industrial Relations', in *British Journal of Industrial Relations*, Vol. XIII, No. 3 (1975).

Currie, Robert, *Industrial Politics* (Clarendon Press 1979).

Dore, Ronald, *British Factory – Japanese Factory: The Origins of*

National Diversity in Industrial Relations (Allen and Unwin 1973).

Fox, Alan, 'Industrial Relations: A Social Critique of Pluralist Ideology' in J. Child (ed.), *Man and Organization: The Search for Explanation and Social Relevance* (Allen and Unwin 1973).

Fox, Alan, *History and Heritage: The Social Origins of the British Industrial Relations System*, (Allen and Unwin 1985).

Hill, Stephen, *Competition and Control at Work* (Heinemann 1981).

Hyman, Richard, 'Pluralism, Procedural Consensus and Collective Bargaining', in *British Journal of Industrial Relations*, Vol. XVI, No. 1 (1978).

Parkin, F., *Class Inequality and Political Order* (Paladin 1972).

Willis, Paul, *Learning to Labour* (Saxon House 1978).

2   Coercion and its limits

In bringing a closer focus to bear upon the managerial problem of securing employee compliance or, more ambitiously, moral involvement, we need to be clear about why such a problem should emerge in the first place. Many of the explanations offered over the years by persons of position and status, and still popular today, rest explicitly or implicitly upon the belief that rank-and-file employees lack the capacity to feel moral obligation, loyalty and commitment, or that they wilfully withhold them out of stupidity, irrational prejudice or political spite. It is understandable that those who most benefit from, and most identify with, our social and economic system should be loath to acknowledge even to themselves the possibility that the employee behaviours they deplore are an outcome neither of moral infirmity nor of stupidity, but of reactions to the social and work situations to which the system allocates most members of the wage-earning and lower salary-earning classes. Such an acknowledgement would leave the critics only the two alternatives of either stoically enduring the behaviours they deplore or changing the essential nature of the very system which endows them with their superior advantages and status. Since both are disagreeable there is a strong disposition to believe that these behaviours need not be stoically endured and can be transformed or at least changed markedly for the better by managerial strategies which leave the essential framework, character and values of the system intact.

Already, however, our discussion has brought out the argument that it is this framework and character of the industrial enterprise, and in certain major respects the society that contains it, which must bear the main responsibility for the failure to command to any substantial degree the moral adhesion of rank-and-file members. It is at this argument that we must now look more closely before we go on to examine the managerial strategies and assess the reasons for their relative success or failure. A fruitful way to begin, perhaps, is to explore further the possibility referred to in the preceding chapter –

that rank-and-file employees may come to see themselves as being used for the purposes of others.

Problem-solving and win–lose situations

The full implications of this for their attitudes and behaviour can be brought out by comparing such a situation with a very different one. Let us suppose that we join as equals with a number of others in the pursuit of a common purpose. We soon discover it necessary for some to act in a leadership and co-ordinative capacity. Given the common purpose, we accept them and feel able to trust them in those roles. This is not to say that disagreements will not arise with respect to means. But given the shared ends, these disagreements can be handled in what is often called a 'problem-solving' manner. This means that attention will be directed to clarifying the facts, searching for the best methods, and elucidating the probable consequences of alternatives. The parties do not seek to trap, bluff or score off each other, for they all have an interest in pursuing the same objective. For the same reason, they do not conceal, distort or manipulate information and ideas. Communications are open and unscreened, for the parties trust each other. This problem-solving pattern can be described, in fact, as a high-trust pattern.

We are using the notion of trust here to refer not to the degrees of trust or distrust that are embodied in our *personal* attitudes towards each other, but to what might be called the 'institutionalized' trust that is expressed in and through the roles, rules, and structured relations which we apply to others or have applied to ourselves. When we impose rules, for example, that leave a person with only minimal discretion, there is an important sense in which, though we may regard the person as honourable, we believe that the effective pursuit of our purposes requires us to bind him or her closely. In other words, for any one or more of several reasons we do not 'trust' the person to behave in the desired ways unless certain narrowly and precisely defined requirements are imposed. The example offered in the preceding paragraph, on the other hand, describes a situation where, because purposes are seen as shared, we repose confidence in leaders and behave accordingly – we 'trust' them.

This may be compared with a situation in which men are conscious of submitting to superior power in being directed towards the pursuit of ends they do not fully share. Those in positions of dominance are clearly unlikely to command the full confidence of those they dominate, for their policies and decisions are directed to purposes which to some degree differ from those of the rank and file. In such a situation those who are controlled are conscious of being used as means to other people's ends. This is not a formula for high-trust relations. While those who are controlled may see the controllers as personally honourable men who practise straight dealing, this does not preclude a conviction that they must be carefully watched and ways found, if possible, of influencing certain aspects of their decision-making. In place of the open problem-solving and free communications between equals that are possible in the situation of shared purposes, we are likely to see power manoeuvres between unequals which display all the characteristics of low-trust relations – mutual suspicion, bargaining, gamesmanship, defensiveness and distorted communications. This is the pattern which in its more marked forms becomes a 'win–lose' situation where each party automatically defines a gain for the other as a loss to itself, and vice versa.

Asked to apply these two contrasting sets of notions to industry, the manager may urge that the former should be seen as the more appropriate. His reaction would be understandable. Who, in running a large complex organization, would not prefer that the rank and file fully share his purposes and thereby feel able to trust his leadership, accept his authority, and extend full compliance with the rules, decisions and policies bearing upon them? Such hopes are rarely realized. More often he confronts some degree or other of low-trust response, and may be tempted to attribute it to stupidity, ignorance or moral weakness. We are none of us wholly free of these failings, but he would do better to take as his starting point the probability that, although they may trust him as a person, they do not feel fully able to trust him in his role as manager. What are the factors likely to generate this rank-and-file consciousness of being used as a means for the pursuit of other men's purposes – purposes with which they feel unable to identify?

What prevents rank and file identifying with management?

In the search for answers to this question we may usefully begin by recalling those national differences of culture and values, with their deep roots in history, that were briefly noted in the preceding chapter. Social forces and influences resulted in substantial sections of both the organized British working classes and the employing classes bringing to bear upon each other a wary zero-sum stance of attitude and behaviour which bred ingrained and almost automatic relationships of mutual suspicion.

The term 'substantial sections' is used advisedly. We are trying here to explore and explain those textures of employment relations which domestic and foreign observers alike have consistently considered over more than two centuries to be the most characteristic in the major industries of Britain. In degree, however, they have always varied considerably, and continue to do so today. There have always been some employers who, from religious conviction, ethical principle, shrewd insight, or hard-headed intelligent calculation, have managed to assert themselves against conventional assumptions and expectations, and build up what for them was a much more satisfactory pattern of relations on a foundation of mutual confidence. They might well need luck – an especially favourable market and profit position; an inexperienced workforce; a location somewhat removed from the principal arenas; a less alienating technology; a local tradition of deference and social peace. In more recent times, subsidiary enterprises managed by foreigners who come in with very different managerial styles and assumptions can sometimes succeed in creating a different pattern, especially if they combine a new and modern technology, a newly recruited workforce, and an indifference to the many class distinctions which help to preserve the British texture of industrial relations. The successful formula may be even simpler. An implacable resistance to trade unionism combined with pay, conditions, and fringe benefits significantly superior to prevalent local standards can work wonders, especially if combined with one or more of the features just enumerated. No feature or combination of features, however, can guarantee immunity in the long-run from the widespread textures we have been examining.

Among the historical reasons for the growth and persistence of those textures has been the predominant stance of governments and state agencies. The formulation and practical expression of the relevant attitudes and behaviours on the part of the working classes was made possible, ultimately, by the governing class's preferred strategy of rule. Given its members' determination, for their own good reasons, to avoid centralized autocracy, there was not forthcoming in sufficient measure the will, the ideology, or the state apparatus necessary for systematically inculcating in the lower orders the submissive habits of thought and behaviour evident in some other countries. Consequently the employee distrust which developed in workplace relations had a somewhat greater opportunity to express itself through self-protective and collective resistance to employer prerogative. In Germany and Japan, by contrast, autocratic rule and the ideology of loyalty and submission to authority that it enforced not only made such resistance more difficult, but even, to some extent, sapped confidence among the rank and file that resistance was legitimate. The greater the effort made by powerful and successful rulers to project an authoritarian ideology, the greater the degree to which the lower orders are likely to 'internalize' the message and to suffer a weakening of their will to resist.

In other words, faced with the organization structures and property relations of an emerging capitalistic order, the British working classes were more fortunately placed for collective self-protection than their counterparts were later to be in other industrializing countries.

Given these potentialities for 'adversary' perceptions, what features of work design and organization were likely to arouse impulses of challenge and resistance among the lower ranks? One way of approaching this question is to ask ourselves what changes in their position would prompt us to expect with some confidence that henceforth they would feel more ready to identify with top management's purposes and values. We would surely expect such identification if – after the appropriate training and personal adjustment – their jobs were to be redefined to embody much greater discretion, responsibility and autonomy, their position in the organization changed so as to ensure them individual treatment based on personal respect, and their whole pattern of rewards and status shifted much nearer to those of top management. In such circumstances they would be far more likely to feel included as trusted and fully participating members of a collective effort, and far more able, therefore, to identify with that effort and those who lead it.

What we have described, of course, are the circumstances in which most middle and senior managers, higher-level administrators and professionals of all kinds pursue their occupations. They are usually observed to be more identified and morally involved with their work situation than most wage- and lower salary-earners. The profoundly different low-discretion work circumstances of the latter cause them to feel excluded from more significant and responsible participation, and therefore not really trusted. Their inferior rewards (and the resistance usually offered by top management towards enlarging them) confirm their sense of being low-status 'hands' who are not seen as full members of the higher corporate effort. The old terminology of 'hands' and 'staff' embodied this crucial distinction. Current attempts to conjure with a new terminology which designates all groups as staff are unlikely to evoke the sought-for spirit of involvement so long as the realities of job, subordination and rewards remain the same. Rank-and-file members will continue to feel used by top management in ways which, by excluding them from significant participation in its purposes, render it unlikely that they will identify with those purposes. Admittedly it is not impossible for men who are totally excluded from significant participation in high purposes to identify with those purposes and behave accordingly. But such cases are rare. The private soldier who, in battle, identifies with the purposes of a High Command he never sees and which treats him as expendable is hardly an appropriate model for factory workers making pots, pans, cars and television sets for an anonymous commercial market. Their situation makes it all too probable that they will see top management's purposes as being in some respects alien to their own. Whether the purposes for which they feel used relate to private profit, managerial empire-building or some remote abstraction like 'the public interest', they are conscious that their needs and aspirations are being actively cultivated by management only in so far as this contributes to, or is at least compatible with, its own top priority purposes. What *are* their needs and aspirations? Their inferiority of treatment along all the dimensions of well-being, together with the circumscribed nature of their role and their exclusion from the centres of power, knowledge, responsibility and control, are likely to push them towards a preoccupation with such aspects of their personal stake in the organization as pay, working conditions, job arrangements and security.

This is not to suggest, as we hardly need reminding, that in being exploited by management to serve ends with which their lowly position and treatment make it difficult for them to identify they will necessarily be oppressed and totally deprived. Grossly ill-treated labour is not necessarily profitable or productive labour, though the history of slavery demonstrates that vast fortunes can be built on it in appropriate circumstances. More commonly the labour factor of production has been found to yield a higher return if certain of its interests and needs are considered. Strategies deriving from this discovery, such as industrial welfare and that of 'treating the worker as a human being', have often, as we shall see later, been hailed as

of surrendering protective work practices which, once lost, may never be recovered. Certain of these situations have multiplied over the past few years as world recession and Thatcherite monetary rigour have squeezed out many businesses or plants and have stiffened management policies towards labour.

For much of the time, of course, the issues are less dramatic than this. Many employees conscious of a divergence between management's objectives and their own simply become unable to feel any strong commitment to managerial rules, policies and decisions, still less to identify with their job in that spirit of dedicated loyalty which management would find so welcome. They respond indifferently to some rules, flout others, and generally manipulate management's system of organization in the light of their own divergent interests except when subjected to close supervision. Acquiescence by employees in the broad general principles of work organization is therefore quite consistent with their positive challenge of some rules and decisions and their negative indifference towards others. Thus develops management's awareness of its problem with respect to compliance. What are the means by which different managements have sought and currently seek to solve this problem?

Control through coercion

Anyone trying to engineer full compliance with a given policy can choose between two basic strategies, or rather between different blends of those strategies. These are coercion and consent. At one theoretical extreme he can try to rely on an overt exercise of naked power to force men to do his will even though they would like to resist. Alternatively, at the other extreme, he can abjure the use of coercion thus defined and seek by some means (which may still require the exercise of power, though in less obvious and direct ways) to engineer their 'voluntary' observance of the policy in question. Between the extremes lie graduated blends of the two methods. Overt coercion comes in degrees, and in practice all members of work organizations are controlled by a mixture of methods, though a person moving up an organizational hierarchy will in general be conscious of a diminishing coercion being used against him. For the moment, however, we shall examine the use and likely consequences of seeking control through heavy reliance on undisguised coercion.

Many of the forms of power required for this purpose derive ultimately from relationships of dependence. If someone is able to do me physical violence or subject me to physical constraint and I believe him to be prepared to use this advantage, my dependence for physical well-being and freedom on his goodwill is obvious. It is no less so if he controls resources to which I need access (for example, for a livelihood), or if I want his respect, friendship or approval. Whatever it is I value, the degree of his ability to control the supply is the measure of my dependence upon him, and the measure of his ability to use it to pressure or coerce me into forms of behaviour I would not otherwise have chosen.* Dependence rarely exists, of course, wholly on one side – in the first case I may be able to inflict at least a minimal violence upon him, in the second the resource controller may need something from me as well as I from him, and in the third the desire for respect, friendship or approval may be mutual. The important question is always, therefore, where the *balance* of power lies. Whose dependence is the greater? This is determined by the strength and urgency of the need on both sides, and the availability of alternative sources of supply for each of the two parties.

Whatever the nature of the dependence, it creates a power relationship. The fear of violence or physical constraint, of being deprived of access to desired resources, of having respect, friendship or approval withheld – these are only selected examples of dependence relationships in which the advantaged party enjoys a position of power that he can exploit, if he chooses, to compel me to behave in certain ways. What do we mean here by 'exploiting' power? He does not actually have to deprive me of whatever it is I depend on him for – the threat is usually enough. Nor do we mean by 'threat' that he continually needs to express it in words or gestures – a belief on my part, derived from experience or hearsay, that he is prepared to exercise his power if necessary is often adequate to ensure that I study his preferences with some care. It is where the superiority of power confronting me is greatest that I shall be most careful in considering my actions, and where the power-holder may least need to make it visible or manifest. In personal relations the effects of power can be traced even further. The power-holder may, without even being aware of it, reveal signs of displeasure which I prefer to avoid by taking appropriate steps to prevent the cause. The effects of power are thus all-pervasive, and its manifestations range from brute

* The term 'coercion' is sometimes fallaciously confined to the context of physical force. In fact, of course, any form of dependence is susceptible to being exploited to a degree experienced by the victim as coercive in its severity.

physical violence to the subtlest nuances of facial expression and tone of voice. All can be found achieving their effects in work organizations if we include those based on slavery.

The advantaged party in a power relationship may not, of course, exploit his power. I may become convinced that he would never, in the slightest degree, use my dependence upon him to determine my behaviour in any way. Such situations do exist. The rare plantation overseer may have made it plain that he would never use his whip, the rare employer that he would never exploit the threat of the sack, the rare colleague that he would never use my need for his respect to influence my behaviour. More commonly those with power use it; some crudely and blatantly, others with subtlety and restraint.

The exercise of power varies greatly in the degree to which it is publicly visible. We are keenly aware of the strikers who picket a factory and prevent it from operating, for we see them on every television news programme. We shall be much less aware of those who, six months later, decide to close it and throw them all out of work, for they are unlikely to be displayed on our screens. When a group of workers manifest power by forcing through a wage increase after a strike publicized with banner headlines every day for a month, we note this as a further twist to the inflationary spiral. When manufacturers, business executives and professionals 'adjust' fees, charges, prices or their own salaries they are far more likely to remain remote and anonymous. Wage-earners who impose stress and suffering upon a non-unionist by refusing to work with him can rarely avoid attention from the media. A dozen men round a boardroom table taking decisions which result in another company being forced out of business are not considered news. Even if they were, they are far better equipped to preserve their privilege of privacy.

In other words, some uses of power in our society are far more obvious and attract far more notice than others very much greater. Employee groups can affect management decisions on their own wages, working conditions, and sometimes production methods. In this they are the frequent subject of public comment, usually adverse. Far smaller executive and directorial groups take decisions on production programmes, prices, international plant locations, foreign trade, capital movements, credit terms and the money supply which significantly shape the fortunes of economic regions and indeed entire countries. Their activities come under much less public comment and what comment there is usually takes a measured, matter-of-fact and uncensorious tone. They are mostly presented as legitimate behaviours only to be expected from companies pursuing their legitimate interests within the rules of the system. It is difficult, for example, to recall any condemnation by the media of those who have greatly aggravated Britain's successive balance of payments crises by making profits out of currency movements against sterling. It is much less difficult to recall denunciations of strikers as selfish sectional groups using power unpatriotically to assert their own interests.

The point in noting these differences is to indicate what a distorted picture they create of the distribution of power. Reminded so often of such power as organized labour can muster, yet so rarely – and in such different terms – of the far greater power wielded by company boards in manufacturing, commerce and finance, we can be forgiven perhaps for accepting too readily the view which some were recently eager to offer us of organized labour usurping rightful authority and becoming the over-mighty estate. We shall not be able to think straight about such matters, however, unless we bear in mind that the palpable and visible exercise of coercion which tends to attract our attention is only one of the more obvious manifestations of power. Those uses of power which attract least notice are often the greater.

In Lukes' words, 'is not the supreme and most insidious exercise of power to prevent people, to whatever degree, from having grievances by shaping their perceptions, cognitions and preferences in such a way that they accept their role in the existing order of things, either because they can see or imagine no alternative to it, or because they see it as natural and unchangeable, or because they value it as divinely ordained and beneficial?' Here lies the relevance of the mass media, the processes of socialization, and the information technologies which modern governments have at their disposal for the management of opinion.

The exercise of control through coercive power has of course always played an important part in the rule by the few over the many. Its application in work organizations can be identified in its more blatant forms by recalling characteristic utterances by employers and foremen down the ages which have passed into the folklore of industrial life. They include: 'If you don't like the wages I pay then go elsewhere – there are men queueing up at the gate for a job'; 'You're not paid to think; you're paid to do as you're told'; and 'If you can't work harder than that there are plenty who will – go and collect your cards.' For every man directly assailed by such open threats there have been a hundred who did not need this experience to tell them where power lay and what its basis was – employer control over productive resources and therefore over access to a livelihood. Even though the power relationship might not be overtly manifest, the awareness of it shapes the behaviour of both parties.

Time has wrought some change. In many situations a more effective union organization at the workplace, or the protections introduced by dismissal procedures, or, until recent years, a tighter labour market, have modified power relations in ways which often oblige management to mend its manners and act more circumspectly in its handling of employees. Yet the essential power relations remain and the same processes continue, veiled sometimes by the politer euphemisms deemed desirable for public relations. Men are 'declared redundant', become 'surplus to requirements', or are subject to a 'labour shakeout'.

Conditions of effective coercion

Post-war labour scarcity and the managerial need to accommodate to increased employee independence, power and aspirations produced a reaction against the harsher, cruder, and more overtly authoritarian modes of rule. Much fashionable management writing appeared to suggest that these modes are invariably less effective in terms of practical results than the more urbane and manipulative ways of exercising power we shall be examining later. No universal proposition on these lines can be sustained. Given simple routine tasks requiring little exercise of discretion, judgement or initiative, and a large supply of weak defenceless labour, coercive power can achieve considerable results provided there is enough of it and that it is used sufficiently ruthlessly. The extreme case has already been mentioned. The vast fortunes of some of the English landed aristocracy were derived from plantation slavery in the West Indies and elsewhere, so their descendants could be permitted a smile at the proposition that naked coercion does not pay. Even short of that extreme, which included, of course, physical violence, coercion was able to secure perfectly adequate results for many an entrepreneur during the Industrial Revolution in Britain and elsewhere. What have just been suggested as the conditions in which coercion can be a perfectly viable instrument of policy if profits or output are the only criterion were in fact exactly those prevailing in some industries during earlier industrialization – thus the origins of the term 'wage-slavery'.

Both the conditions referred to above are indispensable. Coercion is well known to evoke all those negative responses referred to collectively as 'alienation', along with resentment, frustration and a disposition to evade performance of duties except when under immediate supervision and threat of punishment. These do not necessarily, however, destroy or even seriously detract from the profitability of the system. Having 'enough' power means being able to maintain constant supervision and punish instantly any tendency among employees to allow their negative feelings to have adverse effects on their work performance. If we translate this into modern terms we must imagine a power disparity so extreme that the employer feels free to discharge at once any employee guilty of absenteeism, lateness, obstructiveness and anything less than maximum performance. Few can indulge in such luxury today, but there have been situations in our industrial history which bore some approximation to this pattern for varying periods of time. But even this does not indicate the full degree of power necessary for a policy of total coercion. If those being coerced, though weak as individuals, are able to mobilize enough *collective* strength to strike back in some manner at their exploiters, the latter must set against the benefits they derive from the system the costs which result from this retaliation. It then becomes conceivable that the costs may in time begin to outweigh the benefits. The employer's power superiority must therefore be sufficient not only to crush all individual resistance to his coercive rule if the policy is to succeed, but also to destroy all collective challenges as well.

This brings us to the second condition. If the tasks to be done call for a significant measure of discretion, judgement or initiative, the limits of usefulness of the coercion strategy are much more quickly reached. A man can be coerced into performing routine physical movements with regularity and speed. But he cannot be coerced into making good judgements, exercising initiative or using his discretion creatively in the service of another person's objectives. Good judgements and creative initiatives spring from co-operative high-trust responses which involve his mind and spirit as well as his physical self. Faced with the aggressive, low-trust hostility and attempted compulsion embodied in the coercive exercise of power, his self-protective and defensive responses predominate instead. The greater the discretionary content of the job, therefore, the greater the likelihood that authoritarian patterns of management and control will, by alienating the occupant, render him incapable of those states of mind and spirit desirable for the quality of decisions sought by management. Conversely the lower the discretionary content the less it matters for management, other things being equal, what the state of mind of the job occupant is. The more the job can be reduced to routine physical movements involving only minimal discretion, the more coercive control can be applied, for the less it matters to management if the employee's resources of mind and spirit are impoverished and alienated.

When does coercion fail?

But in a world of change other things do not remain equal. Rising aspirations among occupants of low-discretion jobs for dignity and self-respect dispose them to be more resistant to coercive methods and policies. As individuals they may, if the state of local labour markets permit, manifest their dissatisfaction overtly by being resistant and obstructive or reveal their alienated indifference through high absence, sickness and wastage rates, or in the extreme case vote with their feet by getting work elsewhere. Where they find collective organization possible, they challenge the terms and conditions of employment which management seeks to impose on them, and may be supported in this by legislation, public policy and public opinion. These responses raise the costs for management of blatantly authoritarian methods and styles and prompt a search for other means by which it can pursue its ends without incurring such costs.

There is another reason for a shift in managerial perspective. In some industries it has become increasingly difficult for management to rest content with passive indifference among its rank-and-file labour force. Even on the assumption that its power superiority is sufficient to continue enforcing compliance with low-discretion, routine task behaviours, changing circumstances may call for more than passive uninvolvement even among those performing these humble jobs. Quickening foreign competition and accelerating technical change may require, from management's point of view, a ready and co-operative acceptance by rank and file of adaptation and flexibility. But such responses are unlikely to be forthcoming from those conscious of being coerced in their work roles by superior management power. Rank-and-file attitudes and habituated behaviours bred of earlier coercive work relations may prove costly for management when the need arises for accommodative responses which cannot be wrung from them by sheer power (even assuming it to be available). Management's requirements may change in yet other ways. Not only may there develop a need for ready acceptance of new technologies, but the new technologies themselves may require a greater involvement and sense of responsibility on the part of the employee if they are to yield management their full potential return.

The reasons now become apparent why management may find an overtly coercive strategy inappropriate to its needs. In the first place, the changing nature of the required task behaviours can render them quite incongruent with such a strategy. The more top management requires of a given job role that the occupant display judgement, initiative, commitment to top management goals and identification with the organization the less likely it is to use open coercion in its dealings with him. The nearer we direct our attention to the top of the hierarchy, the more we find seniors being treated by top management not as persons to be subjected to authoritarian discipline but as members of a fraternity who are assumed to be sharing certain objectives and who must be handled with respect.

Underlying this strategy are, in the final analysis, power considerations. For top management to subject the occupant of a high-discretion role to authoritarian discipline is to run a risk, not simply that he will fail to exercise his discretion in the service of top management's interests, but that he will exercise it actively in opposition to them. Special importance is therefore attached to his identifying with top management goals and values. For this reason alone, if for no other, we would have to expect the occupant of a role in the upper strata, possessing as he does greater individual autonomy to act for or against top management interests, to receive far more generous treatment than those in the lower strata. In other words, by virtue of the very job role allocated him, he has power against top management in the sense that he could, if he chose, use his job discretion – perhaps for some time before the fact was discovered – in ways which could do it considerable harm.

By contrast, the occupant of a low-discretion job at the bottom of the hierarchy has far less opportunity as an individual to effect such damage. To be sure, his ability to raise the cost to management of openly-coercive strategies has in many situations increased. As we have noted, such responses as high turnover, absence, sickness and wastage may emerge as individual forms of protest (though they can have additional or different causes) which are not easily suppressed, in the present context of social values and attitudes, by methods of naked coercion. But top management only begins to feel the power of these responses when they are practised by significantly large numbers of employees – when they begin to approximate, in other words, to something like collective expressions of protest. The individual by himself can make little impact on management through such behaviours. Similarly his discharge of his actual job tasks affords him, as an individual, far less scope for injuring top management's interests than is available to occupants of high-discretion roles. His freedom of choice is much smaller, and in any case should he use it in ways damaging to top management objectives his actions will be more quickly detected. These facts simply describe a situation in which he has far less power than the occupant of a high-discretion job and is that much less likely to have his interests carefully and spontaneously considered by top management. It is for this reason that he feels he has to combine with his fellows to bring collective pressure upon management if his interests are to be fully considered.

Historically, this kind of collective response has led many employers and managements to feel that in their own interests they must moderate their use of coercion and authoritarianism and search for other ways of promoting compliance among rank and file. Thus whether we are examining high-level, high-discretion jobs or low-level, low-discretion jobs, power considerations play a major part in inducing top managements to seek other methods.

How have these issues been affected by the mass unemployment that was allowed, and to some extent encouraged, to emerge under Labour and Conservative governments during the 1970s and 1980s? The disappearance of labour scarcity manifestly strengthened many managements and this created the possibility of their increasing the use of coercion in workplace relations. Much research will be necessary to obtain reliable judgements as to how far this possibility was seized; meanwhile the preceding analysis suggests the likelihood of a mixed picture. Undoubtedly in some industries and in some places, managements have paid off old scores with an exuberant use of their regained strength. It has long been a lamentation of some British observers that, under the trade-cycle pendulum swing of the balance of power, management and the managed take it in turns to squeeze from the other such advantage as they deem fit. As we shall see, some senior executives made no concealment of their exultation at the turn of events and their determination to use it for purposes of reducing overmanning and of reasserting managerial authority generally.

Any assumption, however, that there has been a return to heavily coercive management on a universal scale would be false. Collective employee strength at the workplace was certainly muted but it was very far from being destroyed. The new managerial stratum of industrial relations and personnel specialists certainly contains some who will have warned their line colleagues against too fierce an exploitation of coercive possibilities, on the grounds that there is a future as well as a present. Firms who enjoy what they judge to be a satisfactory pattern of labour relations may well have chosen not to prejudice it for the sake of short-term advantage. Managers who were conscious that effective performance depended heavily on employee goodwill and co-operation may have used their increased power circumspectly.

In other words, while there has unquestionably been a widespread quickening in managerial initiative and assertiveness on labour issues, there must be considerable doubt as to whether there has been the wholesale, once-and-for-all transformation that has figured so largely in Thatcherian rhetoric. Here and there managements may have sought to rid themselves altogether of the union presence in their workplace – a ploy not necessarily regarded by personnel management specialists as either expedient or even ethical. Others may have hoped to draw employees into 'participative' and co-operative relations with management, but on an individual, not a collective, basis, with the union and shop stewards having no recognized role in the process. Many shop stewards no doubt considered it judicious to moderate their claims and tactics; to make some accommodative gestures; to postpone some of their ambitions. A union rout, however, has not been apparent. Even if the effect has been to increase management strength it could never be a programme for full coercion; work cannot be organized in the modern industrial state on such a basis, if it ever could. It is time to turn, therefore, to a consideration of ways by which employers and managers have sought control while reducing their use of methods perceived by the controlled as coercive.

Further reading

Bendix, R., *Work and Authority in Industry* (New York and Evanston: Harper Torchbooks 1963)

Fox, Alan *Beyond Contract: Work, Power, and Trust Relations* (Faber and Faber 1974)

Lukes, Steven, *Power: A Radical View* (Macmillan 1974)

Martin, Roderick, *The Sociology of Power* (Routledge and Kegan Paul 1977)

Rothschild, K.W. (ed.), *Power in Economics* (Penguin, 1971)

Yoshino, M.W., *Japan's Managerial System* (Cembridge, Mass.): Massachusetts Institute of Technology 1971)

3   Industrialization and the strategy of consent

Control through consent

We have seen that a coercion strategy which may serve top management well given an abundant and defenceless labour force and tasks requiring mainly routine physical movements is likely to lose its appeal when these conditions are no longer met. If task definitions change in such ways as to require more of the individual than the repetition of physical movements, the alienating consequences of coercive strategies may well preclude him from being willing or able to offer the greater contribution required. Even if tasks remain the same, an increase in the power of those performing them – achieved through combination or labour scarcity or both – makes possible retaliatory behaviours of a wide variety of kinds such as trade unionism, indifferent performance, obstructiveness, higher turnover, absence, sickness or wastage rates.

But what is the alternative to coercion? Earlier we noted the alternative as being a strategy of seeking consent. In practice, management strategy is always a blend of consent and coercion, though the nature of the blend varies as between companies and between the various levels within each company hierarchy. The 'mix' usually reveals relatively more coercion at the bottom, relatively more consent towards the top. Consent covers a wide range of diverse forms and this chapter will be devoted to some of the more important. But first we need to note some considerations bearing on the notion of consent itself.

The essential meaning of power, as the word was used earlier, carries the connotation that sanctions are being used to pressure or coerce men into submitting to certain systems of rules and patterns of behaviour against their own preferences. But this is manifestly not the only basis on which men may work to systems of rules and patterns of behaviour. They may accept these without being coerced and without needing constant supervision, inspection and direct control by higher command. Here we examine the opposite theoretical extreme to that of total coercion. In this situation we might say that men fully legitimize management's rule. In other words, they offer full consent to it and to the policies and decisions through which it is expressed, so that management no longer needs to coerce. Spared the need to coerce, it avoids the negative consequences and retaliatory responses which so often result. We might say that the implication of employees giving full consent is that they 'authorize' management to govern them, thereby giving a special significance to the term 'authority'. Management can govern without this authorization by employing coercion, but it faces at best passive indifference and at worst militant hostility. The value to management of consent is therefore apparent.

The most attractive picture of consent, so far as management is concerned, bears the characteristics of the model sketched in the opening pages of the preceding chapter. This envisages the members of an organization pursuing common objectives and, in the interests of this shared purpose, willingly accepting leadership, direction and co-ordination by those appointed to serve these indispensable functions. Any disagreements are clarified by rational problem-solving methods to which the relevant parties contribute facts, ideas and alternative proposals, the ultimate resolution being made by reference to what will best serve the common objectives. In such a situation, management's authority, as we have defined it, prevails throughout. Coercion is unnecessary, for this is required only when employees would otherwise pursue goals, policies or behaviours different from those preferred by management, and this by definition is not a characteristic of the type of situation now being described.

We have noted that by the time the rank-and-file employee takes up his first job he is already, to some extent, socially conditioned in this direction. A wide diversity of influences have accustomed him to offer a generalized legitimization of many aspects of managerial rule and of the type of organization within which he is to earn his living. But issues and problems arise which are specific to the actual organization in which he works and about which he may well be disposed to challenge management policies. Moreover the very nature of the work he does, limited as it is in terms of discretion, judgement, autonomy and intrinsic interest, and far removed from the centres of power, involvement and privilege, can well fail to arouse the positive commitment hoped for by top management. Additional efforts are thus felt to be needed at the organizational level to supplement and reinforce the influences brought to bear in the wider social setting.

So now we must review the more important means by which employers and managements have sought to promote full compliance with, and legitimization of, their rule, including if possible that positive involvement and identification which is often their ideal. Most of these means are still to be found in use to some degree, so in taking a retrospective view we shall also be taking stock of a wide diversity of strategies currently being applied.

Pre-industrial work relations

For our starting point we can usefully go back to pre-industrial times. The pre-industrial workshop with its master, journeymen and apprentices, served a society marked by much poverty, deprivation, disease and superstition – and indeed by much brutal exploitation – but this is not all that needs to be said. The division of labour was, by our standards, minimal, and the small scale of operations made possible a personalized set of relations between the master and, as they were often called, his servants. To be sure, personalized relations are not necessarily good relations – the small master could sometimes be harsh and tyrannical. But at its best the system could display a not ignoble reciprocity by which the master exercised a diffuse concern over his employees, taking into account their moral and physical welfare as well as the development of their craft skills, and they returned a diffuse loyalty going beyond the narrow calculation of self-interest characteristic of a purely contractual relationship. These manifestations of reciprocal goodwill softened the edges of the essential core of master-servant relations – the doctrine of obedience. The very terms carry the message so vehemently asserted by all those in positions of authority – that subordinates owed unquestioning deference to the commands of their masters.

In suggesting that an approximation to this pattern survives here and there today we refer, of course, to the spirit of diffuse give and take which can sometimes prevail in small establishments. These are often marked by characteristics which make it possible for the employer, should he choose to do so, to foster personalized relations of a sort very much to his advantage. The small scale of operations often results in jobs being less specialized; employees enjoy greater variety and discretion in their work; and relationships can be less structured and more informal. They are also likely to be more diffuse, and this brings us to the spirit of give and take. What we usually mean by this phrase is that the two parties to the relationship do not try to hold each other rigidly to some predetermined set of specific contract terms. One may request a favour in the confident knowledge that the other will not demand immediate and equivalent reciprocation, but will grant the favour knowing that in the long run it will be returned when an appropriate occasion arises. Thus an employee may agree to work overtime without extra pay to complete a job, confident that if later he seeks an afternoon off without loss of pay to pursue some private purpose he will not be refused.

In such situations the parties trust each other to observe a diffuse (that is, non-specific) pattern of mutual obligations. The nature of what each owes the other is not precisely defined and each trusts the other to maintain a reciprocity over the long term. Of course either side may betray this trust. The employee may repay considerate treatment with indifferent work; the employer may repay long, devoted service with a lay-off during a slack time. Such failures of reciprocity are likely to destroy the bond. But otherwise the reciprocal honouring of trust maintains and, over time, strengthens it. Such are the features of what we might call a high-trust relationship.

An idealization of the past?

Our selective picture of pre-industrial workplace organization was designed to serve as a basis on which to erect a theoretical model rather than as an adequate historical account – which would require much more to be said. For example, in a wide range of acknowledged crafts many journeymen were already acquiring, during the medieval period, a set of wary low-trust dispositions and restrictive rules designed to protect their skills, status and earnings against masters who sought, individually or in combination, to cut costs by breaking down traditional work patterns.

Such situations exhibited the sort of power relations that could result where subordinates enjoyed a capacity to exert some strength against their masters. In many other pre-industrial workplaces, and in many small workplaces today, the absence of this capacity may make possible an appearance of harmony which is upheld only by a grossly unequal power relationship. 'We are all one big happy family here', says the small-scale employer of his non-union workforce.

The reality may be very different. If we see a group of men

co-operating as equals in the pursuit of a common purpose, some accepting the functional need to subordinate themselves to leadership and co-ordination by others, and all being prepared to meet each other's temporary contingencies in a spirit of give and take, we are right to consider this a high-quality pattern of human association. It is a high-quality pattern because it is a high-trust pattern. But the small work establishment may fall far short of this noble ideal. The handful of employees may be economically heavily dependent upon the employer. Yet the personal relationship he has with each makes it difficult for them to combine against him. The mutual reinforcement, anonymity and depersonalization which facilitate unionization in the large factory are denied them. Each stands in a face-to-face relationship with the man on whose favour their security depends. It is not easy for a person in such a position to pit himself against his employer in that stance of potential challenge which effective trade unionism implies. Instead he adapts to his position of weakness, feeling – though not necessarily from conscious calculation – that if he cannot secure his interests through an assertion of strength, he must do so by identifying with his employer and hoping that this will evoke in return an adequate measure of consideration. The employer, if shrewd and well-disposed, encourages this pattern. By extending humane treatment and promoting reciprocal give and take he builds up among his employees sentiments of loyalty and commitment which serve him in good stead.

Such a pattern of human association is not to be despised. There are many worse patterns. Yet it is open to the criticism which can be made of all relationships which rest on a highly unequal dependence of one party upon another. They are potentially demeaning to the weaker participant. He cannot take part as a free and equal agent in the mutual determination of the relationship. His weakness leads him to subordinate legitimate needs of his own to the interests of the other, to anticipate over-anxiously the other's wishes and preferences, and to adapt his own values and aspirations in such a way as to evoke approval. All these behaviours are gratifying to the ego and interests of the power-holder, who is apt to see them as spontaneous tributes to his own excellence rather than as manifestations which would still be forthcoming even were he half-witted. They betray, however, the highest standards of achievement in human relationships, which have to be defined in terms of equality of power and thereby of dignity and respect. Failing this equality, the moral standard of the relationship must always be suspect.

However much master–servant relations or employer–employee relations display outward characteristics of mutual trust and respect, they remain subject to proof if they rest on highly unequal power relations, for they have never been put to the test. And the necessary test can be expressed in the question: would the weaker party be content with the same pattern of relations — with the same allocation of rights and obligations, privileges and duties, status and respect – were he suddenly to find himself vested with an equal degree of power? If there is reason to believe he would not, the relationship stands revealed as resting on nothing more noble than the ability of one man to dominate another. A central principle of Western liberal culture – that the priceless value of the individual personality demands social institutions which provide free and equal scope for its expression and development – is being manifestly dishonoured. The situation would be one in which the individual, freed from the constraints imposed by weakness and seeking now his full stature, finds his present roles and relations cramping and demeaning. Only equality enables him to make this judgement – or to decide, conversely, that his aspirations and purposes are such that he can legitimize on a free and equal basis what he might be thought to have accepted previously only from weakness.

We see, then, that judgements on the quality of human relationships are more complex than they may seem. The pre-industrial workshop has often been judged a good deal more wholesome in this respect than many modern work situations, and perhaps it was. Certainly it is often suggested to us that the mutual respect which, at its best, marked the relationship of master and man, squire and labourer, parson and villager, was superior to the competitive conflict of today. Yet evidence is abundant that when the weaker parties to these relationships found themselves in a stronger position or were able to mobilize themselves collectively, they were prompt to demand changes in at least certain terms of the relationship. Perhaps the same would prove true today of many workers in small establishments where, on outward appearance, they seem fully to legitimize the rule of the employer and to be willingly receptive of their position and its rewards.

The impact of industrialization

Assuming it were true that such diffuse, high-trust reciprocations as did redeem pre-industrial work patterns rested on a basis of very unequal power relations, then we would have to say that industrialization proceeded on a similar basis, and moreover rendered these diffuse relations in many cases increasingly difficult to maintain even where employers would have liked to do so. Industrialization took many expressions, but prominent among them were an increasing division and mobility of labour, a growing scale of operations, the development of larger and increasingly impersonal markets (including that for labour), the quickening of competition, and the emergence of ideologies which legitimized and encouraged the pursuit of individual self-interest in the acquisition of money, status and power.

The combined effect of these and other associated features was greatly to weaken such diffuse relations as prevailed between master and man. The timing of this effect varied widely between different industries and trades for the obvious reason that industrialization proceeded at greatly differing speeds throughout the various sectors of the economy. Moreover the old traditional pattern of relations sometimes survived in vestigial form even in the face of growing size and new technology – there were always some manufacturers and businessmen who sought to preserve a paternalistic concern for their employees' welfare in the belief (sometimes justified) that this would ensure their loyalty and devoted service. But in substantial sectors of economic life there began to emerge what was to prove the characteristic pattern of employer–employee relations in British industrial society – a pattern marked by increasingly impersonal and narrowly contractual attitudes and behaviour, by mutual distrust and grudging calculation, and by the decay of whatever diffuse bonds of obligation might have mitigated the harshness of power relations in earlier times.

The reasons why the hard lines of power domination were now showing through more clearly and strongly can be traced to the structural changes just enumerated. The increasing size of work organizations represented a growing concentration of economic resources which meant correspondingly greater power for those in control, and the exercise of this power was less and less muffled by whatever traditional obligations might have restrained it in the past. It was directed towards constructing and upholding organizations marked by increasingly impersonal relations between master and man, by a division of labour which defined subordinate tasks ever more narrowly and specifically, and often by close and harsh supervision for the enforcement of these low-discretion task rules. The diffuse work roles and relations which had been acceptable to –

and perhaps even appropriate for – employers in the days of minimal division of labour, local personalized markets and relatively static traditional communities were not acceptable for pursuing profit in a world of expanding markets, large factories and increasing division of labour. Employers sought rather to make job definitions more specific, work rules tighter, authority relations more clear-cut and discipline more impersonal.

There was little room in all this for personalized bonds between master and man. Even where an employer saw value or benefit in trying to build up diffuse obligations of loyalty between himself and his employees, he found it difficult – and the results of his efforts increasingly artificial – in the circumstances of the large factory. Many nineteenth-century employers were, of course, only too glad to be assured that the general welfare of employees was no concern of theirs. Such an assurance was offered them by the social philosophy now favoured by many. It saw the employer and the individual worker as free and equal agents who bargained the contractual terms of their relationship as 'economic' men unfettered by irrelevant non-economic ties, bonds or obligations. Beyond observing the terms of the contract, employers owed no further debts to employees. They could abandon the notion – vague though it might be and honoured perhaps as much in the breach as in the observance – that they were responsible for the general welfare of their workers.

There were, however, some social observers, and even some employers, who fought a strong rearguard action against this abandonment of what were now idealized as traditional patterns of social relations. Critics like Coleridge, Southey, Carlyle and Ruskin feared the effects of competitive individualism and impersonal contractualism on the social bond – on the ability of the superior classes to maintain control, social cohesion, order, and civilization. In certain industries, such as the Lancashire cotton industry, some of the larger-scale employers sought to foster, during the latter half of the nineteenth century, more personal bonds with their workforce and with their local community. But there was never a critical mass capable of changing the texture and grain of British society. Unlike Germany or Japan, where authoritarian paternalism had deep historical roots as a national system of rule and was to be exploited by employers for their own purposes, Britain continued predominantly as a highly individualistic and contractualist society with a weak and relatively non-interventionist state.

Contract and master–servant relations

But, if the spread of the spirit of contract was gradually releasing the employer from traditional obligations towards the employee, it brought no such gains for the employee. For his part, contract was being interpreted as requiring him to go on offering his master a general and diffuse obedience along with a spirit of loyal and devoted service. In other words, injected into the notion of contract were all the traditional 'status' conceptions of master–servant relations. The status of the master and the duty of obedience which were read into the employment contract were urged upon the employee in the hope that he would thereby legitimize the employer's rule and comply willingly with his commands and policies. This was tantamount to hoping that although the employer was imposing more narrowly defined job roles, closer supervision and more restrictive discipline, the employee would continue to return the same diffuse loyalties as had been possible under earlier work patterns.

We can express the same proposition in terms of trust relations. In describing traditional work patterns we characterize the situation at its best as one of high-trust relations. By this was meant that on the basis of simple technology, minimal division of labour, high-discretion jobs, personalized face-to-face contacts, local markets, and only the mildest of competitive pressures, master and employee could, if they chose, conduct their relations on a basis of give and take. Neither party felt driven to calculate his rights and duties with respect to the other on a narrow contractual basis. As industrialization proceeded, however, the employer increasingly imposed on the employee what the latter felt to be a low-trust pattern of work. That is to say, the employer chose less and less to rely on the employee's spirit of give and take, but sought the output or work performance he wanted by imposing more tightly defined, low-discretion job roles, programmed work sequences, closer supervision and harsher discipline. Yet, while asserting a low-trust pattern over the employee, he hoped for a high-trust response in the form of willing compliance, loyalty and a ready confidence in his leadership.

The employee response

It was not forthcoming. Men respond to low trust with low trust. In an increasing number of situations, employees responded by withholding moral involvement in their employer's objectives; working indifferently and with little personal commitment, seeing the employer as pursuing his own interests to the exclusion of theirs; feeling used, therefore, in the service of goals not their own; manipulating the work situation for their benefit if opportunity permitted; practising restrictionism and obstructionism; organizing themselves collectively, if they could, to force the employer to pay attention to their needs as well as his; and in general by refusing to conduct their relationship with him in the full spirit of high-trust problem-solving. Like him, they adopted the stance of contractual calculation. They preferred not to rely on his goodwill, if they could possibly avoid it, for what they sought from the employment relationship. Many of them, for much of the time, could not avoid it. Such is the meaning of weakness and dependence. But while the employer's power might be able to suppress open challenges, individual or collective, by his employees, it could not coerce them into willing loyalty and co-operation, for as we noted earlier such responses cannot be evoked by coercion.

Even as the work patterns characteristic of Britain's industrialization were emerging, therefore, they revealed features by no means to the liking of manufacturers and businessmen. Employees too often failed to offer the desired motivation and commitment, remaining alienated and increasingly showing signs of organizing themselves against their masters. It is perhaps hardly necessary to add that only the occasional social observer traced their behaviour to their perceptions of those structural characteristics of the productive system which subjected them to low-discretion roles, minimal rewards and punitive discipline. For the most part employers avoided the uncomfortable implications of such an analysis, much as they do still, by blaming the rank and file for their moral weakness, laziness, irresponsibility or sheer stupidity in being unable to grasp the economic facts of life.

Here and there there were employers sufficiently motivated to seek ways of avoiding or minimizing what for them were undesirable employee responses. In Britain this search was quickened by developments beginning in the closing decades of the nineteenth century. Competition from industrial rivals such as Germany and America made many manufacturers more sensitive to the costs of, and the yield from, their economic resources, of which labour was of course one. Trade unionism took a stride forward not only in industries and trades where it already had a secure foothold but also in many where it had not. Rising standards and mass education were stimulating the beginnings of that upward curve in all rank-and-file aspirations which has continued ever since. Astute observers at all social levels were aware that irreversible changes were beginning to take place in the social position of labour – changes expressed also in the extension of the franchise to urban and rural wage-earners and in the recognition of poverty and deprivation as a social problem worthy of public discussion and calling for a public policy.

Within this total context two sets of ideas developed, each of which claimed to offer employers a useful strategy for handling their labour in such ways as to overcome the potentially alienating effects of modern large-scale work organization. One became known as Industrial Welfare, the other as Scientific Management.

Employer responses: industrial welfare

Sometimes referred to as 'betterment', the welfare approach concerned itself with such matters as the comfort, convenience and attractiveness of working conditions; providing cheap nourishing foods in works canteens; appointing welfare supervisors to support and counsel employees in their personal problems; promoting social, sporting and cultural activities; and, in some cases, offering good low-cost housing for company workers along, perhaps, with other fringe benefits such as pensions and medical care. Some expressions of this approach embodied no more than a belief that the complex mechanism that is man works better and harder if tended with care. Here the strategy merged with what later became known as industrial psychology. In its beginnings this worked to a view of the individual as a machine needing careful study to establish the optimum conditions of its physical environment. Heating, lighting, ventilation, working hours and rest-pauses were all deemed relevant to individual fatigue and, by the same token, to the working efficiency of the human machine. Many welfare measures contained no rationale more subtle than this.

In some of its expressions, however, welfare was informed by a strategy of greater significance for our present analysis. This was no less than the search for a renewal of the reciprocal, diffuse bonds of obligation and loyalty believed to characterize earlier patterns of work organization. If the employer manifested a concern for the interests and well-being of the employee – a concern for his physical, social and cultural welfare – would not the employee reciprocate with concern for the interests of the employer? Surely a demonstration by the employer of being ready to go beyond the narrow terms of the employment contract as ordinarily conceived would evoke a correspondingly generous response from the employee? Thus would the stark cash-nexus that was generating such bitterness come to be enriched into a relationship of new depth in which the employee offered willing compliance and loyalty to his employer.

It was not difficult for the employer with this conception to become convinced that he was treating his employees as ends in themselves, rather than as means in an exploitative relationship. Yet all that the welfare movement really demonstrated was a conviction that self-interest on the part of the employer did not necessarily require that employees be treated harshly and inhumanely. If this was so then good management seemed to require that employees be handled on generous and humane terms up to the point at which this policy was judged to be yielding diminishing returns. Short of this point, the employer – and even more his welfare manager or supervisor – might be able to assure himself of his moral virtue, which by definition was not yet being put to the test.

As we have seen, there had always been some manufacturers who tried, by paternalistic policies, to maintain a grateful and loyal labour force. Among them were Quakers like the Cadburys and Rowntrees, who were convinced that good morality was good business. Fair, humane and enlightened treatment of employees could not but benefit the company, it was felt, in the long if not necessarily the short run. And there were indeed situations where this seemed to be true, especially when the company appeared to face a prosperous expanding future. At a time when so many wage-earners were undernourished and overworked there might be economic advantages in a strategy which, by offering superior and genteel treatment, made it possible to select the most respectable applicants and promote their close attachment to the company by means of what, for the times, were considerate and humane terms of employment. That many aspects of this strategy were condescending and paternalist was of no consequence if the employees concerned accepted this view of their social status. No cynical calculation by such employers need be assumed. It was possible for a man with sincere religious convictions to want to succeed in business and to treat his employees kindly at the same time. If he were lucky he could do both, and it is naturally these happier coincidences which are likely to be recorded in the history of welfare. Many other employers, no doubt, would have liked to be kind but found their competitive circumstances such as to make them feel unable to afford such a luxury.

Even where they could, the welfare strategy was not necessarily successful. The greater the degree of conscious calculation which underlay it, the more likely was such manipulative intent to show through and promote cynicism among the very people from whom it was designed to evoke trust. In any case, while welfare at its best might maintain a tolerably grateful, firmly attached labour force which thought well of the company – and such characteristics were not to be lightly dismissed – it could not seriously be expected to fulfil the more extravagant hopes entertained for it. Welfare policies were not the natural extension and reinforcement of a diffuse high-trust relationship developing between master and man as they worked alongside each other. They did not spring from a personalized relationship made possible by a simple division of labour and small-scale operations.

Had they done so they could indeed have knitted bonds of personal loyalty by expressing a concern which evoked a reciprocal commitment from the employee. Instead, welfare policies were an after-thought grafted on to the steely outlines of the modern bureaucratic work structure, within which rank-and-file employees, pursuing their highly subdivided roles, were subjected to elaborate mechanisms of supervision, inspection and control; were far removed from the centres of power, responsibility and important decision-making; and were conscious of being used for other men's purposes which they had no share in formulating. If company welfare policies convinced them that their employer was a considerate humane man of paternalistic benevolence they might prefer working for him – and be prepared to speak well of him. But to expect them to be significantly affected by these sentiments in the intensity of commitment with which they applied themselves to their anonymous, fragmented daily work routines was to misunderstand the nature of human motivation in work. Men can apply themselves freely and willingly to a task in either of two types of situation. The task itself may involve them as whole persons, calling upon a range and depth of their skills and qualities. Alternatively, though their task may be a fragmented one they may be strongly committed to the end to which it is a contribution, feeling they are offering a willing involvement in a common purpose. The modern work organization provided too many of its rank-and-file employees with neither, and while welfare could both express and reinforce a relationship of reciprocal support which was generated and underpinned by one or other of these situations it could not by itself generate such a relationship in their absence. It could provide the icing on the cake, but it could not determine the quality of the cake itself.

In the event, the welfare strategy offered little lasting satisfaction for either party. For employees, the gradual rise in living standards as the twentieth century progressed, along with a slow improvement in the standards of treatment offered by an increasing number of employers, served to reduce the relative superiority of the pioneer welfare companies. Moreover, welfare itself in the cultivated paternalist sense was becoming less and less acceptable to its recipients. The heightened status of labour consequent on rising social respectability and aspirations, the increased coverage of trade unionism, an enlarged political role and the toehold of participation in governmental decision-making conceded during the First World War were rendering the paternalist concept outdated. The status implications of the father–child relationship, with the employees in tutelage to what the employer thought good for them, had begun to jar. Men started to wonder why they should not have the money value of welfare in their pay packet to spend how they liked – if necessary on a widening range of social and recreational facilities now increasingly available outside company boundaries.

These responses ensured that from the employers' point of view, too, welfare would never become a universal strategy even in its limited role of icing on the cake. Most of its practitioners soon decided that it did nothing significant to promote that unity of earnest endeavour which was the more ambitious purpose defined for it, and now even its lesser designs were showing diminishing returns. With the working week down to forty-eight hours, and with those lucky enough to have jobs usually receiving adequate nourishment by comparison with earlier times, there was less obvious return for the employer from policies designed to increase the physical efficiency of his human machines by tending them more carefully. Welfare, in short, was like any other resource available to management: it would be used in so far as management believed it to contribute in some fashion or another to managerial purposes, but would decline from favour as that belief became weakened or destroyed.

Later years saw some revival of the fundamental notion underlying welfare, this time focusing on the fringe symbols of status. The first step in this approach was to draw attention to the persistent differences of treatment, sometimes as between manual and non-manual employees, sometimes as between higher salary-earners on the one hand and wage-earning and lower salary-earning employees on the other, in such respects as pensions, sick pay, holidays, clocking-in, canteen facilities and various other fringe characteristics of the work situation. These status differences of treatment were then related to differences in the degree to which the respective groups were integrated into the organization in the moral involvement sense. The observation that superior status treatment in terms of these fringe characteristics is usually accompanied by greater moral involvement was then presumed to have direct causal implications. If lower-rank groups could be assimilated to the higher-rank groups in respect of these treatments, perhaps this elevation in terms of status would evoke an equivalent in terms of moral involvement? Some companies accordingly introduced schemes of 'staff status' for all or selected categories of lower-rank employees.

Such schemes were sometimes but one element in a wider programme which included other organizational changes such as the redefinition of jobs and the restructuring of supervision, so there would be difficulty in gauging the effects of so-called staff status alone. There is reason to believe, however, that like many other strategies in this field the staff status approach by itself is notable more for its hopefulness than its logic. To suppose that the greater involvement of higher-rank employees derives significantly from superior treatment in these fringe characteristics reveals the same neglect of the more fundamental differences in work situation that we noted in the earlier welfare approach. There is no cause to doubt that manual workers when offered tangible improvements in their terms of employment, such as pensions and sick pay, will grasp them with alacrity and may feel a stronger attachment to the company if these features distinguish it from others. And management may be seeking no more than this. But there is little sign that workers read into such changes a degree of symbolic status which is sufficient to elevate their moral involvement in the company to a significantly higher level. Far more basic changes than this are likely to be required – changes in discretion, responsibility, autonomy, sense of individuality of contribution, consciousness of membership of the high-trust fraternity. Possibly the only significant consequence for top management of equalizing fringe benefits and status symbols was a sense of grievance among some white-collar groups at losing the consciousness of privilege which they derived from these traditional superior benefits. Combined with other tendencies such as the depersonalization and intensified routinization observable in certain white-collar situations, this could contribute to a net loss of moral involvement.

Thus welfare is no more likely in its current manifestations than in its earlier forms to offer a major contribution to the problems of management we are concerned with here. If welfare could not fit this bill, still less could the other set of ideas with which we are concerned in this chapter, namely those underlying Scientific Management.

Employer responses: Scientific Management

At first sight there may seem cause for surprise that Scientific Management could be conceived by anybody as a possible basis for willing employee compliance and moral involvement. The reason for surprise is evident when we recall the practical techniques with which it is usually associated. Time and motion study, piecework and bonus payment systems, cost accounting methods and a wide range of other efficiency devices – these are redolent of a view of labour as needing to be programmed, graded and dragooned rather than as a potentially eager and willing partner in a common enterprise. Yet underlying the efficiency techniques of Frederick Taylor and the other Scientific Management pioneers was a philosophy which they saw as ushering in a state of industrial harmony, fruitful co-operation and mutual advantage if only employers and employees could be persuaded to break with the attitudes so often generated by industrialism. These can be summed up – to recall the terminology used in the previous chapter – as those of a win–lose game. In Taylor's view, employers and employees too often adopted towards each other a stance of opposition and conflict – the former acting on an assumption that low labour costs required low wages, and the latter, similarly, acting on an assumption that pursuit of their own interests required 'victory' in a struggle against the employer. Within the context of these mutually impoverishing sets of attitudes, employers practised unscientific rule-of-thumb methods and imposed arbitrary dictatorial government on employees, while the latter responded with unco-operativeness and restrictionism.

Taylor's solution called for a complete 'mental revolution' on both sides. In place of the mutually antagonistic win–lose attitudes, they were to adopt what was referred to earlier as a problem-solving approach to their joint relations. They must grasp the fact that if they dropped their hostile defences in favour of full collaboration they could between them so enlarge the total product that the fight about shares would be transcended in the knowledge that there was ample wealth for all. This 'mental revolution' was the essence of Scientific

Management for Taylor, who went out of his way to insist that it:

> is not a new system of figuring costs; it is not a new system of paying men; it is not a piece-work system; it is not a bonus system; it is not a premium system; it is no scheme for paying men; it is not holding a stopwatch on a man and writing things down about him; it is not time study; it is not motion study nor an analysis of the movements of men . . . it is not any of the devices which the average man calls to mind when scientific management is spoken of.

Rather it was an appeal to management and men to join in a unity of purpose on the basis of 'economic man' – on the basis, that is, of maximizing financial reward. To be sure, the description of Taylor's vision as a problem-solving situation might seem to some extent a misnomer, for he planned no creative role for labour in his proposed scientific transformation of work methods. Taylor's opinion of the rank-and-file employee was unflattering. His view was that most men were naturally lazy, evasive of responsibilities and of limited ability. They had to be motivated by the external goads of the carrot and stick – by financial incentives and punishments. But motivated along what patterns of work behaviour? These were to be programmed by the minority elite of planners, thinkers and analysts who were capable of self-motivation and self-control. They were to design the best methods and impose them on the rank and file. The proper destiny for labour was to seek maximum money rewards by submitting to scientifically designed work systems and incentives devised by the elite.

Yet a problem-solving spirit among employees could by no means be dispensed with even under this arrangement. For smooth and fruitful working it required employees to offer a willing and co-operative recognition of the job rules and programmes laid down for them – a recognition which derived from acceptance that these were the best rules discoverable for serving their own interests as well as management's. In other words, the problem-solving spirit was implicit in this very readiness to accept work methods which aimed supposedly at promoting the joint advantage of employer and employee. The suspicious obstructionism, wary manoeuvring and bargaining gamesmanship characteristic of the win–lose approach were to be dropped in favour of the trusting receptiveness, flexibility and open communications of the problem-solving scene. The employer also, of course, had adjustments to make. His contribution was that he, too, had to submit to the scientific designs of the work engineers and planners. He had, moreover, to rid himself of any

the economic system or the means employed to serve those ends, certain benefits in respect of living standards were filtering down which they could be presumed to welcome. Among men of power and influence, therefore, few were likely to feel driven to turn a searching eye upon the system which favoured them, and to see its basic features as responsible for the responses, at best often lack-lustre, at worst alienated and hostile, of rank-and-file employees. Less disturbing and more convenient was to see these responses as caused by foolishness, moral weakness or subversive agitators, and as being curable by managerial action, attitudinal changes or marginal modifications in the work situation which left the fundamental features of the structure intact.

Social man and the Human Relations approach

It is with these considerations in mind that we turn to examine the Human Relations approach. Taylor's hope of conjuring away the collective employee challenges and obstructions to management rule remained only a dream, but this very capacity among workers for group sentiment, cohesion and action was to prove the vehicle of the next managerial strategy for seeking employee involvement without essentially changing the system. It had been evident for a long time that employee work groups could evolve their own norms and values and thereby strongly influence the attitudes and behaviour of their individual members. Craft custom and practice among groups of skilled apprenticed men constituted a painfully familiar example for some employers. Some of the attitudes and work rules imposed by the group culture upon the members might benefit management, but there were many which it found restrictive and irksome. For the most part, in fact, group control of this kind was a tiresome constraint upon management, for its purpose was to defend earnings, job security, craft skills and group cohesion against threats presented by management in the course of pursuing its own objectives. Sooner or later, however, the notion was likely to emerge that the ability of group norms and values to influence individual attitudes and behaviour was a resource which management could turn to its advantage. At present the informal leadership and norms of such groups often ran counter to top management objectives and policies. But what if management could divert the leadership and allegiance of these informal work groups into its own hands? Norms and values could then be introduced into the group culture which favoured management's purposes. The springs of human motivation, loyalty and involvement which at present were so often directed along oppositional channels would be harnessed to serve management ends.

But how was this to be done? For one prominent group of researchers and theorists the answer was suggested by their explanation of why employees formed informal groups in the first place. The explanation was in terms not of 'economic' man, but of 'social' man. It was argued that industrialism and urbanism were destroying the small, close-knit, traditional communities within which every man had an acknowledged place and function, saw that his function, however humble, had meaning for his group, drew identity and recognition from his discharge of it, and derived satisfaction from his participation in the group's purpose. These, it was argued, were basic social needs felt by all men even more keenly than their economic needs. Yet these social needs were being ignored in modern work organizations. Management, in failing to direct planned effort towards the creation of the right social conditions of work, was denying employees all sense of identity, of belonging, and of participation in a group or community purpose. Since men cannot long endure this atomized and isolated state they try to meet their social needs by forging informal group links, acknowledging informal group leaders, and evolving informal group norms and values. Since this structure is developed by employees themselves out of frustration at management's neglect of their needs, it was likely to be oriented towards opposition to management. Hence the diversion of energy, commitment and loyalty to purposes divergent from management's.

The desirable strategy thus seemed to be apparent. Management itself must meet these social needs in a consciously organized manner and recruit group affiliations for its own ends. Managerial leadership must be substituted for informal (and potentially subversive) leadership by training managers in the arts and skills of winning men's allegiance. Such leadership skills were especially important for first-line supervisors and foremen, for they were in close daily contact with rank-and-file work groups. Included in these so-called 'social skills' was the ability to extend sympathetic consideration to employee needs and feelings, to offer supportive and consultative rather than punitive supervision, to promote in the individual a sense of group belonging and identity by recognizing him as a person with a contribution to make, to invite co-operation rather than extort obedience, and to promote a sense of group purpose in which all could participate. With the members of the work group now turning to him as their leader and offering him that spirit of commitment and identification which all men need and want to offer, the manager could use that spirit as a resource in the service of managerial ends. Such, briefly stated, was the essence of the Human Relations message for management. Properly and imaginatively interpreted and applied, such a strategy could, it was felt, construct for the atomized and isolated individuals of industrial society a social context at the workplace within which they could reknit the social bonds they needed and live satisfying lives. Thus could management both serve its own interests and strengthen the social fabric at the same time by consciously planning for a healthy harmony and common purpose, rather than allowing their organizations to drift by default into disharmony and unhealthy conflict.

This could seem an attractive message even for those with no direct axe to grind. For those few managers interested enough to listen it could seem a very attractive message indeed. Like the grander versions of industrial welfare and Scientific Management, it held out the picture of a unity of purpose which might still be recoverable from the hatreds and prejudices into which the work organization had fallen. These were due to management not yet having realized that willing co-operation in the conditions of modern industry could not be left to chance on the assumption that it would emerge spontaneously. It had to be actively promoted, and this required special management skills. All these skills required, by their very nature, to be exercised through communication with others. Projecting a democratic, supportive and consultative leadership, transmitting sympathetic consideration towards employee needs and feelings, expounding aims and purposes in a manner designed to evoke active co-operation from others, conducting processes of working through disagreements in such a way as to clarify the common purpose while elucidating the errors of fact or reasoning which had created the disagreements – all these called for careful cultivation of the skills of human communication. Thus it became – and in many quarters remains – fashionable to argue that the frictions and apparent conflicts to be found in industry were essentially caused by failures of communication. Management had not sufficiently developed its social skills. The special sin of trade unions was that, given management's default, they exploited these communication failures by deliberately organizing employees in a conflict stance, thereby rendering more elusive the spirit of shared purpose which nevertheless still remained within reach, given management will and ability.

Here, then, was a doctrine of good cheer for management. Admittedly its opening proposition might not seem to fit that description. The emphasis on informal group norms and values as the major determinants of individual attitudes and behaviour implied that the management-designed formal structure, with its rules, controls and incentives, was of lesser consequence. And indeed one result of the Human Relations approach was a concentration of research and theorizing upon small-group dynamics rather than upon the effects on behaviour of such formal aspects as technology, work-flow, control systems and pay structures, and their interaction with the organization's environment and wider social setting. Yet, though this opening proposition might seem initially lowering, the gloom could be quickly dispelled with the assurance that, given cultivation of the right skills, management could capture leadership of the informal groups. Reinforcement was also offered, for those managers who wanted it, to the notion that trade unions were essentially mischievous agencies with an institutional interest in sowing and aggravating distrust. But accompanying this reinforcement was the implication that they could be kept at bay provided management applied the necessary arts to evoke the willing participation and identification which, in their hearts, all men needed and wanted to give. Conflict was a symptom of faulty management styles, not of deep-seated perceptions by employees of divergent interest as between themselves and management. The central message which seemed to emerge from the whole approach, therefore, was that the arts and crafts of man-management as commended by the Human Relations approach constituted the most important determinant of employee behaviour.

The fallacy of social man

The first step in our critical examination of the Human Relations approach is to note the fallacy at the heart of it. Its theorists singled out for special attention the fact that employees showed a marked tendency to relate themselves to each other in informal groups whose culture then greatly influenced their individual behaviour. In answer to the question 'Why?' they explained these spontaneous group affiliations in terms of men's social needs. Employees came together in this way because they wanted the satisfactions and the sense of identity and belonging which could be derived from group membership and participation. The significance of this type of explanation was crucial. For if the objectives which men pursued through their involvement in groups were simply the *intrinsic* satisfactions of membership and participation, then by definition they might find one type of group goal as acceptable as any other. The vital condition for them would be that they involved themselves in a community of endeavour, and the exact nature of the endeavour might not be all that important.

The implications for the informal work group are plain to see. The Human Relations theorists had noted that it was often oriented in opposition to management objectives. But if the essential satisfactions for members derived not from the fact of the group pursuing anti-management objectives but simply from the fact of being integrated into a group *per se*, then the group could be oriented to pursue pro-management objectives without loss to its members. They would gain the same satisfactions from the latter situation as from the former. Provided management could offer them the same experience of group involvement, they would be as ready to follow pro-management as anti-management leadership.

If, on the other hand, the primary reason why men came together in groups was not to secure the *intrinsic* satisfactions derivable from membership, but to combine in order the more effectively to pursue certain *extrinsic* objectives, then the forgoing chain of reasoning collapses. The group would then be seen by its members predominantly as a means to certain specific ends. To be sure, members might also derive intrinsic satisfactions from their mutual co-operation, trust and fellowship which they would be sorry to lose, but these would not be the reasons why the group evolved. The basis of group affiliation would therefore be totally different from that postulated by the early Human Relations school, which envisaged members valuing the group not as a means to an end, but as an end in itself. If, then, cohesive work groups with their own norms and values developed, not to bring their members intrinsic social satisfactions, but to secure certain of their extrinsic economic interests against management rules, policies and decisions (or indeed against threats from other work groups), any management hope of winning the groups' allegiance was bound to seem forlorn.

Such a line of argument was disagreeable to the early Human Relations theorists. It suggested that the structural conditions of the business enterprise were such as to generate employee perceptions of certain divergent interests which might not easily be dispelled by management's social skills and sophisticated communications techniques. It drew attention to the conflict aspects of management/worker relations, whereas they preferred to stress the underlying harmony which they thought could be revealed by the correct managerial style.

The argument of this book has, of course, been that given the structural nature of the enterprise, and given the probable perceptions and aspirations of its members, along with the institutions and values of the society in which it is embedded, the prevalent stance among those performing lower-level, low-discretion tasks is likely to be of the sort described here as low-trust. In some industries, in some places, and at some times, management may succeed in creating a more forthcoming and malleable workforce. But for a succession of observers, domestic and foreign, down the centuries, this has not been the characteristic mode in British industry, and is unlikely to be described as such today. Management's imposition of detailed subordination and control is likely to be reciprocated by employee suspicion and often collective resistance. Managerial attempts to persuade employees to comply willingly in the interests of a common purpose have often foundered on the employees' experience that their welfare would be considered only in so far as this served, at best, management's enlightened, long-term interests, at worst a ruthless pursuit of short-term profit. Accordingly they have, where possible, frequently drawn together into cohesive groups and trade unions and, to the extent they felt necessary, resisted or obstructed management rule covertly or overtly in attempts to defend themselves within their work environment. If we apply this analysis to the Human Relations approach it leads to the proposition that the primary impulse behind informal group structure, in so far as its members evolve norms and values which run counter to management purposes, is to pursue the extrinsic goals of defending and advancing their job interests as they see them. Thus management is unable to rally such groups to its support by the techniques of Human Relations, since they spring from a distrust of management which they naturally turn upon the Human Relations techniques themselves.

So management continued to be faced with the same array of employee responses as before, for while, as always, exceptions were to be found, the return on these techniques was at best small and temporary. Meanwhile, in the post-war period, research increasingly documented a wide diversity of factors which could bear upon the perceptions of employees so as to shape their attitudes, the nature and degree of their grievances and resentments, and their manner of expressing them. This evidence seriously damaged the Human Relations notion that the nature and quality of management/worker relations depended primarily on management's skills in meeting employees' social needs (as this approach defined them). Increasingly apparent was the fact that work-group behaviour might be shaped by many other influences besides management's social skills. Indeed this much could be deduced simply from the observation that informal group behaviour was often strongly oriented not towards social needs but towards economic and job needs. This meant that all those factors affecting their economic and job interests, including not only those internal to the enterprise with their roots in organizational design and company policy, but also many which were external to the enterprise, might be relevant in explaining why employee groups behaved as they did. No outside observer of a particular enterprise at a particular time could explain its members' behaviour without detailed empirical inquiry, but he could be helped in making such an inquiry by knowing what lines of investigation it would be sensible to pursue.

Employee perceptions and their determinants

Reference was made in the preceding paragraph to factors bearing upon the perceptions of employees. The notion of perceptions is so crucial as to need a little elaboration before we explore the structural influences of enterprise and society upon work behaviours. We may begin by noting the obvious fact that observers wearing differently coloured spectacles see the same view in different terms. If we substitute for the spectacles the notion of a frame of reference which is a distillation of the observer's background, experience, values and purposes, the reason is soon apparent why, when we try to understand his responses, we must remember that they arise from *his* perceptions of the situation, not our own. A work group on a mass-production assembly line whose members have abandoned any aim they may have had of intrinsically satisfying work and who seek only to maximize earnings will conduct itself differently from one whose members would be ready to sacrifice some money in exchange for a more interesting job.

This emphasis on perceptions and frames of reference is crucial in the light of attempts by some post-war researchers to demonstrate that each given type of material technology or productive system evokes certain predictable patterns of behaviour from those operating it. The phrase 'structural determinants of behaviour', used in its strong sense, embodied this belief that generalizations could be made about how work-group dispositions towards their work, towards management, and towards the employing body were determined by such features as the technological system, job design, work flow, and other structural characteristics of productive arrangements. As empirical research was extended it revealed the weaknesses of this approach. Mediating between the work group and the objective work environment is the particular set of spectacles through which the members view it, and it is these perceptions to which they respond. The elements which enter into this frame of reference are many and diverse. Some of them have behavioural implications which are not too difficult to predict. If men's experiences at the hands of family, school, friends, job and the mass media sharpen their aspirations for a rising material standard of life but do not encourage a search for intrinsic satisfactions in work, there need be no surprise if they become especially aggressive and competitive about money rewards at the expense of other kinds. If their present standard of life is dependent upon remaining in work they can be expected to resist, if they can, being rendered unemployed. Other contributory factors to the frame of reference are more complex. Work groups with different attitudes to the control and decision-making structures of industrial organizations may react differently to the same type of technology. This effect becomes especially noticeable in international comparisons. Societies in which the workforce has to some extent been constrained to internalize a strong cultural tradition of deference to officially constituted authority offer a more favourable environment for managers in certain vital respects than do societies where attitudes are less respectful. This does not mean that societies in which the workforce is more independent-spirited are necessarily everywhere racked with overt conflict. If, in such a society, the managers in a particular industry, using a particular technology, feel able to offer employee spokesmen a foothold in decision making which approximates to their expectations, there may well be a greater acceptance by the workforce of the company and its technology than in other countries where the same industry using the same technology denies employees the voice they seek.

Many other factors are filtered through the individual or work-group frame of reference besides management's material and social technology. Some are external to the workplace. Employee behaviour in terms of turnover, absence, sickness and other forms which can often be expressions of discontent may be affected by the availability or otherwise of suitable alternative jobs. Some local communities have a tradition of militancy and hostility towards employers; others a tradition of accommodation and peace. Government action on, for example, labour legislation, incomes, taxation and rents can sometimes affect union or work-group behaviour, whatever management may or may not do. Trade unions to which the employees belong may have national or district policies, traditions, characters or styles which affect either favourably or unfavourably their members' receptivity of management initiatives.

All these are examples of external factors which can shape the values, attitudes and behaviour of the groups which the Human Relations manager tries to woo for his own purposes. Already it becomes evident that even these could be sufficiently potent in some cases to become the major determinant of work-group action. Such influences as the manager brings to bear on their behaviour through the arts and crafts of Human Relations man management might easily be swamped by other, more powerful forces shaping their responses. The case becomes even clearer when we add to these external influences a range of structural features *within* the organization. It is then apparent that work situations vary widely in the extent to which employee behaviour is susceptible to managerial modification by social skills alone. Some may be highly so, others not at all, and since the outsider with no special knowledge cannot predict a given situation in advance the manager is dependent in his choice of strategy upon an informed analysis of his own particular case.

Even though the manager may realize that a wide diversity of other factors besides his social skills can affect employee behaviour and that many of them are under his own control, it does not follow that he feels free to choose whatever material technology and work arrangements might seem to offer the best results in terms of employee attitudes and behaviour. There is always *some* extent – varying according to industry – to which management can choose, but the choice is always within certain limits. In every industry management is likely to feel that, to pursue its goals successfully, it has to accept the industry's own particular types of constraints. A decision to develop prototype electronic equipment in an environment of ever-changing technology and markets is also a decision to accept technology, work organization and group structure which need, for success, to be different from those seen as more appropriate to mass-producing rayon yarn – which in turn are different from those likely to be chosen for the continuous refining of oil. Each of these three production systems can exist in a number of variants – probably more numerous than most managements suppose – but each set of variations will differ from the other two. And management is likely to believe that should it attempt to go beyond these limits and constraints it will pay a price in terms of output, costs, profits or whatever other yardstick it works to. In other words, what is being recognized here is that even if certain forms of work organization and group structure could offer management a potential benefit in terms of employee attitudes and motivation, many managements might be conscious that adoption of these forms would involve costs in excess of the benefits – costs produced by the use of organization patterns which were uneconomic for the particular job in hand. This is to say no more – and no less – than that the organization of work according to society's present institutions and values often constrains management into constructing work systems which may subject rank and file to frustration of their social and psychological needs. Although this may seem a statement of the obvious it was denied by the dictum which could so easily be drawn from the Human Relations approach: that 'the happy and contented worker is the efficient worker' and *vice versa*. It was a dictum responsible for many disappointments. It ignored the possibility that the technological conditions which made a worker economically productive might also make him unhappy and discontented. Despite the hopes of a few, the stubborn truth remained that the technological and organizational forms which best served economic ends were not necessarily compatible with the social and psychological fulfilment of the rank and file. Stress-related illnesses, by popular myth the special affliction of top executives and managers, are in fact more widespread throughout the lower ranks. It is tempting for the liberal-minded observer, noting the costs of such illnesses for the national economic effort, to believe that they outweigh the material benefits of present production techniques and organization. In the absence, however, of any precise appraisal it is sentimental to assume that there is necessarily a felicitous full compatibility between man's various needs. Here, as in other spheres of life, full compatibility is less apparent than the need for trade-offs. This alerts us to the important questions of how and by whom the trade-off points are determined; what influence is exerted, if any, by those whose lives are most affected by them; and how, where they do have influence, their preferences were formed in the first place. For the answers we have to revert to the debate about the structure of social power and to the differing interpretations, noted in preceding chapters, of how our society works.

Economic man and his significance for management

Whatever conclusions we reach from these debates about the social forces which shape our values and priorities, it can hardly be denied that economic ends and means rank high among the preferences which result. The informal or formal rules and objectives of the work group are normally related, not to social needs as the Human Relations approach defined them, but to economic welfare, economic security, and freedom from arbitrary rule in pursuit of these ends. This is not to say that employees are conscious of having no other interests in their work situation. Needs conflict within individuals as well as between them, and many employees have social and psychological interests in their work situation which they could only pursue by forgoing economic interests. Usually they share the priorities of their managers in putting their economic interests first – hence a prime source of conflict.

This brings us, then, to further sets of structural influences on employee behaviour. We have just seen how different technological, engineering and related organizational factors can evoke different employee responses with respect to the formation of attitudes, grievances and the manner in which they are expressed and pursued – differences for which Human Relations techniques had only a partial and limited relevance. Now we need to note that employees' economic needs interact with pay systems and pay structures in ways which often create problems that certainly call for management skills, but not those skills described by Human Relations as 'social'.

There is hardly need to emphasize that people doing work from which opportunities for intrinsic satisfaction have been largely excluded are likely to view their jobs principally in terms of the extrinsic rewards of pay and the security attending those rewards. They will not necessarily be discontented with this situation. There is reason to believe that large numbers of wage-earners and lower salary-earners, seeing no practical alternative, come to terms with their presumed destiny by adapting their aspirations accordingly. They expect, or teach themselves to expect, no more from work than the pay packet and perhaps good relationships with a few fellow-workers. Given adequacy along such dimensions, many will declare that they experience 'job satisfaction'. Absence of moral involvement and identification does not necessarily, therefore, mean dissatisfaction for men conditioned not to expect them. It is, however, likely to evoke from them an especially exclusive preoccupation with the cash nexus. Such attitudes are sharpened by the plenty which industrial society displays before them. They are strengthened further by inequalities which we shall examine again later.

Given this central role of pay in the jobs of many wage-earners and lower salary-earners, there is no cause for surprise that managements can be found intensifying the vicious circle by manipulating pay as a direct and immediate incentive to evoke desired behaviour. There is less need for this in high-discretion work. In jobs which have not had the potentiality for high intrinsic involvement designed out, the possibility exists that such a potentiality will generate within the individual a capacity for internal self-discipline which needs neither the stick of close supervision nor the carrot of direct economic incentive. But few rank-and-file jobs retain a significant quota of these potentialities and possibilities, and the role of the financial incentive has become even more marked in one form or another. Certainly, with pay as the central feature, people performing such jobs respond to direct financial incentives in a way they rarely do otherwise. Work pace under payment by results tends to be markedly different from work pace under payment by time, though the former system can display off-setting disadvantages which have become increasingly apparent.

Employee responses to payment by results systems have thrown up some of the most familiar examples of group behaviour antipathetic to management interests. Employees may be interested not only in financial rewards but also in the security of those rewards. Fearful that too unrestrained an effort by each to maximize his earnings would result in individual members of the group being found 'surplus to requirements' or in management finding some excuse to cut piece-rates, work groups have often imposed controls over the effort and earnings of their members, supporting these rules with informal sanctions which expressed group approval or disapproval. The early Human Relations school viewed these efforts not as rational responses to understandable fears but as largely irrational gestures arising from employee frustration and resentment born of management's neglect of their social needs. This view was of a piece with the desire to see the enterprise as needing only the right managerial social and leadership skills to become an integrated structure which provided its members with identity, recognition and a sense of meaning and belonging. To regard what became known as 'restrictive practices' as rational responses to understandable fears they would have had to take much more seriously the notion that work groups might reasonably see some of their interests as divergent from management's – not a notion which accorded happily with the Human Relations approach or the social philosophy underlying it.

Neither were Human Relations techniques adequate in themselves to deal with another potent influence on employee behaviour – the dynamics of pay structures. This category of problems was referred to earlier as economic in nature, but this is only partly true. Many of the disputes with which we are familiar are not, in the deepest sense, about money but about something else. A simple example will suffice. If we are told that, on account of our specially valued contribution, we are to receive a salary increase of £750 while colleagues are receiving only £500, our mood is likely to be a cheerful one. If, on the other hand, we discover that while we are to receive £1000, they are to receive £1500, a certain moroseness would no doubt be evident. What would we be morose about? Clearly not the absolute size of the increase, for we would have been cheerful with less. Our grievance would derive from the *relative* deficiency, which would no doubt cause us to feel a sense of injustice or shock at this evidence of our low rating. In other words, differentials in money rewards, rather than the absolute size of the money rewards themselves, are the really explosive issue.

This makes 'fairness' a crucial concept in management/worker relations. It would present much less of a problem were there to be a criterion of fairness on which all could agree. In fact there are many conflicting criteria. To management it may seem only 'fair' that the 'loyal' employee should receive more than the indifferent, the strong and hardworking more than the weak and indolent, or the married more than the unmarried. To employees, who may have learned by experience that such principles can be used to divide and weaken them, these criteria may lack all moral validity. But these are the simplest of divergences, and there are many others. Should we compensate men according to manual skill, responsibility, bad conditions, intrinsically unrewarding work, seniority, organizational profitability, job discretion, training required, cost of living, general principles of reducing inequalities, or any other item in a list which could still be extended? All are advanced as criteria of fairness and all are capable of offering different answers to given problems of differentials.

These problems extend, it is hardly necessary to remind ourselves, far beyond organizational boundaries. Suppose it is thought fair for a police constable in rural Dorset to receive the same rate as a constable in Oxford, or for a railway porter in Cornwall to be on a par with a porter in Coventry. This might be defended with the slogan: 'The rate for the job'. Yet at the height of car-production prosperity the constable in Oxford and the porter in Coventry were poor relations alongside the highly-paid car assembly workers in the same cities. They could well have considered it unfair that even an unskilled labourer could receive as much as themselves by the mere accident of a job in an industry which was able to pay such high rates simply through the freaks of market and technology. Yet the redress of grievances of this sort would only transfer them to Dorset and Cornwall, for why should porters and policemen be fobbed off with less simply because they live in the country?

Such are the endless dilemmas of money reward. In a society where money can buy so much these dilemmas are inevitably invested with strong emotions, yet there is widespread failure to grasp their full significance. Economists, government spokesmen, employers and other members of the favoured classes are apt to set store by calculations which show that if all very high incomes were distributed equally it would raise standards per head by only a small margin. They offer such calculations as arguments against egalitarianism. There seems difficulty in grasping that the egalitarian attacks great inequality not only on grounds of absolute standards but also on grounds of moral offensiveness.

Clearly the skills which will serve management best in coping with these complexities are not those required for ministering to employees' needs for identity, recognition and a sense of belonging, but those required for an objective, patient appraisal of the economic aspirations and perceptions of different groups, for an analytical examination of facts and trends in rates and earnings, and for a shrewd judgement of power relations among, and the mood and temper of, the groups under its rule. Lacking access to such skills, management may find the structure of pay and earnings within the organization so overtaken by anomalies, inequities and contradictions as to become itself a potent source of disorder and disruption among work groups. Social skills as defined by the Human Relations school will not help management here. That these pay systems and differentials can be an independent structural influence in their own right on employee and group behaviour can be demonstrated by means of an example. We may imagine two plants exactly identical in product, technology, labour force and every other sense except that one is governed by a pay structure which management, by a judicious blend of rational argument, persuasion and power, has preserved as a stable, coherent system largely legitimized by its employees, and the other by a structure which management has allowed to become riddled with what are seen by employees as inconsistencies and anomalies. It is a fairly safe prediction that despite being identical in every other respect the two plants would differ sharply in their record of disputes and distrust.

The same reasoning can be applied to the rest of management's personnel and labour relations policy. If this takes the form, not of a planned and consistent overall strategy, but of piecemeal, hand-to-mouth expedients to meet a succession of emerging problems and issues, the resultant contradictions and confusions can only become another addition to the structural influences which can make management's task of governing more difficult. And, as with the other factors, solutions satisfactory to management are likely to require analytical ability, negotiating flair, insight and courage rather than social skills.

Organizational character

Even a manager well-endowed with these qualities and abilities meets a special problem when he takes over a new command, for he inherits a situation created by predecessors. This proposition may seem as unexceptionable as it is obvious, yet we are apt not to grasp its full significance. Inheriting a situation created by predecessors means inheriting sets of attitudes, assumptions, hopes, fears and expectations among employee groups which others have played a major part in bringing about. One's subordinates, and for that matter one's colleagues and superiors, have a dimension in history which has led them to expect certain things for themselves and to expect certain behaviours from others. These established attitudes and expectations within the organization play a considerable part in shaping the behaviour of new entrants – including the new manager. The way people perceive and behave towards us is often the major factor in determining how we perceive and behave towards them. If they act with suspicion and distrust it needs a considerable conscious effort on our part not to respond in the same manner.

This tendency illuminates one of the ways in which an organization may be said to have a character. Applied to management/worker relations, it means that employee attitudes and expectations brought to bear upon a new manager represent a distillation of their previous experience. In other words, the frame of reference through which they perceive, interpret and evaluate the manager's behaviour and policies will to some extent, however much they aim to 'give the new man a chance', reflect the attitudes and expectations, good or bad, created in them by his predecessors. Unless the newcomer is socially aware to an unusual degree and consciously aspires to break with established patterns of behaviour, he will tend to be drawn by them into certain reciprocatory responses which ensure that the established patterns in fact continue. Thus is the newcomer socialized into the character of the organization. Social mechanisms of this sort contribute to continuity in organizational processes, a continuity which we all have occasion sometimes to applaud, sometimes to deplore. In some respects we approve the fact that habitual patterns of perceptions and responses ensure the ongoing continuance of organizational life, in others we may wish that behaviour were more flexible and quickly adaptable to change. But whatever the balance of our preferences, the tendency of habitual behaviour to persist remains a fact. This is why historical depth is an indispensable dimension of understanding and insight in the field of management/worker relations, as in other types of human interaction.

With this structure of established attitudes and expectations, existing in the form of a diverse set of organizational subcultures, we acknowledge yet another determinant of employee behaviour, the last of which we can take notice of here. We have been led into this brief review of some of the more important behavioural influences by the need to examine the message which so often seemed to be projected by the Human Relations approach; that the nature of employee behaviour and of relationships with management depended most importantly on management's social skills. Even the limited sketch we have provided for ourselves here indicates that attempts by management to draw employee work groups into an integrated structure of problem-solving co-operation towards a common purpose are likely to meet with strongly resistant counter-tendencies. What is clear is that many job structures created by the industrial revolution, as perceived by their occupants, generate resistances, grievances and claims which have their roots not in the occupants' need for a sense of belonging and meaningful participation in the organization, but in the need for furtherance of their economic interests and security and for protection against arbitrary rule and injustice. Indeed, it is precisely the manifest failure of the work organization as we know it to convince the rank and file that the latter needs will be adequately respected that has so weakened their motivation to behave as willing and co-operative participants. The argument has led us back, in other words, to the proposition that the modern, large-scale work organization fails, in general, to secure the moral adhesion of its rank and file – which is only another way of saying that it fails to draw them into an integrated community of purpose with top management.

The Human Relations approach, like other strategies we have examined, represents an attempt to retain the economic benefits of hierarchy, extreme division of labour and elaborate authority structures while avoiding their costs as manifested in a largely indifferent or actively hostile rank and file. It seeks to draw them into an integrated community of purpose without, however, changing the basic structures of job design, reward, decision making and authority relations within which they are located. The failure of this approach produced a gradual increase in readiness to look somewhat more searchingly at the nature of the employee's job in its structural context. The attempt to integrate employees purely by means of management styles, personal leadership techniques, and other devices which left work and decision-making structures virtually intact, had not offered the hoped-for return. Perhaps it was time to think whether marginal modifications in such structures could be devised which strengthened employee compliance and motivation but did not involve offsetting losses in technical efficiency. As ideas developed along these lines it became increasingly clear that what was centrally involved here was decision-making and the widely varying degrees to which members of the organization participated in it. Our task in the next chapter will be to develop this notion and what it logically implies.

Further reading

Baritz, L., *The Servants of Power* (New York: John Wiley and Sons 1965)

Child, J., *British Management Thought* (Allen and Unwin 1969)

Friedmann, G., *Industrial Society* (The Free Press 1964)

Gallie, D., *In Search of the New Working Class* (Cambridge University Press 1978)

Goldthorpe, J.H., Lockwood, D., Bechhofer, F., Platt, J., *The Affluent Worker: Industrial Attitudes and Behaviour* (Cambridge University Press 1969)

Goldthorpe, J.H., Lockwood, D., Bechhofer, F., Platt, J., *The Affluent Worker in the Class Structure* (Cambridge University Press 1969)

Robinson, D., (ed.), *Local Labour Markets and Wage Structures* (Gower Press 1970)

Tillett A., Kempner, T., Wills, G., *Management Thinkers* (Penguin 1970)

5   Consent and participation in decision-making

Prescribed and discretionary aspects of work

The 1960s and 1970s saw a heightening discussion of 'employee participation'. The emphasis came both from 'progressive' management thought and from the radical left. This is itself enough to demonstrate that participation meant very different things to different people. On the left it was seen by some as a move towards 'workers' control'; by others more modestly as a way of strengthening management accountability to employees and their unions. Those deemed to be in the vanguard of management thinking and practice saw it, ultimately, as a means towards enhancing the legitimacy of management, improving relations, and avoiding 'wasteful confrontation' in an age of rising employee expectations. For the latter group the importance of doing something about participation was greatly enhanced, given the radical flavour of the times, by the need to pre-empt dangerous demands coming from the left. For the relevant functionaries of the European Economic Community, especially, it was necessary to display leadership and initiative by promoting 'harmonization' (a euphemism for the less appealing notion of a contrived uniformity) among member states on the basis of employee representation on company supervisory boards and work councils.

The discussion here, however, will be broadened by conducting it in terms of participation in decision-making viewed in its widest sense. This requires us to recognize that decision-making is not, as some appear to believe, an activity pursued only at managerial levels. Much discussion seems to assume that decisions are made only by managers. If this is the starting assumption, participation in decision-making by the rank and file comes to seem simply a matter of their participating in other men's decisions – namely those of supervisors and/or the various managerial ranks arrayed above them. This has the consequence of shifting discussion almost at once on to the theme of employee representation on managerial or directorial boards and committees. For although the individual employee may be able to participate directly and personally in certain of the decisions made by his immediate supervisor, the stage is soon reached when his involvement in decisions at higher levels has to be indirect, through representatives. Thus debate tends to revolve round the nature and extent of this indirect, representative participation in which only a tiny proportion of the rank and file are personally involved.

It will be convenient, before exploring the inadequacy of the indirect representation approach, to note the range of managerial decisions which, in theory if not yet in practice, are open to this mode of participation. The discussion can be simplified by means of a crude categorization which serves to illustrate the possibilities. There are what might be called 'personnel' decisions covering such issues as wage rates and salaries, hours of work, hiring and firing, promotion and transfers, overtime pay, shift arrangements and holidays. 'Social' decisions might be thought to bear on the administration of welfare programmes, health and safety regulations, pension funds and the like. The notion of 'economic' decisions could be used to cover (*a*) 'technical' issues concerning methods, materials, organizational arrangements, production planning and control, division of labour and the design of jobs, and (*b*) 'business' issues such as organizational objectives and priorities, markets and sales, expansion or contraction of operations, rationalization, capital investment, distribution and use of profits, changes in plant organization, mergers and so on. No significance attaches to the names given to these categories, and the allocation of items to categories is in many cases quite arbitrary. Moreover it is often difficult to treat the categories as separate, for an item in any one may be bound up with items in either or both of the other two. Nevertheless they give some notion of the range over which participation could conceivably extend.

An even wider perspective on participation is afforded, however, once we remember that to see decision-making solely as a managerial activity is fallacious and is bound to distort subsequent discussion. Every job in the organization, however humble, involves making decisions. Decision-making is simply a process of choosing between alternatives, and no job can be performed without making choices. The chief executive and the board have to decide, for example, the rate and allocation of capital spending; the office cleaner has to decide what degree of thoroughness is appropriate if the job is to be completed before the staff arrive. In making choices between alternatives the employee, at whatever level, is exercising discretion.

Without the opportunity to choose between alternatives there can be no decision-making and therefore no discretion. Thus since every job calls for choices, every job may be said to have discretionary content. Discretion is always exercised within certain prescribed limits which leave the occupant no discretionary choice and therefore involve him in no decision-making. The decision has already been made. It comes to him in the form of a prescription and he is required only to obey it. The chief executive and the board make choices within limits set by contractual obligations, collective agreements, company law, insurance stipulations, health and welfare legislation, and a host of other constraints which in effect deprive them of discretion over a wide sector of their behaviour. The office cleaner works within prescribed limits set by arrival and departure times, by the areas of responsibility allocated, and by the implements and materials supplied.

The difference between the prescribed and the discretionary aspects of work can also be presented in terms of specific and diffuse obligations. The prescribed elements impose upon the job occupant certain specific obligations – as when the manager instructs his secretary always to keep in stock a specified number of the appropriate postage stamps to deal with the day's posting of mail. Discretionary elements, on the other hand, impose diffuse obligations. There are no specific definitions laid down and the job occupant has to make a personal judgement as to what is required (in other words, make a decision) – as when the manager instructs his secretary only to be careful to keep 'enough' stamps in stock and leaves it to his or her discretion how many is enough.

Thus in designing a job, or in other words defining the nature of its duties, the job designer has to decide which aspects of the job to leave to the discretion of the occupant, and which to prescribe for him in the form of choices already made (decisions already taken). Prescriptions can be embodied not only in contractual and legal obligations and negotiated commitments, but also in machinery, jigs and patterns, programmed procedures, budgetary controls, and operating rules of many diverse kinds. From this point of view, the organization can be seen as a continuing series of decision-making events within prescribed limits, and we can ask of it the all-important question: How are these powers of decision-making distributed throughout the system? Or, to put the same question another way: In what diverse ways and to what diverse degrees do the various members of the organization participate in this total process of decision-making that constitutes the organization as an ongoing concern?

We are thus now using the language of 'participation in decision-making', but with one important difference. As we have noted, this phrase usually refers to some form or another of participation in other men's decisions, as when supervisors and managers practise so-called 'participative management' by inviting the subordinate to contribute in some way to their decision-making, or when employees serve on consultative or policy-making committees with management, or participate as representatives on directorial boards. The present analysis, however, emphasizes that the individual's own job also determines, by the degree of discretion it carries, how far he participates in the total process of decision-making which the organization requires.

With this in mind we can ask of any employee two crucial questions: first, how many, and what quality of, decisions is he able to make in his own job; and second, what degree of influence does he have upon other people's decisions in which he may feel to have an interest?

Decision-making and moral involvement

The significance of these questions for the themes explored in this book has been implicit in some of the propositions advanced earlier, but it must now be made explicit. There is growing reason for believing that, in our kind of society, the degree of moral involvement and identification generated within the individual towards his work situation bears some relation to the degree and nature of the discretion it affords him. This is not a simple and direct connection. There are some who are temperamentally averse to this kind of involvement in work, or who have been irreversibly conditioned by family, sub-culture and their own work experience to expect or demand none. These may opt for low-discretion work and resist any change in it. Moreover enlargement of discretion does not necessarily affect the job-occupant's behaviour. Yet observation does suggest a widespread capacity among men to develop a moral involvement as their job makes greater and deeper demands on them, and conversely, to become to some degree alienated and indifferent if it requires only mechanical performance of routine activities planned and designed by others. Should this be so, there would be no occasion for surprise. The greater the extent to which one's job requires only the performance of tasks already programmed and decided upon by others, to the relative exclusion of choices made by oneself, the less one's individual self is involved in the activity. The old term 'factory hands' can thus be seen to be highly appropriate, for the mind, heart and spirit are not being invited to participate. The faculty most in demand is that of obedience to prescribed rules – given, of course, whatever training may be needed. This does not seem the sort of job situation likely to evoke from most people subjected to it a contribution of moral involvement and personal identification. Such a contribution is more likely, for most of us, to be evoked by a situation in which we are called upon to express our individual and unique self through the exercise of choices in a process of decision-making about issues to which we attach significance.

Here we can establish links between the language of discretion and of trust relations. As already noted, this use of the word 'trust' refers not to the personal relationships involved in face-to-face contacts, but to trust – or distrust – in so far as it is embodied in the rules, roles and other policies and arrangements which some men make for others. The greater the degree of discretion extended to a person in his work, the more he feels that the relevant rules and arrangements embody a high degree of trust. This high trust suggests to him that those controlling his work destinies see him as one of their own fraternity, to be treated with respect as an individual person whose interests must be considered. Such a relationship is likely to generate in him something of the personal involvement being discussed here.

Conversely, the occupant of a job of low discretion, hedged about with prescriptive rules, checks, controls, inspection and close supervision, is likely to feel that his job definition embodies low trust. This may suggest to him that his masters are excluding him from their own high-trust fraternity – that they see him as no more than an instrumental and inferior means to their purposes, who need not be treated any more favourably than labour market forces demand or than collective pressure with his fellow-employees can exact. Here we move towards the impersonal, contractual, low-trust relationship which yields so little of the moral involvement we are discussing, thereby exemplifying the specific type of relationship as against the diffuse kind more characteristic of high-discretion work. It must be repeated, however, that the use of 'trust' terminology in this discussion does not rest on its ordinary sense of personal relationships. Industry has had more than enough of well-meant admonitions that its participants must be nicer to one another. It cannot be too strongly emphasized that this is not what is being suggested here. The proposition is that, quite apart from personal trust or distrust between particular people, there can be said to be 'institutionalized' trust or distrust which is embodied in the social arrangements, decisions and policies which men seek to impose on each other.

It is not, to be sure, inevitable that a low-discretion role has a depersonalizing, alienating effect on the occupant. We noted earlier that a person may willingly apply himself to the humblest role in a spirit of strong personal commitment provided he shares the objectives of his leaders. He may not derive much zest or fulfilment from his actual task activities as such, but he discharges them conscientiously in the knowledge that they serve a cause which he supports and respects. We also observed, however, that such attitudes do not seem common among the rank and file of modern large-scale industry. Preceding chapters have shown how employers and managers, increasingly conscious that the great benefits of modern material and social technology were being partially offset by a shortfall in rank-and-file commitment of this kind, have tried to induce in employees a sense of common interests and diffuse, high-trust relations. Welfare programmes, the philosophy underlying Taylor's strategy of Scientific Management, the early Human Relations approach via social integration – these have been examined as attempts to retain the advantages of large-scale organization, extreme division of labour, hierarchy and full managerial control, while at the same time avoiding their disadvantages. Although not wholly without their benefits for management, they have generally failed to evoke the spirit sought by their more hopeful exponents, for the reason – as this book would argue – that they aspired to generate a high-trust response from what employees experience as a low-trust situation. The structure and definitions of work roles and of organizational decision-making in general remained essentially unmodified.

Events were to show, however, that other shots could yet be found in the managerial locker. A few diverse initiatives began to explore the possibilities inherent in the notion of participation in decision-making. But still the strategy remained one of effecting only minimal changes in the orthodox, managerially-dominated structure. The fear persisted that greater participation by the individual rank-and-file employee in terms of an enlarged discretion in his own job would threaten the economic advantages of division of labour, hierarchy and managerial control. The policy of trying to secure what was seen as the best of both worlds therefore continued. Since the tried and tested advantages of bureaucratic organization were being marginally offset by negative responses from the rank and file, the rigours of hierarchical bureaucracy were to be softened somewhat in the hope of strengthening employee compliance, loyalty and involvement. No significant enlargement was to be made in the employee's participation in terms of decision-making in his own job. But he was to be given a limited influence, often necessarily an indirect one through representatives, upon the decision-making of supervisors, higher managers or perhaps even directors. The theory rested on the assumption (certainly valid for some cultures but not necessarily all) that a degree of participation in decisions affecting them, even if only limited and indirect, disposes men to comply more readily. This limited influence might require management on some occasions to bend from its first preferences, but the calculation was that this danger could be sufficiently contained.

Given, then, that after the Second World War discussion was turning to the possible value to management of a limited and contained employee participation in managerial decision-making, one might suppose that the already deeply-rooted institution of collective bargaining, by which representatives of both sides negotiate decisions about terms and conditions of employment and the settling of employee grievances, would already have been welcomed long ago by employers as a major contribution to the promotion of compliance. And indeed by some it was. Yet it is doubtful if many managers, called upon to direct their thoughts to the subject of participation in managerial decision-making, turn first to collective bargaining. Rather they tend to think first of participative management, participation in terms of representation on advisory or consultative committees, or a minority voice on directorial boards. What accounts for this selective interest? In suggesting answers to this question we shall find ourselves exploring some of the principal characteristics of these various forms of participation and the responses they evoke from management and employee collectives.

Participation through collective bargaining

Participation in decision-making through collective bargaining has become by far the most widespread and important form in Western industrial societies. Although there has always been, and there remains, a tradition of resistance to it among some employers and managers, it has come to be seen by many as a valuable and even indispensable mechanism for negotiating and preserving order over the large aggregates of employees and complex occupational structures increasingly characteristic of industrial society. With this growth of organizational scale has come a managerial need for complex patterns of rules and usages governing rewards, work arrangements, hiring, firing, discipline, and the handling of individual and group grievances. These in turn have raised problems of securing employee compliance with rules, their detailed application, and possible alteration.

It is in this context that some managements have come to see the representative procedures of collective negotiation and grievance settlement as having a positive contribution to make in promoting consent among the governed and serving as an instrument of bureaucratic administration. Certainly this has become established as the received view of most governments, relevant agencies and specialist opinion in Western countries.

This does not necessarily imply that managements will see collective bargaining as the only, or even the main, strategy for handling their labour force. From their point of view it may have certain inadequacies or indeed positive disadvantages which partially or wholly offset its usefulness. In the first place, compliance with rules is not the same as high moral involvement in an identification with, and commitment to, one's work situation. Collective bargaining can promote compliance by virtue of being a process through which employees secure, indirectly through representatives, a voice in the making of decisions immediately important to them. Such a process can, given the conditions noted in the first chapter, strengthen the legitimacy of the rules in the eyes of the governed and thus increase the chances of their being accepted and obeyed. It also offers a channel of communication that may be more effective in articulating problems and grievances than the line of managerial authority. There was no reason to suppose, however, that collective bargaining would generate within the individual employee that positive moral involvement in his job which management might be seeking. The fact that someone is participating on his behalf in other men's decision-making does nothing of itself to enrich the importance and quality of the decisions he is currently called upon to make in his own job.

Moreover, for some managements, collective bargaining might seem more than simply inadequate to promote moral involvement; it might appear to them to be positively opposed. After all, the very concept of bargaining implies perceptions of divergent interests. Admittedly there is scope for wide variations in the degree of divergence, conflict and mutual hostility. While this may, at one extreme, be so severe as to threaten organizational survival, it can take a form sufficiently mild as to approximate to the problem-solving type of situation that we examined earlier. But collective bargaining can never be pure problem-solving as management would like it to be, since the trade union or work-group collective can never concede that there exists a total unity of interests between itself and management. There always persists, in the collective's view of events, an element of 'us' and 'them', a perception of 'the two sides'. This is likely to make the group's participation in decision-making somewhat threatening for management, for here are employees as a collective force taking up an oppositional stance on what may prove an ever-widening range of issues which might end in a fundamental challenge to management's basic prerogatives. Such considerations convince many managements that, useful and necessary though collective bargaining may be, it has to be supplemented by efforts to overcome or minimize its divisive influence. Hence the search for a strategy, to be operated in parallel with collective bargaining, which will, as far as possible, integrate rank and file into a common team effort with the higher levels under management's leadership. Could they be drawn into such an integrated involvement in a way which, besides minimizing the threat to managerial power presented by collective bargaining, also minimized changes in job design and the distribution of decision-making which might threaten the benefits of division of labour and managerial control? There seemed to be a number of possibilities.

Participative supervision

The Human Relations approach had thrown up an idea later developed as participative, consultative or permissive supervision. If, as this approach urged, the unco-operative responses so frequently found among rank-and-file employees were due to management's failure to provide for the expression of their salient need – the need to feel they were making a valued contribution to a group purpose – the answer seemed plain. Management must contrive that this employee need, which was presumed to be all-important for motivation in work, was somehow satisfied. Employee commitment and loyalty would then become focused upon this source of satisfaction. The way would be clear for supervision and higher management to harness the moral involvement thus offered and direct it along pro-management instead of anti-management channels.

But this was easier said than done. How could the employee doing an anonymous fragmented job on extreme division of labour principles be persuaded that his role was a significant and individually meaningful one? The possibility mooted was that his supervisor, suitably trained in Human Relations techniques, might draw him into some degree of consultation and participation in the decisions immediately governing his work life. Perhaps even the small work group of which he was a member might be so involved as a collective unit. The hopes reposed in such. manipulative techniques led to a proliferation of Human Relations courses for supervisors and middle managers.

Why has this approach been given a label so pejorative as 'manipulative'? Why should an attempt to enlarge, however slightly, the individual's insight into, and influence over, his work situation be described in terms carrying an overtone of disparagement? The answer is that the ultimate reason for offering the employee this minimal consultation in supervisory decision-making was not for what it might contribute to the fulfilment of his own purposes and personality, but for what it could contribute to management's objectives. That this was so became apparent as soon as the possibility was envisaged of the employee making an 'unsuitable' or 'inappropriate' contribution or response to supervisory decision-making – that is, one which ran counter to management's interests. To be sure, he might only rarely have the opportunity to do so even under a Human Relations strategy. In practice its application proved more likely to be confined to explanations of why a particular managerial decision or policy took the form it did. Here and there, however, employees might be allowed to make rather larger choices than previously – for example, to vary the speed of a conveyor belt during the shift. Only if, over a period, they made the 'right' choices and the experiment threw up no incidental problems was it likely to be continued. It was always a safe prediction that 'mistaken' initiatives or inconvenient choices would be at best kindly 'corrected' and at worst simply overridden.

In fact, most of the Human Relations literature tactfully passed over such embarrassing possibilities. The assumption was either that employees could always be brought, by skilful 'leadership', to use their participative opportunities along lines acceptable to management, or that if this seemed unlikely then management would realize the circumstances to be 'inappropriate' for participative supervision. What justifies the description of this approach as manipulative is that it sought to exploit a presumed human need for purposes which were rarely explicitly stated. The literature often spoke of treating employees as ends in themselves, but the underlying assumption was clearly that the whole approach only made sense in so far as it served managerial purposes. For all the talk of a recognition by business of its social and moral responsibilities, rank-and-file employees were no more being treated as ends than in the harshest years of pioneering industrialism. They were still handled instrumentally as means; all that had changed (for a small minority) were views as to the most effective methods of handling employees.

In the event, participative supervision was to prove no Holy Grail. Some of the reasons are identical with those advanced in the last chapter to explain the more general weaknesses of the Human Relations approach. But there are others. Employees conditioned to expect and accept authoritarian rule were as likely to be bewildered as gratified if the style suddenly changed. Bewilderment was likely to pass into suspicion when it became clear that the new style was not an open-ended invitation for employees to participate in ways which might conceivably lead anywhere, but a technique by which management sought to pursue its ends more effectively while at the same time convincing the managed that they were being given a significantly greater voice in their work experience. With respect to this as to many other techniques of personnel policy, management showed a greater capacity to deceive itself than to deceive employees. Some managers no doubt convinced themselves that they were introducing a new concept of treating employees as significant ends in their own right. Perhaps they felt that a genuine ethical development was being frustrated when their superiors indicated, as many did, that disappointing results, the return of bad times, or the danger of the new style getting inconveniently out of hand, rendered desirable the resumption of more conventional patterns. We need to recall what we have noted elsewhere, that individual managers may well be allowed, indeed encouraged, by their seniors to pursue, and to speak with full ethical conviction about, policies which for them have a genuine moral content – provided these are viewed by seniors as compatible with 'organizational interests'. Those with the ultimate power of decision are likely to have no objection to subordinate managers harbouring moral convictions about how employees should be treated – so long as these convictions appear to serve what they define as organizational well-being.

Participation through joint consultation

Participative supervision caught on more in America than in Britain, partly because the hope of stemming union influence by means of integrative personnel policies had remained more widespread and vigorous there. But this is only a matter of degree: Britain, too, witnessed managerial practices which sought to strengthen the integration of the lower ranks into managerial purposes and values. One which received special emphasis for some years after the Second World War was joint consultation. Government and progressive management circles hoped that employee consent could be strengthened and motivation quickened through the voluntary adoption of formally constituted committees, representative of management and employees, which met regularly and discussed common interests in a problem-solving manner. Whereas bargaining focused on the issues that divided the parties, joint consultation was to promote constructive co-operation on the issues presumed to unite them – such as those matters relevant to the economic success of the organization and its ability to supply all members with a rising standard of living. This share in the managerial process beyond the range normally covered by collective bargaining would, it was hoped, release the potential for creative involvement which resided within the rank and file. Existing job structures and organizational design would not be affected, and managerial retention of control seemed ultimately assured by the fact that the the committees were no more than advisory bodies through which management 'collected the voices', ideally before rather than after making its decisions. In these respects the movement was an expression of the Human Relations belief that the postulated rank-and-file need for co-operative involvement could be met – and managerial benefits derived thereby – without conceding any real change in the power structure and organizational design of the enterprise.

Joint consultation proved no more than a panacea, however, than all the preceding and succeeding devices about which such great hopes have been entertained by a minority of enthusiasts. Here and there a company might count modest gains – joint consultation could sometimes be fruitful where it constituted a further expression of an existing relationship of confidence between the parties. But as a universal key for releasing the co-operative potential of the rank and file it passed through the usual stages of being greeted with fashionable enthusiasm and then declining to the role of just another technique which companies might or might not find marginally worth having, depending on history, personalities and circumstance.

The reasons for disappointment can be deduced from the preceding analysis. Whatever the joint consultation process might do for those few who as representatives actually took part, there seemed no reason to suppose it would transform the perceptions and motivations of their constituents, whose jobs and subjection to hierarchical authority and control remained unchanged.

If joint consultation offered little to the wage-earner on the shop floor or the clerical worker in his office, there was not much of enduring value either for the trade union officer or shop steward. At worst it might seem a device by which management hoped to undermine rank-and-file loyalty to their collective organizations and thereby weaken them. At best it was only really valuable to the extent that management could be induced to commit itself to a mutually-agreed policy on issues important to the unions and their members. But the further the situation moved in this direction the more it had to be seen as a bargaining relationship rather than as an advisory and consultative one. Admittedly there might be matters in which employee representatives had an interest but on which they lacked the strength to press management into making a binding commitment. Here it could be useful for them to have an extra channel of communication through which to urge upon management certain views and opinions. But as shop-floor representatives gained confidence and strength they pressed not simply for management's ear but for its readiness to enter into binding commitments on the issues important to them. As against merely 'making representations', which management might choose to ignore, or helping management to solve its problems, which might guarantee employees no enhanced share in any favourable outcome, the union or work group might want management to *commit* itself on certain wider issues of policy just as it did on such conventional bargaining matters as wages and working hours. Given such rising aspirations there was little value for them in what they were increasingly likely to see as a talking-shop from which management emerged committed to nothing.

Management was saying, in effect: 'Contribute your constructive proposals, offer your opinions, advance your judgements – and then trust us to fashion the best policies in the interests of the company and all its members.' But this was precisely what the rank and file felt unable to do. As instruments towards other men's ends, they felt the need for specific, defined protections and returns. In this way they expressed the low-trust responses which their job situation engendered in them. From management's point of view, however, the forging of specific commitments converted what it had hoped would be a problem-solving activity into a win–lose bargaining process.* Where management persisted in opposing this trend, the employee representatives could well lose interest and allow the consultation machinery to become moribund. Where it accepted the trend, the distinction between consultation and bargaining lost whatever practical reality it may have had and logic pointed to the abandonment of separate consultative forms. For a time it seemed as if joint consultation, as Britain's industrial relations system had known it, was disappearing permanently from the scene.

Another device sometimes included in the category of participation is profit-sharing. The belief persists, for example, that to give employees an ownership stake in the enterprise or a share in profits will arouse the desired spirit of involvement and commitment. This is to offer increased participation, not in decision-making, but in the outcome of the organizational effort. There is no evidence, however, of any lasting effect upon the employee whose job remains highly prescribed and subject to hierarchical control. The destinies of the enterprise are moulded, as he well knows, by events and decisions, both within and without the organization, which lie far above and beyond any conceivable control or influence of his. His role is simply not strategically important enough in discretionary terms for him to feel that any extra commitment from him will have significant effects on the total outcome. His effort becomes swallowed up in the complex aggregate of other men's efforts, many of them vastly more influential than his own.

If the persistence of profit-sharing ideas could be said to represent the triumph of hope over experience, rather different reasons must be offered for a certain revival of practical interest in joint consultation during the 1970s. As workplace union power reached its peak, some managements turned in desperation to what took on renewed

---

* It will be recalled that a problem-solving approach works to an assumption of shared ends and concentrates on clarifying the facts, searching for the best methods, and elucidating the probable consequences of alternatives. The parties do not seek to trap, bluff or score off each other, and do not conceal, distort or manipulate information and ideas. These are characteristics of a high-trust situation. In bargaining relationships the parties are conscious of divergent ends and therefore bring pressure to bear on each other, using gamesmanship, bluff and concealment or manipulation of information and ideas. These are characteristics of a low-trust situation.

attraction as a way of engaging employees in 'constructive' dialogue outside the negotiating framework. On the employees' side there emerged the paradox that in many establishments the workplace union organization now seemed so secure and unassailable that shop stewards relaxed their fears that joint consultation might be exploited to bypass or subvert the union presence. Recent research confirms that joint consultation has mainly grown not at the expense of, but as an adjunct to, union recognition and organization. How this partial revival has fared under mass unemployment, the weakening of workplace strength, and Thatcherian encouragement of macho-management remains to be empirically explored.

Participation through employee directors

During the 1960s Britain witnessed a quickening interest in the idea of employee directors on company boards. This was fed by assumptions derived from envious glances at West Germany and other European countries. Entry into the European Economic Community enlarged somewhat the awareness that West Germany, for example, makes legal provision for labour representation on company supervisory boards which oversee the management boards responsible for day-to-day business, and in certain industries for labour representation on the management boards themselves. This knowledge contributes to a certain picture of labour relations in West Germany, a picture with some basis in fact but losing nothing in journalistic heightening and adornment. It was a picture of management/worker harmony, keenly motivated workers offering willing co-operation in order to maximize economic growth, and a happy absence of opposition-minded shop steward organization on the shop floor. We cannot attempt here to assess the validity of this view. The crucial point is that, with the usual tendency to draw over-hasty conclusions about cause and effect, the assumption was made that the allegedly halcyon state of labour relations in West Germany was a direct consequence of the arrangements for labour participation in managerial decision-making. This contributed to interest in the idea of employee directors as introduced in a few cautious experiments in the private and public sectors.

Both top management and employee collectives might feel they had something to gain from this innovation. However vigilant managers try to be in keeping their ears to the ground, differences of status and authority often prevent their getting a full picture of feeling and opinion among rank and file. Employee directors could be expected to make a contribution in this respect. Moreover, they could supply an extra dimension to management's appreciation of rank-and-file attitudes and behaviour – a sympathetic understanding of the *reasons* for those attitudes and behaviour – not a dimension along which management is usually well endowed, and one which could be crucial in shaping a successful personnel and labour relations policy. Information and insight of the right quality could enable management to gauge better the probable consequences of alternative policies and to formulate more appropriate strategies of response to the expected outcomes.

There was the more fundamental argument that, given the ever-pressing need for flexibility and change, management would be better equipped to carry the workforce with it if opportunities were given for participation in strategic policy-making discussions at board level as well as in lower-level decision-making. This admission of employee representatives to the highest counsels could inspire a new relationship of confidence from which might flow a fruitful co-operation and a release of constructive energies from the lower ranks.

The experiments conducted so far had limited employee directors to a very small minority on the board, and among organized labour even those who favoured the idea had somewhat less glowing hopes. Nevertheless, it might yield something. Given the appropriate relationship with the employee directors – a crucial condition – they would have a voice in deliberations about policy. True, it would be no more than a voice, and a minority voice at that. But they could use it both to seek information and to offer reasoned statements in support of preferred policies, though admittedly the managerial directors could choose to be niggardly with the first and dismissive of the second. As with conventional joint consultation, this was not a process through which either side entered into a commitment with the other. A meeting of a directorial board or committee of management is not a process by which management seeks to secure employee acceptance of, and commitment to, certain agreed policies and decisions, or *vice versa*; it is a problem-solving and programme-determining process by which management fixes the policies and decisions it wants to apply. Employees might be aware that 'their' directors were not in a negotiation situation; that they constituted one voice among many; and that they had no power to press their interests and views with any force, but they might nevertheless think it useful to have this voice.

Many leaders and activists thought otherwise, holding to the traditional union distrust of such devices. In a few cases the objection was doctrinal. Employee spokesmen must not enter into collaboration with the class enemy, helping thereby to uphold an exploitative economic system. More often the objection was practical. Employee directors, occupying their minority position, would be heavily subjected to managerial logics and definitions. Perceptions of what were seen as appropriate 'questions'; assumptions about what must be taken as 'given'; identification of 'relevant' search processes for 'realistic' answers; selection of 'significant' data with which to support statements of both problems and solutions – all of these would be supplied by managerial specialists serving the board, and would be imbued with logics, values, and priorities very different from those of the organized workforce. Employee directors could be overwhelmed by this expertise and possibly unable to fight their way through it. As a consequence they might well acquiesce in policies highly detrimental to employee interests. If their role was defined as representative, the position of the union and the organized workgroup would be deeply compromised. How could their spokesmen subsequently fight an unpopular decision when other spokesmen had already submitted to it? Such were the arguments that had tradition-ally been mounted to support the idea of trade union independence of managerial functions and decision-making. Aloofness from any commitment to managerial policies was essential if the unions were to preserve their oppositional role. But were not such arguments only relevant if employee directors were defined as representative? In the event that they severed their links with the organized workforce and behaved entirely as individuals, union independence would not be prejudiced. But this did nothing to enhance their usefulness to the union cause. Even more certainly they would be drawn into the ambit of managerial perceptions and values. They would be tolerated on the board only in so far as they smoothed the path of the company's labour relations policy by contributing special insight and judgement on the subject of employee attitudes and dispositions.

The argument about preserving union independence did not go unchallenged. Was it not the case that unions would be totally ineffective if they really attempted to maintain independence of management? Did they not, by entering into joint regulation with management on pay, conditions, and many detailed features of the work situation, not to mention procedures for handling disputes, already share in the making of managerial decisions? And were they not inevitably involved, too, in the administration, and if necessary the enforcement, of those regulations, being required to co-operate in their application to particular cases and in ensuring that members honoured them? How could this be described as independence of management? The traditional argument rested, it was said, on an inadequate analysis of the union role.

Though this critique was sound so far as it went it did not meet the instinctive fear of many leaders and activists that they must not become too deeply involved and committed in top-level decision-making. Where, then, did the critique fall short? It failed to recognize that the real argument was not about the *principle* of union involvement in managerial policy-making and enforcement but about the *degree*. Union officers had always had to accept that, given a sector of joint responsibility with management over pay and a range of workplace issues, they might sometimes have to try to impose unpopular agreements on their grumbling members. But this did not mean they relished the prospect of a massive widening of that sector to include major strategic company decisions. Where would such a process end? Even their present position was ambiguous, as their rank-and-file critics were always pointing out. Even given the present limited coverage of collective bargaining, they could often be attacked for seeming to line up with management against their own members. If they allowed themselves to be drawn into ever-widening sectors of policy-making, would they not become defined ever more fully and clearly as a subsidiary arm of the managerial function? British trade unionists were not notable for their meek acceptance of official union authority. Further absorption into joint decision-making might well render union discipline even more problematic and strengthen unofficial militant leadership.

Despite these doubts in some sections of the movement, the official TUC position during the 1960s was positive if cautious. Its written submission (1966) to the Donovan Commission considered that 'to say that trade unions cannot limit or control management if they become part of it is to play with words'. Compulsory legislation on representation at board level 'would prove very difficult to draft', but permissive or discretionary legislation which made experiments possible 'would be widely welcomed'.

By 1974 a new document, *Industrial Democracy*, revealed that the tentativeness had gone. The 'impact of closures, rationalizations and redundancies has become much more widespread, and the inability of trade unions to prevent or mitigate the effects of these in most cases has been a major deficiency. The time has come when a mandatory system needs to be proposed.' Major decisions on company planning, allocation of investment resources, plant locations, closures, take-overs, mergers, and top managerial appointments were generally taken at levels not reached by collective bargaining and were perhaps not readily covered by that method. 'New forms of control were needed.'

The phrasing indicated that the inspiration behind this resoluteness was not the vision of a joint pursuit of efficiency and growth, primed by a release of constructive energies from all ranks, but a resolve to strengthen the protective role of the unions by securing the formal responsibility of the directorial board to employees as well as to shareholders. Employee directors were to be appointed through the medium of trade union machinery; they were to be defined as employee representatives though they need not themselves be employees; and they were not to be required to give up lay or full-time union office.

The TUC favoured the existing European preference for a two-tier system, with a supervisory board periodically appraising a management board that conducted the everyday business. One half of the supervisory board would be appointed by the employees through trade union machinery: a structure which would give employee representatives 'a degree of joint control over all the major decisions of the company: closures, redundancy, major technological changes, mergers etc.' Again, the protective stance was manifest. Other things, too, were manifest. The emphasis on the unions as the appointing bodies expressed the long-standing principle of Britain's unions that there must be one and only one channel of representation. European unions had often been forced by weakness to accept works councils which gave a role to non-unionist employees; which worked to notions of 'company interest'; and which were susceptible to managerial manipulation. In Britain these had made comparatively little inroad into union functions and there was a determination to maintain this position. The insistence by some employers' spokesmen that board representation must be married to a system of works councils therefore came under union suspicion as probably deriving from a hope of weakening the union presence and influence.

That the intention in pressing for board representation was to enhance union control was further confirmed by the TUC statement that 'there is no necessary conflict between worker representatives arguing the case at board level, and then pursuing it at negotiations, representing workpeople's interests, at a later stage'. This reassurance was obviously directed at trade unionists who feared a sell-out by employee directors, rather than at managers hoping for a creative problem-solving spirit. The danger, as traditionally perceived, that a minority of employee directors, having no structured connections with the union, would be drawn into commitments later deemed damaging by the workforce, was to be avoided by means hitherto considered by 'responsible' opinion to be out of the question. A claim for equal representation with shareholders on the board; for the unions to control appointment; and for the conventional bargaining machinery to serve as a long-stop for contesting unwelcome board decisions, would not have been taken seriously until the mid 1970s, with their radical mood and the unions at the peak of their power. It was this consciousness of strength that convinced many, though certainly not all, union leaders that given control over employee directors they could ensure that board representation would not be exploited to weaken them and undermine collective bargaining.

The European Economic Community had contributed something to the atmosphere which made this conviction possible. In September 1972 the Commission circulated among member states a draft 'Fifth Directive on Company Law'. This proposed general adoption of the two-tier system and offered two alternative systems for the supervisory board. The Wilson government which took office in 1974, hard pressed for union co-operation in incomes policy, considered it judicious to acknowledge this trend and in 1975 appointed the Committee of Inquiry on Industrial Democracy, chaired by Lord Bullock. Its narrowly drawn terms of reference required it to accept 'the need for a radical extension of industrial democracy . . . by means of representation on boards of directors'; to accept also 'the essential role of trade union organizations in this process'; and to confine itself to considering 'how such an extension can best be achieved . . .' Its members included Jack Jones, then General Secretary of the Transport and General Workers Union and a formidable advocate of greater worker participation. Its majority *Report* of 1976 accepted as axiomatic that any attempt to bypass the rapidly growing represen-tative structure of unionism at the workplace would be seen as an attack, would be fiercely resisted, and would doom any programme from the outset. The 'single channel of representation' was therefore to be preserved by vesting in trade union machinery the appointment to a single-tier board of directors equal in number to those representing the shareholders; both groups co-opting an agreed third group according to the so-called '2X plus Y' formula. The system would become mandatory if requested by employees in a secret ballot. It would create 'a new legitimacy for the exercise of the management function'; a legitimacy 'essential for the long-term efficiency and profitability of the private sector and for the ultimate success of the economy itself'.

These proposals were supported, however, only by the three union spokesmen, a sympathetic industrial-relations academic, a sympathetic academic lawyer, and the chairman. The solicitor member submitted a note of sharp dissent calling for a majority of shareholder directors, and the three employer spokesmen signed a *Minority Report* diverging fundamentally from the proposed system.

Reception of the report was remarkable for the vehemence of hostile reaction from the Confederation of British Industry, whose leaders probably found resistance a valuable institutional bonding device. There was, no doubt, relief in government quarters that they were absolved from action on the proposals by the manifest evidence not only of empatic resistance from leaders of some large and powerful unions, still persuaded by traditional arguments, but also of apparent indifference among much of the rank and file. The report sank without trace, and after 1979 and the first Thatcher administration the issue became not whether the unions could extend their power and control but how much they could preserve of what they already had.

Although the issue has, for the time being, disappeared from view, it has been worth examining for what it reveals of the profound ambiguities underlying the debate, especially in Britain, about extending employee participation and, indeed, about industrial relations generally. There is no mistaking in the Bullock majority *Report* the note of optimistic hope that here might be the mechanism which at long last would release the constructive and co-operative energies of British labour. Equally, there is no mistaking in the TUC statement, *Industrial Democracy*, revised in 1977 to include its evidence to the Bullock committee, the emphasis on the need to create a management accountability to its organized workforce on a range of issues which, though increasingly perceived by trade unionists as crucial to them in a context of highly aggressive international capitalism, had so far eluded effective challenge. Both the majority *Report* and the TUC emphasized the importance of maintaining full communication between employee directors and their constituents, but for different reasons. For the former such links would provide the channels for the new relationship of legitimation and confidence; for the latter they would ensure that employee directors were held to their responsibility to shop-floor constituents.

The difference of emphasis was detectable, too, in references to the role behaviour of employee directors. For the committee, it 'would be unreasonable and unrealistic not to expect the employee representatives . . . to argue strongly at board level for the interests of their constituents'. But they must not be mandated delegates, and there must be no 'change in the law which at present prevents the mandating of a director to vote in a particular way'. An employee director would be 'in breach of his duty' if he did not pursue his own conclusions about which policies would 'work for the greater good of the company'. The TUC document, by contrast, referred to the 'primary responsibility' of employee directors as being to their constituents. 'The aim must be to give legal rights to workpeople of collective participation and control over decisions which the collective bargaining and consultative process have not given them. It is no use doing so and then requiring that worker directors should behave like any other directors.' They must be 'workers' representatives on the board' and not simply 'worker directors responsible only to themselves'.

It is not surprising that many employers and their associations feared that implementation of the Bullock proposals would, whatever the committee's hopes, too often facilitate the invasion of the board room, if not by the formal institutions of collective bargaining, then certainly by the adversary, zero-sum spirit which both sides in Britain had so widely helped to promote. Issues of a highly sensitive and strategic nature, hitherto successfully preserved from joint regulation, would be put before the scrutiny of union-appointed directors. Should they present threats for the organized workforce, there was a strong likelihood that conflict would be joined, possibly with the third group of directors holding the balance. The prospect was raised of an extension of adversary relations to a far wider range of issues than before. Although the result was unlikely to be a dramatic increase in open conflict, it was not a prospect relished by many British employers. They visualized these strategic, sensitive issues as being far more likely to come under zero-sum wariness than positive-sum co-operation. Why, then, run the risk of accepting a scheme that seemed to offer them so little?

The likelihood is, however, that both the more ardent supporters and the more ferocious critics of the majority proposals overestimated the changes that would have resulted had they been implemented. The unions might well have suffered disappointment at how little employee directors were able to achieve in terms of securing management accountability to the workforce, dependent as they would probably be upon management sources for the definition of 'problems', for the search process for 'solutions', and for the selection of data to support both. Except in the unlikely situation of employee directors being supplied with their own supportive expertise in the specialisms of business economics, cost accounting, and company strategy, they would be poorly equipped to mount informed resistance to managerial proposals and to offer credible alternatives. Those hoping for a fresh constructive spirit in British industry might equally have been disappointed to find that while employee directors themselves enjoyed a much hightened sense of involvement, little of it became communicated to their constituents, who continued to perform their low-discretion tasks in the same spirit as before.

Nevertheless the whole debate and the nature of the partisan behaviour accompanying it had been revealing. It had illustrated yet again the habitual reflex postures and expectations into which much British industrial relations behaviour has been cast by the unbroken continuities of our history, traditions, culture, and institutional development. It had illustrated, too, the diversity of meanings and purposes covered by the term participation.

The full diversity ranged, of course, far wider. It could refer to a style of supervision or management which seeks to foster a sense in the subordinate of being consulted, but which is often little more than a manipulative exercise designed to mask the authority relationship. It could describe the activities of group or departmental employee representatives on somewhat remote and infrequent committees whose role is limited to receiving the decisions of higher authority *after* they have been made. Both the first (or direct) and the second (or indirect) forms are subject to significant variations. The subordinate may be allowed a degree of genuine freedom of decision by his superiors, who may or may not find this innovation useful and allow it to continue. Representatives on committees or boards may be allowed to press views and preferences upon higher authority *before* final decisions are made. Within collective bargaining procedures the participation of employee representatives results in higher authority binding itself, after negotiation, to certain agreed courses of action. We shall be taking note later of aspirations categorized under 'workers' control' or 'workers' self-management'. It is not difficult to appreciate that, given these and other variations which can be found, the notion of participation is but the crudest of blanket terms. Confusion is compounded by its application to systems of profit-sharing or co-ownership.

Participation through enriched job discretion

It was suggested earlier in this chapter that the conventional view of participation which studies it only in terms of participation in *managerial* decision-making can usefully be broadened to cover the degree and quality of decision-making in the subordinate's own job. As we have noted, there are grounds for believing in fact that in our society the individual's degree of identification and involvement tends in many cases to be associated with the degree of discretion his job affords him. Compared with this, the significance of such forms of participation as direct influences on the decisions of immediate superiors, or indirect influences, through representatives, on the decisions of more distant authority, seems relatively marginal so far as moral involvement in the individual's job is concerned, however important they may (or may not) be in promoting compliance with the rules and support for the system in general.

The decades following the Second World War saw growing interest in an approach to motivation which does concern itself with the nature of the individual's job. This approach received widespread discussion and a limited degree of practical application under the name of job enrichment. To enrich a job in this context is to vest it with wider and more significant responsibilities – to change it in ways which can be summed up as an enlargement and enrichment of discretion. By the same token, such changes would, it was believed, enlarge and enrich the individual's participation in the decision-making of the organization. The expectation was that, given a keener consciousness of personal involvement as a consequence of this enlarged role, the employee would respond with a stronger commitment.

The 1960s and 1970s saw widespread discussion of this so-called 'humanization' of work – more in Scandinavia, America, Japan, Australia and Continental countries than in Britain. It became a major theme in the so-called 'Quality of Life' debate and, particularly in the 1970s, enjoyed some governmental support. In Scandinavia job redesign became a public issue; in France it was discussed almost obsessively in magazines, journals, and the serious press; the West

German and Norwegian governments provided grant aid for local experiments in new forms of work organization. Social scientists in many countries undertook research and theorizing with much enthusiasm. Some consultants adopted it as a specialism. Inter nationally, the EEC Council pronounced in favour of 'work humanization' and in 1975 the Organization for Economic Co-operation and Development (OECD) also expressed support.

The motives inspiring these activities were, of course, mixed. Many social scientists who came forward with philosophies and practical company schemes, far from being mere management hacks, were convinced that they were contributing their skills and insight to the solution of a genuine and growing social problem – the increasing alienation of many employees, white- and blue-collar, from their fragmented and unsatisfying jobs. Redesign would, it was felt, not only raise the quality of their work experience by reducing alienation, but also consequently enhance the quality, efficiency, and adaptability of the whole organization as an economic and social unit. It was the latter possibility that especially attracted the attention not only of a few 'progressive' company managements and governments, who were conscious that tight labour markets and union strength were enabling the lower ranks at work to assert their discontents ever more freely, but also of consultants, who soon found themselves mining a profitable seam. As we noted in an earlier chapter, employees have, to widely varying degrees, manifested resistance to the work structures and job definitions imposed on them, and job enrichment appeared to offer a way of reducing those resistances.

Under these stimuli, changes in job design – and in the supervisory relationships and organizational arrangements often associated with them – were introduced in a few companies, sometimes by management fiat, sometimes through negotiation with unions and work groups. They were apt to be accompanied by much flattering publicity – a not insignificant benefit at a time when large-scale private enterprise felt ideologically on the defensive. Companies like Volvo and Saab in Scandinavia, Shell and Phillips in Britain, Fiat in Italy and certain General Motors plants in America that were experiencing costly problems in recruiting and retaining an adequate workforce were discussed as the harbingers of a new philosophy of industrial organization.

Sometimes the schemes were combined with the reform of pay structure, overtime arrangements and work allocation in a comprehensive exercise of productivity bargaining. Examples revealed a variety of possibilities. In some cases, mass-production, conveyor-belt jobs, previously fragmented down in approved Scientific Management style into highly-prescribed, minimum-discretion functions each performed by a separate specialist operator, were enlarged in a way which enabled each operator to combine a number of functions. The hope inspiring such changes might be no more than that by relieving monotony there would be a reduction in labour turnover, absenteeism, low productivity, or strikes. Subsequent research has revealed, however, little evidence of a direct and simple connection between job discontents and these negative symptoms. In this as in other ways job enrichment was presented within what is now recognized to be a somewhat simplistic theoretical framework.

The enlargement of discretion effected by such schemes might be small – indeed insignificant. More noteworthy changes were those in which, for example, production workers were trained to carry out maintenance and minor repair tasks, or in which craftsmen were given increased freedom to schedule their own work. Most significant of all, perhaps, were changes which went beyond the individual to his immediate work group. Some experiments vested control over certain decisions within the small group under its own leader – the so-called 'autonomous work group'.

How far such exercises derived their impetus from full-blown theories linking the employee's job discretion with his degree of moral involvement with the company is problematic. In some instances, managements came to believe that · mass-production techniques involving short work-cycles and repetitive tasks were, by evoking job frustration and discontent, generating costs at the margin which threatened the benefits. Employee resistance, either collective and overt or individual and covert, suggested to a few companies that a certain degree of back-tracking from extreme Taylorian principles might improve employee performance in some way that justified the exercise. In other instances, ideas about job satisfaction and employee motivation played little or no part in the calculation. In a society riddled, like Britain, with demarcative and restrictive principles at all social levels, job redesign seemed to offer, at the manual level, a way of reducing costs by increasing flexibility as between the various crafts and between the crafts and non-apprenticed workers. An early but unrealized dream of some senior managers at the Esso oil refinery at Fawley, for example, as they moved towards their famous productivity negotiations, was the vision of the 'refinery mechanic', a fully flexible job category purged of demarcative restrictions.

At a time, as in the 1960s and early 1970s, when unions and organized work groups were approaching the peak of their power, and when progressive managements were casting about for ways of adapting constructively and economically to this rising workplace strength, it was understandable that many of their efforts should have been clothed – sometimes by themselves, often by outside observers – in the language of 'reform' and 'humanization' of work and work organization. This was not invariably hypocritical, but it has to be viewed in the context of the search for enhancement of management control – with control defined in its broadest sense to mean not – or not only – direct and immediate command but also the longer-term shaping of the organization in pursuit of what is deemed its most desirable adaptation to the expected environment.

Within any organization, control is invariably exercised in a variety of different forms using a variety of different sanctions according to the definition of the job, the type of work behaviour sought, and the type of employee response expected. When we see, for example, a senior executive enjoying considerable freedom from close supervision, direct command and technical constraints, we do not define this as a case of top management abandoning their control over him. They are controlling him, probably far more effectively, by a complex of other means – by admitting him to the high-trust fraternity of high status and rewards, and its accompanying socialization, to the prospect of further promotion, and to judgement by the long-term appraisal of technical, professional, or financial results.

In some cases, therefore, job enrichment might be seen as a very modest exercise in shifting the emphasis marginally from one method of control to another. It was hoped that by relaxing technical or supervisory constraints there would occur some benefit, direct or indirect, short-term or long-term, to the company. Sometimes part of the hoped-for benefit might be very indirect indeed. It was possible, for example, for a large 'household name' company to decide, when the competition for able graduates was at its peak, that a reputation for 'social responsibility' – which could cover job enrichment – would help to attract them, and therefore justified full-page advertisements in the up-market press designed to enhance the company image along that dimension.

Recent experience supports the judgement that job redesign may have owed less than was once thought to a belief that enrichment as such would strengthen individual or group attachment or moral involvement at a time of extreme labour assertiveness, and rather more to the attractions of increased labour flexibility, or to the 'needs' of new technology or new forms of work allocation, or to a desire to escape the corrupting effects of systematic overtime. To understand this judgement we must first note that mass unemployment and the weakening of workplace strength has induced many prudent employees to behave in ways which have been interpreted by some excessively hopeful observers as demonstrating a newly-acquired 'loyalty' to the firm, or a new 'realism' in the face of change. The question arose as to whether managements would take advantage of this more subdued workplace situation to design work so as to extract the full benefit of extreme Taylorian principles, confident of being spared the more costly negative consequences. In fact, firms have continued throughout the deepening of the slump to restructure work in ways not necessarily Taylorian. Flexibility within and between work groups and the reduction of demarcations between craft and production workers have even greater appeal given the intensified pressure on costs. Firms pursuing job design may well, however, feel little need in the changed climate to adorn their schemes with notions about job satisfaction and job enrichment that are no longer fashionable.

Job enrichment as a means towards heightened motivation has in fact never been a burning issue at the workplace, and experience so far hardly suggests a change to be imminent. For the unions it comes well down any ordered list of priorities. Indeed, if it threatens to reduce the workforce they are likely to oppose it, and craft groups have cause to view it with suspicion in any case. Company management has shown few signs of sustained enthusiasm. More recently Volvo have opted for only marginally innovatory methods of truck assembly, and in Scandinavia generally little appears to remain of the experiments of the 1960s. Shell's elaboration of a 'new philosophy of management' did not promote the widespread introduction of autonomous work groups and participative management throughout the organization. Comprehensive productivity bargaining exercises of the 1960s showed few lasting managerial benefits in the 1970s.

The fact is that the theory of job enrichment and all its associated variants was often too narrowly confined to the presumed wants, perceptions, and work experience of the individual and of his immediate group, with other possible variables being overlooked. It is true that the evidence, though far from definitive, tends to be consistent with the view that forms of job redesign which emphasize increased discretion and autonomy typically enhance performance, though there are exceptions which may figure large in particular cases and which will be noted later. It does not follow, however, that the actual or potential dynamics of the individual or small group will be decisive in determining the stance towards job enrichment of either management or union (or unionized work group).

For the former, an improved situation at the operative level may be offset by higher costs in some other area. Even with respect to the operative level managers may feel that greater autonomy carries too high a risk from their point of view that it will be 'misused'. A unionized work group, for example, may be able to use it as a tacit or explicit bargaining weapon. In other words, managements are likely to view job enrichment within the context of a much wider-ranging preoccupation with issues of costs, organization, control, and the divergent interests of different groups and functions in the company. Even when the responses of employees seem likely to be favourable, managements may be deterred by other consequential changes – which can include uncertainties about their own powers of scheduling and control. Nor may problems of job satisfaction and job redesign be perceived by management as particularly important as issues of contention. The technical content of jobs is far from being the only source of discontent, conflict and alienation in the organization. Conflicts over pay, workplace custom and threats to it, deeply ingrained attitudes to work, traditions of mutual distrust: these and others may loom far larger. Moreover such conflicts may block the successful application of job enrichment even when management chooses to implement it. Much job enrichment theory was of little help to managers here since it too often overestimated the possibility of reconciling the interests of workers and employers by means of job redesign. By omitting crucial variables it displayed, like so many managerial panaceas, a certain analytical innocence. The approach of some consultants was even more bland, a tendency strengthened perhaps by knowledge of managerial distaste for analytical frameworks which explicitly acknowledge structurally induced antagonisms and conflict.

Even at the level of the individual there is need for a number of caveats. One of them concerns the attitudes, values and aspirations of those to whom the strategy is applied. Here we need to enlarge on a qualification we have already applied to one of the major propositions referred to in this book. Reference has been made to the association between the degree of involvement felt by the individual in his job and the degree of discretion he has. But we have also seen that in explaining these attitudes of involvement we must not rest content with an objective description of the rules, tasks and discretionary content of the work role itself. Equally important is how the job occupant perceives and responds to them. We can imagine people who, placed in a high-discretion role, would respond not with moral involvement and identification but with psychological discomfort and insecurity. Feelings of incompetence might be one cause. Another might be that the person is temperamentally happiest within a highly structured, clear-cut and programmed situation and dislikes the uncertainties, ambiguities and general diffuseness of high-discretion situations which require the employee to make important choices and accept the consequences. But a third cause, and a very significant one for our purposes, might be that the individual in question had already adapted – having been encouraged to do so by family, friends, school and early work experience – to the assumption that work could not be expected to yield any significant intrinsic satisfaction and must be undertaken largely for its pay packet.

This is especially important in that there are grounds for believing that considerable numbers of those growing up in wage-earning families and wage-earning social environments are in fact conditioned to take just such attitudes as these towards work. They are not necessarily irreversible. Those who have not hitherto taken work seriously as a possible source of intrinsic satisfaction may nevertheless be open to such an orientation if opportunity offers; and even if they begin by resisting – or at least being nervous of – greater discretion and responsibility, they may learn by experience of the enriched job that they value the change for reasons additional to any increase in monetary reward it may offer. They might as a result of increased personal involvement feel somewhat more at one with management in certain respects. They may, if the increase in discretion is significant enough, become rather more conscious of being trusted and of being a member of a team. Such responses could take behavioural forms which management would find valuable.

But quite different responses are possible. Some individuals and groups may be so powerfully conditioned to see work purely in terms of the pay packet that for all practical purposes their attitudes are irreversible, no matter what alternative type of work experience they are offered. Another possibility is that they may have become so habituated to take a wary, low-trust stance towards management's purposes and values that they cannot be weaned away by changes in work roles towards a closer identification with their job and the organization.

These considerations remind us that in the ordinary course of events men take up higher-discretion jobs with appropriately matching attitudes and aspirations. The individual singled out for promotion is likely to be ready, indeed eager, for greater responsibilities and to have suggested by his behaviour that he is able to offer an increasing identification with the organization. The technician, scientist, engineer, manager or academic is likely to have been socialized by family, school or university into a conception of himself as pursuing a career which must yield not only the desired material and status rewards but also work which is intrinsically satisfying and meaningful. In industry as we have hitherto known it, therefore, the likelihood of men faced with high-discretion jobs bringing to their task a totally incongruent set of aspirations and values is relatively small. And given that they are motivated to accept and apply themselves to their high-discretion roles, these roles are likely to evoke from them the appropriate attitudes. Hence the confidence with which reference has been made in earlier arguments to the association between high-discretion work and moral involvement.

In the case of job enrichment, however, management is offering enlarged discretion to those who do not necessarily bring to that new situation a congruent set of attitudes and values. Their responses in terms of behaviour will not necessarily, therefore, take those forms of involvement and identification which management hopes for. There is no reason, however, to suppose that such managerial ventures are destined for universal disappointment or anything like it. Certainly one would expect them to encounter setbacks. Individuals so set in their ways that they dread any variation; groups which see the proposed changes as perhaps disrupting long-standing social relationships which they greatly value; groups with an anti-management stance so strongly nourished by tradition and experience that it proves resistant to all managerial wooing – these are obvious possibilities. But equally there are signs of a readiness among some lower-level employees to accept an enlarged discretion in their work and to apply themselves within it in ways that meet management approval.

Even so, job enrichment has not, so far as present evidence appears to carry us, resulted in jobs that are seriously comparable in respect of discretion with those of middle and upper managers, engineers, scientists, lawyers and others of similar high-discretion status. As a consequence, it has not generated among those affected a comparable set of attitudes and values. Even job-enriched groups which demonstrate more positive and favourable attitudes towards their work and towards management show no disposition to dismantle their defences and integrate with management by abandoning trade unionism and collective bargaining, assuming they possess those defences.

Despite all these caveats, obstacles, and disappointments, job enrichment ideas have not disappeared. Recent years have seen the importation from Japan of so-called 'quality circles' – small groups of between five and ten employees who work together and meet regularly to discuss and solve job-related problems – a technique which links motivation with productivity and the economic performance of the company.

Finally, whatever else it has or has not done, the restructuring and redesign of work, whatever the managerial motivation, have led to some brisk disagreements among theorists. Until recently there was a tendency in much Marxist writing, for example, to assume that, given the constant thrust towards capital accumulation, employers and managers would inevitably be driven more in the direction of extreme division of labour, rigorous close supervision, and similar direct devices for extracting the required surplus. Braverman, for example, presented these as the increasingly characteristic techniques of exploitation under industrial capitalism. The various techniques categorized here as job enrichment hardly accord with this picture. Sometimes attempts are made to contrive an accord by dismissing all instances of job enrichment as mere window-dressing, of no significance to the recipients. How far this is true is a matter for empirical inquiry rather than deduction from first principles.

Perhaps some of those who consign job enrichment to instant disparagement do so because they see it as in some way a relaxing of managerial control – a slackening of the exploitation which they take to be inevitable under capitalism. And if even lower-level work were to become more satisfying, would that not weaken one of the factors making for proletarian discontent? To the first point it cannot be repeated too often that top management's search for control in the fullest and broadest sense does not necessarily require an unchanging commitment to any particular system of work patterns and job structures. Already some company employees perform discretionary tasks on a computer in their own home, free of both immediate technical constraint and direct human supervision. The answer to the second point is that it has always seemed regrettable that a supposed emancipation of future generations of labour should be thought to require present generations to remain maximally miserable. Much work has become conspicuously less gruelling and degrading over the past century. Further humanization seems a process to be encouraged rather than discouraged.

The final point, however, has to be that for anyone interested in the wider emancipation of labour, job enrichment is but one element. The shape of work is never, and has never been, accepted wholly passively by workers; nevertheless its basic outlines are determined by those with the predominance of power. It is to the fundamental power structure of society that those who seek major changes in the total experience of work must turn.

Further reading

Batstone, E., Ferner, A., Terry, M., *Unions on the board: an experiment in industrial democracy* (Blackwell 1983)

Blumberg, P., *Industrial Democracy: The Sociology of Participation* (Constable 1968).

Brannen, P., *et al.*, *Worker Directors* (Hutchinson 1976)

Braverman, H., *Labor and Monopoly Capital* (New York: Monthly Review Press 1974)

Bullock, Lord, *Report of the Committee of Inquiry on Industrial Democracy*, HMSO, Cmnd. 6706 (HMSO 1977)

Clegg, H.A., *A New Approach to Industrial Democracy* (Blackwell 1960)

Daniel, W.W., McIntosh, N., *The Right to Manage* (Macdonald-PEP 1972).

Davis, L.E., Taylor. J.C. (eds.), *Design of Jobs* (Penguin 1972)

Emery, F.E., Thorsrud, E., *Form and Content in Industrial Democracy* (Tavistock 1969)

Friedmann, A.L., *Industry and Labour* (Macmillan 1977)

Friedmann, G., *The Anatomy of Work* (Heinemann 1961)

Herzberg, F., *Work and the Nature of Man* (Staples 1968)

must set collective bargaining alongside them) from such devices as participative supervision, joint consultation and employee directors is that they vest the employee collective (union or organized work group) with some degree of control over decisions and with some responsibility for them. As we shall see, the possibilities are various. An examination of their relative merits and demerits cannot be undertaken here, for no discussion of how men ought to perceive their rights, duties, privileges and obligations in the context of particular decision-making arrangements can carry weight unless related to the prevailing structure and distribution of rights, duties, privileges and obligations in the wider society outside, and space limitations render discussion on this scale impossible. All that can be said is that decision-making arrangements which might appear to facilitate sectional, self-regarding behaviour by the employee collective (to the detriment, say, of consumer interests, or the technological or commercial viability of the organization, or government counter-inflationary policy) might properly be criticized in the context, for example, of a society dedicated to the pursuit of equality, but might be argued to be less open to criticism in a society structured so as to make sectional (or individual) self-regarding behaviour the principal mainspring of a highly unequal, competitive and acquisitive society.

Against the background of these considerations we return to the various alternatives of participatory control, enumerating them after the manner of Blumberg (1968):

1   Employee representatives may have the right to veto managerial decisions:
    a   temporarily, after which management either: (i) remains free to implement its decisions or (ii) must negotiate with employees (the arrangement sought by engineering unions in Britain);
    b   permanently (as in the system operated by the Glacier Metal Company).

2   Employees may have the unilateral right of decision (claimed by some forms of craft-type control, workers' 'self-management' and the like. This system is also receiving a certain limited expression in the shape of the 'autonomous work group', which is proving a favoured form in the discussion of job enrichment. The 'autonomy' granted by management is of course exercised only within a containing framework of managerial control, and depends for continuance upon its serving managerial purposes.)

3   Employees may have the right of co-decision with management.

At this point we turn from our abbreviated itemization of

alternative forms of control and focus on the commonest form of co-decision, which is, of course, collective bargaining. Its commonest context relates to 'personnel' decisions as categorized earlier, though as far as the employee collective is concerned any type of managerial decision is potentially appropriate for negotiation. The sorts of questions which the collective might well need to ask itself with respect to a particular area of decision-making include the following: Is this of sufficient concern for the union or work group that we want to induce management to commit itself to an agreed policy about it? Since an agreement implies a commitment on our side, too, what are we likely to have to commit ourselves to? Can we, and do we want to, carry the members with us on that commitment? What processes of communication and consultation are necessary if we are to carry the members with us – in other words if they are to legitimize the commitment?

The last question is crucial, for union and work-group leaders as well as management have problems of winning consent. If, at all levels above the individual's own job, participation in decision-making usually has to be through representatives, problems at once emerge of constructing and maintaining communications between representatives and constituents. Should adequate relationships not be maintained, the possibility exists of agreements being reached with management which constituents feel unwilling to honour. The issue is worth examining further since the debate about representative participation in decision-making in some form or another will no doubt sooner or later be renewed, and also because the question of constituents honouring the consequent agreement or understanding is widely felt to be of some moment.

One way into the problem is to ask how far management and employee negotiators can regard constituents to be morally, as opposed to merely formally, bound by an agreement in circumstances where, for example, it transpires that the employee representative failed to acquaint constituents with the relevant issues, choices and information, or has committed them on some issue about which they showed no interest at the time but which later proves to affect them adversely. The distinction between being formally bound and feeling morally bound is crucial; if the former is not supported by the latter the weakness is apparent. We need to think harder than hitherto about what procedures are going to be regarded as imposing moral obligations on people when representatives conclude agreements on their behalf. In other words, under what conditions and procedures of participation are we going to define constituents as morally bound? The extreme case exemplifies the problem. If an employee representative, be he union officer, shop steward or whatever, takes part in making a decision on an issue without consulting his constituents and without canvassing their opinions in any way, it may prove hollow for union and management if they subsequently insist that 'an agreement has been signed' and that constituents are bound by its terms. If the constituents feel no moral commitment to the agreement and have the power to resist it, the possibilities are obvious. Management and employee representatives have to work out, for their own situation, what are to be the conditions under which constituents *will be deemed* to have bound themselves morally to an agreement, and these must include a pattern of systematic communications between representative and constituent.

We noted in Chapter 1 certain deeper problems concerning employee obligation and the honouring of agreements. It was suggested there that in some industrial situations employee behaviour can only be satisfactorily explained by inferring that they feel little or no sense of moral obligation (as against a sense of expediency) towards the observance of agreements. If men subjected to subordination and extreme division of labour in large organizations consider that, despite trade unions and collective bargaining, they remain under a severe power disadvantage *vis-à-vis* management, their awareness of this managerial domination of the system may preclude their feeling any moral attachment to it. For the most part, trade unions have sought to strengthen membership observance by stressing the claims of honour. Yet even when members have appeared to accept the implied pluralist assumptions, leaders have often paid too little attention to the conditions which must exist if they are successfully to demand and expect their members' adhesion to the agreements concluded on their behalf.

Perhaps the problems of ensuring this adhesion are the more acute *a* the higher the level of decision-making at which representative participation takes place, and/or *b* the greater the extent to which the decisions lie within the 'technical' or 'business' categories without having any *immediately apparent* significance for the 'personnel' or 'social' categories. The danger is that, because employees evince no present interest in certain issues, representatives may agree to managerial measures which, when their full practical implications emerge, prove unpopular. It is these problems of communication and legitimation which require union or employee representatives to be wary about what they commit themselves to, rather than the usual argument of 'Unions mustn't get involved in management because they can't face both ways.'

Collective bargaining and management

That collective bargaining is not a formula for perpetual warfare is well attested by the experience of most Western industrial countries, where compromise agreements negotiated through collective bargaining, usually without disruption, have become the standard pattern governing some of the most central relationships between employer and employed. But although the institution of collective bargaining, far from generating destructive conflict, has always received some managerial support for its contribution to the promotion of employee compliance, it is not, as we have already noted, the open, high-trust, problem-solving relationship which for so many managements would be the ideal. To be sure, negotiating relationships vary widely and few are conducted in an extremity of bitter distrust. But few occupy the other extreme either: indeed the participants in a fully open, high-trust, problem-solving relationship do not see themselves, and are not seen by others, as being in a bargaining situation. Such a pattern is rare, however, between management and lower-level employees and their representatives. Even in the most co-operative of management/union or management/work-group bargaining relationships there is some irreducible minimum of wary mutual inspection, screening of communication and calculated measuring of specific obligations. These are the dimensions of distrust, and they constitute that failure of full integration which has proved so stubbornly irremediable under the numerous strategies applied by management over the past century.

The future would seem to offer little comfort for those managements still hoping for this full integration. Despite membership losses since 1979, the post-war movement towards union organization among white-collar and professional employees has shown that low-trust attitudes and the ability to express them in behaviour have spread vertically up the hierarchy to touch, in some cases, even middle-management ranks. They may not take the full adversary forms often found among manual wage-earning membership. Especially since the mass unemployment and punitive stance of the Thatcher adminstrations, some leaders in the white-collar and professional union field are raising possibilities of a more co-operative approach in their dealings with management, resulting in a relationship somewhere between the extremes of high conflict and full problem-solving. This could well sharpen divergence of policy within the trade union movement, but it would still be an approach which operated through the bargaining method.

Collective bargaining: a standard model

For purposes of analysis we may construct a standard model of collective bargaining which is intended not as a description of any particular reality but as a reference point for further discussion. As we proceed it will become evident that our explorations have moved full circle to take up again the themes touched on in the first chapter.

The standard model is grounded firmly on the explicit or implicit acceptance by both negotiating parties of the pluralistic conception of the organization. The working assumption is made that a distribution of power exists which, while not necessarily equally balanced between the two sides, at least is not so unequal as to induce either side to feel it is being coerced. On this basis, bargaining representatives conclude collective agreements which can rightly claim observance by those covered, not only for reasons of their own expediency but also because a moral obligation rests upon the parties to observe any agreement or contract which has been fairly and honourably negotiated free of duress. Our standard model also includes the notion of 'mutual survival'. Each side has, at any one time, a conception of certain entrenched rights which underpin a definition of its own functions, well-being and development, and these rights are recognized by the other. Thus management has a certain view as to those categories of decision-making which should be reserved for its own prerogative, as against those in which it is proper for unions and work groups to demand participation, and this view is shared by the unions and work groups themselves. Both parties therefore agree on how they define the frontiers of control and influence.

This agreement has obvious implications for the sense of security enjoyed by the parties and conversely for the degree of vigilant hostility they feel it necessary to deploy against each other. Management feels able to participate in collective bargaining and to afford the employee collective the necessary facilities and even encouragement, confident that no attack is contemplated on those areas of decision-making which it currently sees as defining its own autonomous managerial function and prerogative. On the basis of this confidence it tolerates the collective's challenge to its authority within the agreed range of negotiable issues, and tolerates too the fact that within this range the collective presents itself to employees as a rival focus of leadership and loyalty. Conversely, the collective does not examine every turn of events from a stance of deep suspicion such that management will resent and regard as illegitimate its presence in the organization and will seek to exploit every opportunity to undermine that presence. Given this confidence that management fully legitimizes its functions within the agreed range, the collective feels able to be more open and flexible in its communications and policies than if it felt it were constantly under threat of managerial attack and subversion.

A further feature of the standard model is that, within the agreed area of joint regulation, neither side persists in claims that are found intolerable by the other. It would clearly be possible for either side to try to enforce demands on which no compromise proved possible – a demand by the union, for example, that wages be doubled, or by management that wages remain constant for a period of years in the face of rising prices. Under our standard model, however, the aspirations asserted by the parties through the bargaining machinery always prove ultimately susceptible to negotiated compromise.

Given these conditions, the participants in our notional model find themselves able to construct and operate joint procedures of negotiation and dispute-settlement. In so doing they demonstrate that within the management/employee relationship there are areas of dispute but also substantial areas of agreement. Management acknowledges that the union has proper and legitimate functions within the organization and that these include mobilizing employees to challenge its prerogative in respect of certain categories of decision. But equally important, the union concedes that management has proper and legitimate functions that include the exercise of decision-making prerogatives over a wide range of issues which the union does not currently choose to dispute. This makes possible – though of course does not guarantee – a system of dual loyalties among employees by which they are conscious of ties to both company and union which co-exist and need not be in conflict.

These features demonstrate that under the standard model of collective bargaining the employee collective accommodates to the existing system of hierarchy, division of labour, and authority relations. Management's role is certainly modified in ways which are important for those subject to its rule, but the essential features of the work situation and the management/employee relationship remain the same. Under the standard model the collective aims to improve its members' position marginally along a number of these dimensions, particularly money rewards, but does not aspire to changes of such magnitude as could convincingly be portrayed as a qualitative transformation of the system.

Divergence from the standard: management and the unitary frame of reference

Having sketched the principal features of our notional picture, we can use it as a standard by which to measure the widely diverse situations found in real life. Some could be found which approximate closely to the model. Many others would reveal degrees of divergence from it which might not, however, strike us as so significant as to call for different categories of description. But there would certainly be some situations which diverged so significantly as to dispose us to look for new categories. Two extreme cases of this kind will now be examined. Both have already emerged in other contexts during the earlier exposition. One represents the extreme situation where management totally fails to observe the behaviour patterns described in our standard model. The other points to a similar failure by the employee collective.

The word 'failure' in this context does not necessarily imply that the party in question is *trying* to practise the appropriate behaviours but is not succeeding. To be sure, in this sphere of human action, as in all others, men may aim at certain standards yet fail through ignorance, foolishness or lack of foresight. But the possibility also exists that the failure is intentional, that the behaviours in question are not being followed because the party concerned is not pursuing the objectives for which they are appropriate. Here we need to register those situations which diverge fundamentally from our notional standard for the reason that management rejects the whole collective bargaining relationship. By its behaviour it demonstrates that it regards the employee collective as having no legitimate functions which involve it in challenging managerial prerogative in any area of decision-making whatsoever, or in presenting to employees a rival focus of leadership and loyalty which interposes itself between them and management. Refusing thereby to concede any legitimacy to the collective, it remains alert to any opportunity to undermine its position in the organization or weaken its appeal to employees.

Such a stance is likely to issue from a management which not only cherishes a private vision of the organization as a unitary structure with but one source of authority, leadership, and loyalty, but which also seeks to impose that conception in the face of whatever resistance is encountered from employees. Here we have in extreme form the determination to use power to prevent or minimize any union threat to the total integration of the organization. The union is apt to be seen as a purely external, self-seeking force trying to assert itself into an otherwise integrated and unified system. Success in excluding or severely weakening it is thought to preserve those ties through which management exerts its full prerogative and employees offer their undivided loyalty.

This is not necessarily, from management's point of view, a mistaken formula. If the union has secured no more than a toehold in the organization and the labour force as a whole remains relatively amenable and quiescent, there may be no obvious reason why management should lay itself open to union interference and collective bargaining. Free to regulate terms and conditions of employment and administer its policies unchallenged, it may see nothing but gain in taking active steps to maintain this situation by resisting the union presence. Such a strategy may enjoy considerable success when conducted within the context of a paternalistic family concern, or a plant that is geographically isolated, or a company whose policy combines non-unionism with the payment of wages well above the rates prevalent in the locality.

The balance of advantages may look very different, of course, if the spirit of collective challenge among some or all of the various occupational groups becomes so strong as to be a significant impediment to management's bureaucratic regulation of labour conditions and its exercise of prerogative in day-to-day business. Given the will and ability of work groups to contest decisions and impose costs on management unless it makes some accommodation to their needs, the principle of enlightened self-interest may come to point, for management, in the direction of recognizing the union stake in decision-making and seeing systematic collective bargaining as the best means of promoting that compliance which it now finds problematical.

This is not to suggest, however, that this issue is necessarily resolved by the calm application of sweet reason and rational appraisal of costs and benefits. We are dealing here with power relations, and people with power are apt to value it for its own sake as well as for what they can do with it. In other words, power may yield them intrinsic satisfactions as well as instrumental usefulness. Where this is the case the issue of whether to yield to union power pressures for participation in certain types of decision-making may be partly determined by managerial responses which have little to do with calm appraisals of whether union participation will or will not serve management interests. Counsel may be darkened by a primitive impulse to prevent any encroachment on personal prerogatives. Status considerations may also play a part. Resentment at being called upon to explain and justify one's actions and negotiate on them with persons of inferior occupational and social status was a common response among earlier generations of employers, and although few managers today would admit to a sentiment so unhelpful to public relations, the possibility that it survives in some quarters must be borne in mind.

Recognition of these impulses which can prejudice management's rational appraisal of the costs and benefits of union recognition and collective bargaining may have a wider application. Located on the continuum between the standard model and a total assertion of the unitary perspective are many situations which share some of the characteristics of both. Management may be prepared to engage in collective bargaining provided the employee collective confines its challenge within the limits found convenient by management, moderates the size of its claims to a level which enables management to settle for acceptable compromises, and contributes to the handling of grievances and disputes a spirit of give and take which fully recognizes the principle of mutual survival. But the employee collective may not observe these terms. It may on occasion press upon the relevant limits in ways which for management reopen the whole question of the value of collective bargaining. Clearly there may enter into these management responses the same primitive resentments relating to power and status which we have already noted. They help to explain the sudden emotional flare-up which sometimes aggravates the problems of a tricky bargaining situation.

We see here, then, a scale of management attitudes towards collective bargaining ranging from total acceptance (given the pre-conditions) to total rejection, with many companies occupying positions between these extremes and perhaps changing their position according to shifts in employee aspirations or changes in company circumstances. The scene is made still more complex by the fact that although, for convenience, the argument has referred to 'management', there are often differences of stance between different managers within the same workplace or company. These add to the difficulties faced by any company seeking to apply a consistent labour relations and personnel policy.

Finally, as noted earlier, even managers who fully accept the union presence and collective bargaining may also feel the need to try to counter the 'them and us' spirit and to do what they can to strengthen the assimilation of employees to managerial purposes. As a consequence, the language and policies of negotiation and recognition of divergent interests can often co-exist with the language and policies of 'human relations', 'involvement', or whatever other technique of man management is currently in vogue.

Divergence from the standard: the work group and the radical frame of reference

A similarly wide range of possibilities exists for the employee collective. It may, as we have seen, share with management a definition of the entrenched rights of both parties which enables them to conduct their relations in a spirit of mutual survival and therefore mutual security. At the other extreme, we may imagine a collective – perhaps a totally disaffected work group – acting in a manner which allows the inference to be drawn that it has completely withdrawn legitimation from management and concedes no right on management's part to discharge its present functions within the existing institutional framework of industry. To be sure, management may be able, perhaps at some loss to itself, to coerce the group into a forced compliance. But the essential conditions for a stable negotiated peace are not present. The employee collective does not offer that contribution which, along with the corresponding contribution from management, creates the reciprocity of mutual survival.

In the absence of this reciprocity, negotiation as normally understood is not possible. Management finds that the give and take which it sees as normally playing a major part in relationships with rank and file is not present. The collective appears to press every tactical advantage to the utmost, to resist the notion of mutual concession, to work actively against the promotion of mutual trust. This is, of course, simply a mirror image of the behaviour manifested by a management which refuses to concede legitimacy to the union presence. Coming from an employee collective it represents a total distrust of management which can spring either from experience in the particular company or industry concerned or from a generalized ideological rejection of the whole institutional framework of industry *and* society. At this point we return full circle to the theme with which we began: the contrasting images which different people and groups have of society, and in particular the radical stance which withholds legitimacy from management functions as at present socially defined.

But just as management attitudes usually lie between the extremes, so do those of employee collectives. While coming nowhere near denying management all legitimacy, the collective may yet wish to challenge managerial prerogative on issues which lie beyond the limits which management seeks to impose on its participation. Faced with continued exclusion from these issues, which management insists on retaining solely in its own hands, or perhaps grudgingly conceded a limited partipation which management seeks always to restrict and even reduce, the collective finds reason for distrust which may either co-exist with mutual confidence on other issues or gradually spread until it permeates the whole relationship.

The appeal to government and the political power structure

As these considerations show, the standard model of collective bargaining sketched earlier is useful only as a reference point to help us gauge the relative presence or absence of certain selected qualities in real-life situations. Perhaps few relationships between management and employee collective embody the full reciprocity of mutual acceptance displayed by the standard model. But the discussion has shown that in all situations where collective bargaining persists there is *some* body of shared ideas and values. Bargaining institutions prosper only when management recognizes the collective's claim that it has a right to exist; when the collective acknowledges that management must be allowed functions it currently deems crucial; when both can agree that their relationship shall continue; and when both subscribe to certain procedures, modes and values through which to conduct this relationship.

The prevalence of such situations in our society should perhaps reassure the fearful, though doubtless disappoint the revolutionaries with its implication that we are still far short of that anarchy which until recently was so widely seen as characterizing Britain's present condition. There are few signs yet of any widespread disposition to challenge management's hierarchical structures with their highly unequal rewards, status and respect.

Meanwhile, however, it is apparent that the institution of collective bargaining itself can still generate social tensions. Here and there managements try to resist it altogether and evoke deep frustration among unions seeking recognition as negotiating agents. Elsewhere managements may accept bargaining about pay but resist its extension, say, to disciplinary codes. Conversely, until mass unemployment became an issue, and in some places even since, unionized groups at the workplace could arouse hostility from management by pressing unacceptably hard with respect to both the range and the intensity of their claims, flouting agreed procedures for handling those claims, and manifesting too little of the spirit of give and take deemed desirable in day-to-day business.

Each side looks round for allies, and since the greatest potential ally is the state there develops the likelihood of appeals to governments for legislative support. Unions seek legislation which would help them, for example, in securing recognition from resistant managements; managements seek legislation which would help them in curbing those forms and degrees of collective pressure which give them special difficulty. Governments may of course legislate from convictions of their own and not necessarily as a result of pressure from the organized interests. The increased acceptance of responsibility by post-war governments for the health (as they define it) of the national economy has drawn them into an unprecedented degree of statutory intervention in industrial relations. Much of this has simply been an extension of a century-old state concern with peace and order in industry – a concern to encourage and promote procedural and substantive regulation which handles contentious issues in ways that minimize conflict and disruption. As union organization at the workplace grew rapidly in strength after the 1950s, more and more work groups became able to challenge management on issues which previously only a privileged minority of workers had been able to bring within effective control. Where voluntary effort seemed to be inadequate to meet the consequent need of systematic regulation, the state stepped in. Together with its responses to pressure from union or employer interests, this resulted in a substantial volume of legislation on such issues as periods of notice, redundancy payments, unfair dismissal, health and safety, and racial and sexual discrimination. Responses by Labour governments to specific union pressure produced much additional intervention, as did responses by Conservative governments to pressures from employers and management. As will be seen later, the 'national interest' was deemed by governments of both colours to require legislation which pleased neither side of industry.

Expressed in this way the positions of the parties may seem aggreeably symmetrical. The two major interest groups of capital and labour both appear to have access to governments for supportive legislation and an approximation to rough justice is assured over the long term. We may draw upon the analysis of the first chapter, however, to argue that this appearance of symmetry is illusory, just as the whole notion of a power balance is illusory. The legislative struggle takes place over measures designed to strengthen or weaken the ability of organized labour to challenge management only at the margins of the institutional structure of industry. As we have seen, the management/union struggle is not about such fundamentals of that structure as hierarchy, subordination, extreme division of labour, labour as commodity, and massive inequalities of treatment. These are – as yet – almost universally accepted by the rank and file in the sense of being seen, apparently, as inevitable and beyond any power of theirs to contest. Certainly we are all urged by a multiplicity of conditioning influences to see such features as right and proper, unavoidable, beyond the reach of human choice to change.

The struggle therefore takes place at the margins of this structure on issues which seem to employee collectives to be within their capacity to affect. How big the wage, how long the shift, what length the holiday, how heavy the work stint, on what conditions the job transfer, under what arrangements the redundancy – such are the usual categories of decision-making in which employee collectives seek a foothold. And it is legislation designed to influence one way or the other the ability of collectives to participate in *these* decisions which has been the subject of the relevant political struggles as conducted so far in Britain. What have been referred to here as the fundamentals of the institutional framework have remained untouched. The superior power of those concerned to preserve them has always been amply sufficient to daunt even such members of strong Labour governments as might cherish aspirations towards radical change. Thus the political struggle, like the industrial struggle, has so far been conducted largely at the margins of the system, and the reason for this has been the power of those individuals and groups whose interests, objectives or values are served by confining contention to the margins and preventing any more basic challenge.

Here we see at work the least visible and least discussed yet the most important and most significant characteristic of power – the part it plays in defining the issues and problems which come up for private and public contention and debate. Men conscious of relative weakness in a power relationship usually see as a waste of time and resources any aspirations which seem far beyond their capacity to realize. Similarly, most of those who shape and conduct public discussion through the media of radio, press and television are conscious of pressures to seem 'realistic', 'relevant' and 'topical', and are aware too, no doubt, of the influential disfavour apt to be directed at those who encourage 'destructive' and 'irresponsible' attacks by 'extremists' upon the fundamentals of the system. Thus they, too, play their part in determining the limits and nature of the public debate, thereby socializing us in what to see as the important and relevant issues and problems. For all that they pride themselves on their impartiality, it is an impartiality only between parties contesting issues at the margins of the system, not between parties contesting the assumptions, merits and values of the system as a whole.

In many subtle as well as not so subtle ways, therefore, the power structure operates not only, and not even mainly, by determining the outcome of such conflicts as do occur, but also by determining what kinds of conflicts do *not* occur. And in terms of maintaining in recognizable shape the basic fundamentals of the system it is the latter function which is the more crucial. Consequently, in trying to make an overall assessment of the workings of society and how different groups fare within it, it is as important to identify those issues which politics and collective bargaining do not deal with as to identify those with which they do.

The role of trade unionism and collective bargaining in Britain

When we appraise the situation in this light, collective bargaining in Britain emerges as a process through which employee collectives aspire, not to transform their work situation, but to bend it somewhat in their favour. It is not the same everywhere. Some French trade unions, for example, aspire to mobilize workers for radical political and social change, and allow this – not always with their members' approval – to shape their industrial campaigns. The more limited and pragmatic purpose of British unions and their members expresses what they currently see as a realistic adaptation to the facts of power, what they are induced by a multitude of influences to regard as a legitimate aspiration on their part, and what degree of self-confidence they feel in making this or that specific demand.

It is a process often misunderstood by conservatives and radicals alike. The former have sometimes seen it as a threat to the social order; the latter have sometimes derided it as shadow-boxing which, far from changing anything, serves only to prop up an unjust system. It is important, even at the cost of some recapitulation, to identify what is, and is not, valid in this particular radical position. Any wholesale disparagement of the part which can be played by collective bargaining in the work experience of those who feel the need for it reveals nothing more edifying than a total lack of insight into the nature of that experience. Perhaps those who press an extreme view here are not open to the sort of evidence which demonstrates the value that members so often place on their collective – such as the strong resistance they normally offer, given the chance, to any attack on its existence. Yet the limits to the role of collective bargaining have been revealed by our exploration of its very nature and of the values and assumptions on which it rests. It has survived because each party has conceded certain entrenched rights to the other – which for the employee collective has meant submitting to the institutional structure that decrees, among other things, extreme subordination and inferior treatment for its members.

The importance of the negotiation method for the collective's leaders in securing concessions has impelled them to propagate among their members, explicitly and implicitly, the values and assumptions which inform and support that method. Rank and file, as well as leaders, have had to offer a general acceptance of its codes of behavioural restraints and its recognition of what are currently to be seen 'realistically' as negotiable as against non-negotiable issues. Thus we have a situation in which the widespread and influential institutions of trade unionism and collective bargaining figure among those social forces which, far from stimulating rank-and-file employees into ever-rising aspirations and ever-sharpening challenges to managerial prerogative and authority, have served rather to contain them and confine them within those limits currently deemed appropriate for the continuance of the negotiation method. Trade unions have helped, in other words, to socialize their members in what it is sensible to demand of their work situation and in the methods (agreed with management) by which those demands should be pursued. Needless to say, the directions of influence have also operated in the reverse direction. Trade union members draw upon many other sources besides the union in fashioning their aspirations and their view of society, industry and work, and there are many formal and informal processes through which they communicate these aspirations and views to their leaders. Union officers and shop stewards are therefore right to stress that the ends they pursue and the means they employ to pursue them must always be responsive to membership wishes. But this is only half the story, for the union itself and its associated practices, methods and procedures help to shape membership conceptions of both ends and means.

Here we begin to draw close to what is valid in the radical critique of pluralist interpretations of how Western society works. It will be recalled that, starting from the assumption of an approximate power balance between the major interest groups, these interpretations present party-political democracy, trade unionism and collective bargaining as introducing into the system a degree of equity with respect to decision-making sufficient to render it tolerably fair and thereby deserving of respect and support. How many rank-and-file employees would find this picture convincing we do not know. What we do know, with respect to the work situation, is that the institutions of trade unionism and collective bargaining help to marshal them into patterns of aspirations and behaviour which, on the whole, support rather than challenge the fundamental structural features of the *status quo*. This, then, is how the radical critique perceives collective bargaining – as a process by which the rank and file, inferior in power, status and treatment, are allowed to press for marginal improvements in their lot on condition that they leave unchallenged those structural features of the system which perpetuate their inferiority. They are then urged to see the process as affording them parity with management and as thereby justifying the demand that they offer moral adhesion to the system as a whole. From the radical perspective, then, the institutions of collective bargaining and the social propositions which support and derive from it are in no sense neutral or balanced, but are heavily weighted in favour of the *status quo*.

down to the rank and file; they were given the franchise; they raised their status and aspirations. Increasingly, they asserted themselves as citizens who could not be denied, in their work situation, some version of the rights they now enjoyed in the political field. The middle-class sympathy and support once freely offered to employers who openly attacked the unions and collective bargaining became somewhat less reliable. And while there were always those for whom this shift in social values was a matter of indifference, many considered it judicious to change with the times and behave accordingly. Thus what had once seemed an insolent challenge to employer prerogatives and status came to be seen as standard practice which had to be lived with and made the best of. As they became increasingly habituated to the practice over the years, employers and managers found it easier to keep their tempers, provided union demands observed the conditions discussed earlier.

These developments demonstrate that the conception held by employers at any one time as to the extent of their prerogative is not a constant in some presumed pattern of human nature, nor yet a fixed and unchanging element in their definition of the management role. Rather is it an interpretation which, besides varying according to how they respond individually to challenges to their power and status, can be affected by changes in the values of social groups whose goodwill and support they prefer not to forgo. And it is clear that the latter can affect the former. Men may react emotionally when their expectations are violated or frustrated. But they develop these expectations as members of a society, and may change them under the influence of shifts in social values. And when expectations change, events which previously triggered off anger and resistance may do so no longer. Present-day management is far less likely than early entrepreneurs to offer vehement and emotional resistance to an employee demand for negotiation about pay. The logical implication is clear. Perhaps, given further changes in social values, it could become habituated to negotiating about issues which it currently regards as wholly within its prerogative. This possibility is not negated by the current Thatcherite encouragement of a macho-management style. It is by no means certain that Thatcherite modes will continue indefinitely to be seen by predominant forces within the Conservative party as the best and most judicious ways of conserving.

Even so, care must be taken to avoid over-simple projections. There could prove to be items in both the 'technical' and 'business' categories which continue to be seen by management as so central to its function, status and rewards that its resistance to negotiation on these issues stiffens progressively as such core activities are approached. Feeling could be so intense as to rule out any possibility of being influenced by changes in values in the wider society should these show signs of moving in labour's favour. Instead, management might devote considerable resources to attempts at securing that the predominant values in society did not move against them in this way. Such attempts would (on the assumption that they stopped short of state-supported violence) probably take the form of ideological and propagandist campaigns designed to convince as many as possible (*a*) that the latest proposed encroachments on their prerogative would destroy management as a specialist function serving the public interest, and (*b*) that the new demands were therefore essentially 'political' in a subversive sense which called for the mobilization of the sane, loyal elements in society.

What we are now considering, therefore, is the possibility that employee collectives, given increasing strength, rising aspirations and growing confidence in asserting them, might be found pressing hard against the defences of what management defined as sacred ground. In such circumstances there is a strong possibility that employers would condemn this union or work group pressure as fundamentally political in nature. This brings us to the distinction between 'industrial' and 'political' issues: an important one calling for closer examination.

Industrial and political issues

The distinction between industrial and political issues has been a key feature of Britain's industrial relations system, and constitutes another of the joint understandings which comprise the pluralist philosophy informing relationships between the organized forces of employers, trade unions and the party-political structure. These two categories have been deemed each to have their own appropriate procedures of resolution and their own appropriate arenas within which the procedures were conducted. The procedures appropriate to industrial issues were of course collective bargaining, conciliation and arbitration, followed, if these failed, by the strike (or lockout), the overtime ban, the go-slow, the work-to-rule and similar forms of pressure. The arena was industry itself, as represented by the organized forces of the employer or employers and the union or unions, along with such services as might be forthcoming from the government department concerned with these matters. The political arena constituted by parliament discussed these conflicts defined as industrial – definitions about which there was considerable agreement between employers, unions and the political parties – only when they caused widespread disruption. Even then, the common practice was for both Labour and Conservative Members to tread gingerly. The ostensible principle to which all wished to appear to be paying deference was that of saying nothing which might make the situation worse.

We may suppose the Parliamentary Labour Party's motivation here to spring from two major considerations. The first was no doubt an anxiety to appear 'responsible', alert to 'the national interest' and unfettered by exclusive ties to the trade unions. The other was likely to be a general disposition to avoid interfering in what was deemed the unions' industrial business unless specifically invited. The Parliamentary Labour Party was under a strong incentive to observe this convention, for it could then demand reciprocity from the trade unions in leaving political issues to be handled by political methods within the political arena. The conviction was widespread and emphatic within the Parliamentary Party that the unions should not use weapons fashioned for the industrial struggle, like the strike, in the pursuit of political ends, which should be reserved to the procedure and protocol of the Commons and the Lords.

Most union leaders showed no unwillingness to respect this convention, for they too had their reciprocal expectations. But, like the politicans, their interest in respecting it was twofold. Just as Labour politicans saw it as possibly damaging for them if they obtruded their political role too partisanly into industrial conflicts, so union leaders saw as possibly dangerous the deployment of their industrial battalions on the field of political conflict. For the politicians, the threat was to their claim to be a 'national' party; for the union leaders, to their rights and facilities as industrial negotiators. Our concern here being with the industrial field, it is the latter we need to examine more closely. Why should union leaders see danger for what has become their central function in our society, namely collective bargaining, in using their industrial strength for political purposes? In trying to answer this question we shall find ourselves pursuing different implications of the word 'political', one with particular relevance for their dealings with politicians, the other for their dealings with management.

the first case, the unions' deployment of their industrial power to pressurize or coerce the politicians would bring them into conflict with men who could, if they chose, use the legislative (and in the last resort, coercive) processes of the state to limit union rights and strength. There would be much support for this response from those alarmed at the prospect of the country's economic life being disrupted by industrial stoppages in pursuit of political purposes which they deem should receive expression only within the appropriate political institutions. If we ask who benefits most from this arrangement it will seem a reasonable assumption that the exclusion of the unions' industrial power from the arena of party politics particularly favours the more privileged sections of society. Political issues about which the unions felt strongly enough to use their industrial strength would be unlikely to command the sympathies of the well-to-do, who must therefore be reckoned to have a special interest in the convention we are examining. Observance of this convention was a pre-condition of the unions securing legal and some measure of social acceptance. This acceptance would not have survived the belief that organized labour's industrial strength had been 'captured' for 'subversive' purposes. However, the unions would not support such a convention unless it yielded them, too, some sort of return. And the return here lies in the fact that if the unions abstained from applying their industrial strength to political causes which offend the interests of wealth, power and status, then these in turn would not feel the need to use their great reserves of power to cripple the unions.

On this tacit understanding the unions could grow, thrive and have their being within the circumscribed area of action allowed them. The wealthy and powerful continued to enjoy their privileges, subject to yielding certain concessions which nevertheless left the essential structure of industry and society intact, while the unions and their members developed a stake in their participatory role as joint decision-makers with management over the limited area covered by collective bargaining.

Provided their perceptions, values, and objectives underwent no fundamental change, they could find this role sufficiently satisfactory to give them a strong consciousness of having something to lose. They assessed their strategies by criteria which included the need to avoid weakening, and to ward off any threat to, the institution of collective bargaining. Thus derived the fear that to use extreme industrial weapons against the politicians might bring down upon themselves and upon their functions the wrath of far more powerful sections of society. When used to support this conception, the distinction between political and industrial issues bore an ideological connotation in that it underpinned a particular interpretation of the proper role of trade unions in our society – an interpretation which, as we have seen, embodies values and assumptions supportive of the *status quo*.

By this time the reader may be somewhat restless at the preceding references to industrial and political issues on the grounds that no attempt has been made to define them. What makes one issue industrial and another political? There are no objective criteria. Issues have no *intrinsic* quality which lead us to put some in one category and some in the other. The difference simply lies in the methods by which we try to provide for their resolution. Political issues are those we currently handle through the institutions and procedures of national and local party democracy, while industrial issues are those resolved by management, or by unions, or by joint negotiating institutions representative of both.

There is nothing fixed or mutually exclusive about the allocation of issues to these categories. An issue may move from one to the other or finish up in both. It may begin, as in the case of the terms on which men may be declared redundant, by being regarded purely as a matter for decision within industry itself, and later become also a legislative issue at the national political level. In earlier times the determination of wage rates was deemed to be the ultimate prerogative of the state, exercised through annual assessments by local magistrates with reference to the trades within their area. In the nineteenth century the last remnants of this (always uncertain) procedure were swept away by the conviction that such decisions must rest solely within industry's own purview. Even this ideology of *laissez-faire* was enjoying its nineteenth-century apogee, however, governments in Britain were being constrained by the exigencies of opinion and events to legislate certain maxima with respect to working hours. Later came the state concern with factory health, sanitation, industrial injury and wage minima in certain selected industries. The categorization of what are industrial and what political issues is therefore shifting and conventional. There can be said to exist, at any one time, prevailing views as to which issues ought to belong in which categories, but these views are often contested by groups whose opinions do not currently prevail but may become the standard orthodoxy a few years hence. So nothing about the present categorization is sacrosanct, and no objective principles can be advanced to support an assertion of this kind.

We can go further, however, than to say that the two categories are conventional and not mutually exclusive. A case can be made that the whole distinction between the industrial and the political now rests on no more than paper-thin foundations, for its basis has been increasingly undermined by forces that have been at work for many years. Over a whole spectrum of issues ranging much wider than those of management/union relations, history has witnessed an increasing interpenetration of these two spheres of activity. Events of the last half-century have demonstrated that the development and exigencies of the modern national and international economy tend to draw the state more and more into active intervention for the purposes of regulating domestic economic affairs, promoting growth and influencing the nation's external trading relations. Increasingly the fortunes of governments are determined by their success (according to prevalent definitions) in monetary and fiscal management, in maintaining growth while containing inflation, and in striving towards economic viability within the world economy. Thus more and more the political levels of decision-making become involved in shaping many of the forces to which industry has to respond or which in some way limit its choices. By the same token, they shape the context within which trade unions operate. The unions cannot but be aware that political decisions can greatly affect what they are able to achieve for their members.

It has always been true, of course, that the state of the law, and how it is moulded by political legislators as well as interpreted by the courts, establishes a framework within which unions shape their objectives and fashion their methods. But increasingly political decisions affect the economic events to which those objectives and methods are a response. Such decisions have a bearing, for example, on the general level of employment, economic activity and demand for labour; on the state of labour markets in particular regions and even particular companies; on monetary and fiscal measures relating to prices and the cost of living; on the issue of expansion or contraction in particular industries; on the location of new economic development; and above all (in the form of incomes policy) on the constraints which bear upon unions and employers in their bargaining activities. Increasing awareness of the impact of these decisions upon their functions and achievements is likely increasingly to push the unions into seeking a voice in them. If it makes sense – and is justified by the democratic ethos – for a shop steward, as leader of his work group, to press for a say in his management's decisions about piece-rates, then equal sense and justification would attach to an aspiration by his union to participate in decisions affecting the conduct and fortunes of the company, the industry, the society in which they are located, and the economic relations between that society and the outside world – all of which bear upon the work experience, well-being, and destinies of the union's membership.

Political decisions and industrial issues being thus inextricably interwoven, unions can only fully apply themselves to the latter by pressing also for admission to the former. Being organizations with the central function of modifying decision-making, they are under pressure to seek out the highest as well as the lowest relevant levels at which this takes place. There is, of course, a litter of consultative and advisory bodies on which trade unionists serve even now and which touch this wider decision-making structure at certain points. But these commit nobody.

The prospect may seem remote given the strategies of the Thatcher administrations, but governments change and events may yet push unions, government and the organized employers into seeking commitments from each other on certain strategic areas of economic management. And it would be an unwary prophet who asserted that the strike threat and other expressions of industrial strength would never play any part in these processes. Possibilities of conflict would exist over such matters as what issues of high government policy were negotiable, and what the limits of change were for the issues being negotiated.

Thatcher governments and Labour politics

At the time of writing, the predominant weight within the Conservative party lies with those who are determined to contain and if possible reduce the political and for that matter the industrial influence of organized labour. For them, the implications of a 'social contract' – the name given in 1974–5 to an understanding reached between the Labour government and the TUC – are dangerous. In return for union co-operation in restraining the inflationary growth of incomes, the government made a number of concessions with respect to price controls, food subsidies, council house rents, and various social benefits. The bargain did not touch the fundamentals of economic management. The TUC did not aspire to have a voice in those government policy decisions about social, industrial, and military spending which, along with monetary and fiscal strategies, help to determine disposable income and employment for their members. They may, of course, claim such a voice some time in the future, thereby creating new constraints for government but at the same time binding themselves more deeply to attempt control over their members. For Conservatives at present, however, the dangers of such a procedure would far outweigh the possible benefits, for in negotiating for union co-operation they would consider there to be an unacceptable risk that the unions might steadily raise the price of their co-operation. This would continue that constant 'drift to the left' consequent on the relatively accommodating stance of previous Conservative governments; a drift which it was a central feature of the Thatcher strategy to halt and reverse.

Along with this must be noted the Thatcher government's desire to reduce more generally the unions' political activities. Not only have the unions been held at arm's length with respect to serious political consultation; legislative plans are also afoot to require the unions periodically to ballot their members on whether they should maintain a political fund at all. There has also been talk of requiring the individual member to 'contract in' to the political levy instead of, as at present, putting the onus on him or her to contract out, a change designed to deprive Labour Party finances of the benefit of human inertia. This proposal, however, had the consequence of bringing into sharp relief the fact that shareholders have no way of contracting out of subventions made by their company boards to Conservative Party funds. If the unions offer their own formula for acquainting the individual member with his right to contract out they may continue to be left alone on this issue.

The Conservative motivation to consider such changes has been strengthened by the rapid post-war growth in white-collar and professional unionism. Although support for the Labour Party has suffered damaging decline even among manual wage-earners, its appeal to white-collar and professional employees has ordinarily been even more limited. There is consequently thought to be a prospect that majorities in some of these unions may, given the chance, vote against having a political fund – from which all political activities have to be financed. Since the predominantly wage-earner unions are unlikely to follow suit, the possibility exists that TUC unions may become more markedly divided politically than they have been in the past. It is sometimes suggested that as the movement becomes increasingly white-collar in nature – a trend already far advanced – major sections will become increasingly conformist and politically unthreatening to the *status quo*. There is an implication here that in its predominantly wage-earner days it did present such a threat. The threat has never, however, been real, though there have been brief periods (1911–13 and 1919–20) when appearances confirmed some Conservatives in their belief that mass organization among the lower orders must always carry the danger of being used as a vehicle for political radicalism.

The debate on 'direct action'

Given that the Conservative impulse is to restrict the unions' political role, it must not be supposed that Labour politicians are at one in viewing that role with favour. Opinions about the 'democratic' quality or otherwise of the unions' block votes at party conferences, for example, tend to fluctuate according to whether the votes are wielded in directions favoured by the observer. But there are more searching disagreements. One of those receiving special prominence in recent years relates to 'direct action'.

The blurring of the distinction between industrial and political issues has had its counterpart in the increasing scepticism revealed by some Labour radicals towards the conventions just discussed. We are faced here with the paradox that although a popular base for radical social change seems as far away in Britain as it has usually been, radical social analyses which set out to 'de-mystify' the political and social process have become, since the 1960s, more widely disseminated than ever before. Among the results is wider acceptance of the argument that there is a profoundly ideological cast to the convention which decrees against organized labour using its industrial strength in pursuing political objectives. Business and finance are free to use, often relatively unobtrusively, their most powerful weapons – wealth and influence – towards political ends, whereas the political use of labour's strongest weapon – industrial organization – is defined as unconstitutional.

The issue is part of a wider debate about forms of 'extra-parliamentary' action, which are often deplored by those who invoke the sanctity of a parliamentary sovereignty supposedly uncontaminated by the power pressures of the world outside. A measure of humbug is at once apparent, since the history of parliament is inseparable from the history of pressure groups, lobbies, organized interests, and opinion spokesmen, all seeking to exert power upon parliament to move or not to move in a given direction. Sometimes the power is manifest and overt, as when people take to the streets, demonstrate, and try to mobilize opinion against the government. Sometimes it is latent, as when governments act on the awareness that a given policy would 'destroy business confidence', cause a flight of capital, or alarm foreign creditors and international bankers. Every government department is conscious of legislation that its seniors would like to promote but that they are deterred from promoting because of the unacceptably strong resistance it would arouse from organized interests. Every government department presents to parliament proposals for legislation that have already been tailored to meet at least some of the points raised during back-stage consultation with organizations affected. What critics of extra-parliamentary action usually have in mind, therefore, is action by organizations and towards objectives of which they happen to disapprove. Thus it is political pressure by local union or radical groups that is apt to be seen as of dubious constitutionality.

The debate is likely to persist, for, although there is no popular base for major social reconstruction, the post-war period has seen many instances of extra-parliamentary agitation and 'direct action' on certain specific themes, some national, many local. They include the Campaign for Nuclear Disarmament, Upper Clyde Shipbuilders, scores of factory 'occupations', and an abundance of local mobilizations on such issues as union recognition, the women's movement, race, community needs, and pay-beds in the National Health Service. Even on non-industrial issues they may include participation by local union branches or shop steward committees. They spring from a frustrated consciousness by participants that, for all our much-vaunted democratic machinery, matters which are deeply important to them are being handled by decision-makers who are beyond reach, shielded by formal constitutional procedures or by arrogant and unresponsive bureaucracies. The frustration is heightened by the fact that British government is, and has always been, particularly secretive government. Pressures which in other countries have produced Freedom of Information legislation have met little success in Britain, where the Official Secrets Act is freely used, though in recent years not always successfully, to prevent any unwelcome divulgence of information however irrelevant to 'national security'.

Many of the examples just enumerated give the critics of extra-parliamentary action little concern, since they lie at the relatively innocuous end of the spectrum of power. Demonstrations, processions, petitions, and similar forms of agitation can sometimes prove expensive or embarrassing nuisances to the authorities, but their propaganda effect on national opinion can often be countered by the far greater resources available to the state, and they usually impose few constraints on decision-makers. There are, however, certain examples which give the authorities greater unease. They include, on the larger scale, the anti-nuclear movement; and on the smaller scale the stance of health service employees on pay-beds and the apparent readiness to use the strike weapon towards their abolition. The latter raises the age-old spectre discussed earlier. It is a spectre that has troubled and divided the Labour Party, off and on, throughout its existence. The division remains today, between those who are, and those who are not, prepared to condemn extra-parliamentary action. Both sides usually have in mind, though this is rarely made clear, action which goes beyond demonstrations and the like and seeks virtually to coerce authorities, by means which include strike action, in directions they would otherwise not follow. In conjuring up nightmare visions of Britain becoming 'ungovernable' the debate usually ignores the great difficulty of inducing large numbers of people to strike about an issue that perhaps has only limited and indirect bearing upon their workplace situation.

Ultimately the problem arising from these more drastic forms of direct action derives from a clash between two varieties of democracy. One rests upon a conception of elected representatives and appointed specialists who expect, on the whole, to be left free within wide limits to discharge their functions according to their own judgement and to be answerable, if at all, at some future date and through certain defined formal procedures. The other visualizes a more participative situation in that the rank and file, or more precisely, interested groups within the rank and file, expect to have a much more direct and unmediated influence upon decision-makers. The pros and cons of both systems call for a discussion too elaborate and lengthy to be possible here; it must suffice to say that there must be some doubt about the ability of national and local democracy, as at present constituted, to cope satisfactorily in terms of consent with the multifarious 'special-issue' groups and functional organizations that spring up in an increasingly complex society and strive to exert influence over decision-makers. The assumed general consent that governments and local authorities derive from the present constitu-tional procedures does not necessarily cover the grievances, claims, and convictions of particular groups who are in a position, if they feel ignored or affronted, to make life difficult either for the authorities or for their fellow citizens or both. Of course, since no society can ever wholly meet the often contradictory needs of all its constituent groups, frustrations of some sort must persist. They are, however, heightened when the system is unable to provide ways by which certain groups and organizations can fully register their case at strategic levels and derive a sense of participating in the major decisions made there.

The 'politicization' of industrial relations

In few fields of public policy have these problems of decision-making, participation, and consent been more obvious and intractable than in that of post-war pay movements and the struggle to contain inflation. Governments have been elected to office pledged to efficient economic management and counter-inflationary policies. In their pursuit they have had to take note of views and advice which the TUC had no hesitation in urging upon them. But their policies also had to be shaped within a context of commitments and priorities on a host of other issues in which the TUC had no voice and was hesitant to assert one – military spending, obligations abroad, total government expenditure, monetary and fiscal policy, and all the exigencies imposed upon Britain as a result of the determination to maintain an open economy exposed to a highly aggressive and efficient international capitalism. Union leaders were urged to accommodate themselves and – far more taxing – their members within whatever levels of pay increase were deemed by governments or state agencies to be appropriate in the light of policies which the unions were powerless to influence.

The difficulties with respect to consent were acute enough as between government and union leaders; they were vastly greater as between government and the mass of rank-and-file unionists. They, after the 1950s, had been enabled by continuing full employment and the power it bestowed to strengthen and extend the structure of union shop-steward organization at the workplace encouraged during the war. Enjoying, as they did, a considerable measure of independent strength they were often able, given complaisant managements anxious to minimize interruptions to business, not only to push up earnings by a variety of devices well above the limits thought desirable, but also to protect themselves by acting upon the labour supply through restrictive measures usually described as 'custom and practice'.

Labour and Conservative administrations alike fought many losing battles against the ratchet effect of constant inflation and the problems it brought for the balance of payments, the exchange rate, and economic growth – which suffered regular discouragements by measures aimed at reducing pressure on resources. Governments felt impelled to interfere, sometimes with powers of statutory enforcement, in those processes of free, 'voluntary', and sectional collective bargaining which, by one of the tacit understandings so important in British political life, had long been accepted as inviolable except in wartime.

For the Labour Party the compulsion felt by Labour governments to appear 'national', 'responsible', and 'fit to govern' created internal conflicts that became increasingly acute as Britain's economic decline became more and more marked. Labour's right-wing acceptance of the 'mixed economy' and all it was assumed to require involved its governments, as the left wing of the party saw it, in propping up an ailing and inefficient capitalism at the expense of working class standards and of free collective bargaining. In struggling to stem rising levels of earnings and reduce the incidence of strikes, Labour governments were trying to discipline their own class base. It was as if the front line of the economic class struggle ran, not between capital and labour, but down the middle of the Labour Party. For governments of both colours, in other words, as for governments in other countries, what happened in industrial relations had become of acute concern. Conversely, much that governments did was of acute concern to those involved in industrial relations. Industrial relations had become 'politicized'.

The term, however ugly, is useful in that it prompts questions about how Britain's polity is affected by the attenuation of that distinction between 'industrial' and 'political' issues which was an important element in the settlement, slowly forged over a century, between the ruling order and organized labour. Yet it is also a term displaying many ambiguities.

In the first place it permitted of both a strong and a weak sense. Used in the strong sense, it conveyed the fear of some on the right, and the hope of some on the farther left, that economic conflict at the workplace might be translated into political conflict beyond it. Were the British working classes at last being brought nearer that revolutionary temper whose historical absence so many on the left had tried so hard to understand and explain? How could they fail to grasp, now that events were forcing not only Conservative but also

Labour governments to intervene ever more blatantly to hold wages down and reduce strikes, that the whole system was rigged to serve an unjust capitalist and exploitative order? To the revolutionary it seemed they must grasp it all the quicker if the basic nature of the confrontation could be revealed in its maximum starkness and reality. This could be achieved by appropriate leadership, by encouraging employee claims and aspirations on issues deemed by management to be non-negotiable, and by encouraging claims and aspirations on issues that were negotiable to be pitched so high as to intensify the usual difficulties of compromise. Only when the ruling classes are goaded beyond endurance, it was believed, do they reveal the exploitative resolve and violence that otherwise often lie, if not latent, at least decently masked by the mystifications and 'ordinariness' of the system. Given the fiercer resistance that this must evoke from the exploited, who would finally come to see their common predicament in basic political–class terms, there is a prospect of rendering existing institutions unworkable, thereby opening a way for the construction of new ones.

Essentially this strategy seeks to achieve radical social change by testing the existing system to destruction. A system which rests on compromise is weakened to the extent that differences are levered so wide apart as to make compromise impossible. The industrial disruption thus produced, if on a sufficient scale, may also serve as a battering ram with which to coerce government.

The same results may also be produced by promoting claims which bear intolerably hard upon the frontiers of prerogative as management currently defines them. Such claims have always generated genuine alarm. As we have seen, these frontiers protect structural arrangements, principles, values and decision-making roles considered essential to managerial functions and privileges, but common also to most economic, political, and social organizations of any size in our society. Understandably, therefore, management shares with many others the conviction that they are fundamental to the existing social order. Any strong refusal to submit to them is bound to seem 'irresponsible', 'unreasonable' and 'unpatriotic' to those anxious to uphold them. It will also seem 'political'. The charge of being political will always be levelled at those whose aspirations appear to threaten the stability of an established order. The use of the word in a derogatory context therefore serves an ideological purpose. Indeed, in such a context the whole distinction between political and industrial issues is an ideological one, for it serves to discredit those which constitute a challenge to the existing system while tolerating those which do not.

At this stage we can draw from the argument a point relevant to all forms of employee participation in decision-making. We can recognize a distinction between participation activity which is deemed by those in positions of authority to accept the existing system and to work within it, and participation activity which in some respect or another is seen as rejecting the system and seeking to change it. Those who for reasons of personal interest, objectives or values identify with the existing system may tolerate, possibly even welcome, the first. They will certainly oppose the second. Here we establish a link with a point noted earlier. The support offered by management and by those in sympathy with its values and purposes to the notion of participation is never open-ended. It is bounded by the extent to which participation confines its aspirations and pressures within what is currently deemed the essential framework of the prevailing order. The management approach to participation is thus as fully instrumental as the other personnel and labour strategies examined in this book. Employee participation can only enjoy management support and encouragement when it takes place on management terms and can be justified in some way or another as ultimately contributing to managerial purposes and values. When, therefore, employee representatives taking part in decision-making come under familiar exhortations to 'Be responsible', 'Be reasonable' or 'Be patriotic', these can often be translated to mean: 'Limit your claims and aspirations to what is compatible with the stability and continuance of prevailing social values, institutions, priorities and arrangements.'

Those who choose not to observe these limits are pursued hard in the media, some of whose practitioners help to keep alive the old myth of the sinister stranger who arrives on the train from London, secures a job in the local factory, and within weeks has single-handedly galvanized a hitherto contented workforce into a mass strike. Perhaps one of the most persistent misjudgements committed by established authority is its exaggeration of their ability to do this. Revolutionaries might well wish they really did enjoy those powers of creating mass disaffection out of thin air with which they are so freely credited. Detached observers, however, have often pointed to the abundant evidence that while those bent on disruption can often fish successfully in troubled waters, they cannot generate these favourable circumstances wholly by themselves. They can focus and sharpen grievances, encourage militant rather than conciliatory means of pursuing them, and place themselves at the head of aggressive action. They cannot, however, conjure up a mass grievance where none exists, and far more revolutionary hearts have been broken by rank-and-file indifference than have been warmed by a militant readiness to take up the struggle. Even when their troops have followed them on to the battlefield in pursuit of a bread-and-butter grievance which they have managed to adorn with the rallying cries of the class war, they have been mortified to discover that once the bread-and-butter objective is achieved their army soon melts away, leaving the ground strewn with abandoned revolutionary banners. But while established authority often exaggerates the ability of the militant leader to promote and sustain mass disturbance, there is more substance in the tendency to believe that its interests would be furthered by eliminating him and (it is hoped) leaving the rank and file leaderless. Admittedly this too is often questioned by the liberal observer. Experience has shown, he may argue, that a mass grievance is not eliminated by getting rid of the leader who focuses, articulates and organizes it. Authority's obsession with the leader's importance merely expresses its need for the self-reassuring belief that basically the rank and file are loyal if gullible, and that only the interfering and often politically motivated firebrand is responsible for the really serious disruption.

These arguments gloss over an important point. To eliminate the leader who is focusing, articulating and organizing a grievance may represent for management (as for any other ruler) a considerable gain. Certainly the grievance itself is not thereby eliminated, and another leader may spring forward to fill the gap, more bitter and desperate than his predecessor. But the grievance has to be of great intensity to ensure this, and in many situations of a less extreme temper the supply of those prepared to incur the potential strains and penalties of leading a campaign against superior power is strictly limited. Even in the absence of leadership, however, will not the grievance manifest itself in a variety of covert ways no less disagreeable to management? It may or may not; management may believe it can control these alternative expressions or consider them less costly. There is no intention here of supporting any general proposition that management's best policy is always to try to eliminate the troublesome leader. Judged by long-term criteria which take the widest possible view of costs this may often be a mistake. But there are situations where it is not *necessarily* true that for management to suppress an aggressive and disaffected employee leadership does managerial interests more harm than good. Any such assumption is a liberal illusion.

This teasing-out of the implications of revolutionary disruption creates some danger of exaggerating its practical significance. Although in certain circumstances those who pursue this strategy may be able to heighten the difficulties faced by managers in some limited sections of industry, their hope of exploiting such possibilities for purposes of radical social change are forlorn. It is safe to say that, except in the eyes of those on the left or the right who have been determined to perceive events in these terms, a majority among the British working classes have always declined to convert their workplace militancy into radical political categories, even at the peak of their union power in the 1970s. Like owners and controllers in the industrial, commercial, and financial sectors, and like many practitioners of the professions, they are usually prepared to assert their sectional interests with apparently little or no practical consciousness of the claims and obligations of any wider collective citizenship. To expect them to behave otherwise, given the way British society has developed, is part of the humbug in which that society abounds. But to suppose that there is the slightest prospect of this most conservative of working classes being prepared, even given a significant measure of industrial breakdown, to follow workplace leaders towards radical socialism of the type currently on offer can only be described as another triumph of hope over experience.

As a consequence of all this we can talk of industrial relations being 'politicized' only in its weak sense. Because governments felt impelled to try to impose, sometimes by statutory means, what they defined as the 'public interest' upon the outcomes of collective bargaining and upon other aspects of collective behaviour at the workplace, unions and unionized work groups were drawn into disputes and conflicts with political agencies. Industrial relations and behaviour had become, in other words, part of the stuff of politics. This might, and did, mean sharp disagreements and resentments between trade unionists and governments, and between groups within the Labour Party. It did not mean that major sections of organized labour felt driven to adopt left-wing radical perspectives. Even so, the prospect of the strike being used to contest issues defined by government as political was daunting for the authorities even though the motivation stopped far short of being politically radical.

This became especially evident when the situation took on a new dimension with the advent to power of the 'New' Conservatism. Leading members of the Thatcher administrations revealed, in their stated public attitudes and in their legislation (1980, 1982), a determination to reduce the standing and effectiveness of the unions in the nation's economic and political life. Given the step-by-step whittling away of the unions' legal scope and safety; given the transfer of public services and industries to the private sector; given the bit-by-bit withdrawal of the state's century-old support for collective bargaining; and given the studied exclusion of the TUC from serious top-level political discussion, was there not a probability that organized labour would feel driven to use the strike weapon against the government's expressed will? The British Telecom case of 1983 provided an example. Its engineers considered that legislative measures which opened the field to the private sector threatened their own jobs, and withheld the necessary co-operation. Was this to be regarded as a *bona fide* trade dispute, enjoying the immunity, conferred in the 1906 Act, from actions for damages? For the Thatcher administrations it was crucial, not only for this particular case but also for their anti-union strategy in general, that it should not. On the contrary it was necessary that the unions' so-called 'immunities' be ever more narrowly defined so as to deprive them of protection whenever they pitted their strength against the government. Already the 1980 Act had greatly undermined the 'trade dispute' defences by cutting, in the words of leading labour law authorities, 'wide swathes' in the immunities. The 1982 Act renewed the attack by further narrowing the definition of 'trade dispute' in four ways, one of which required it to be 'wholly or mainly' in connection with industrial matters, a stipulation said to be necessary for excluding 'political' disputes. The government's insistence on this distinction, argued here to have become strictly meaningless over a wide area where 'industrial' and 'political' overlap, is itself of course a political act.

The whole question therefore of the relations between governments – especially Conservative governments – committed to national economic management and trade unions committed to defending their members' interests has become even more deeply problematical than it has been in the past. Whether the Thatcher government's 'solution' of imposing its own highly adverse definition of those relations upon the union movement represents a stable settlement is among the gravest issues facing British society.

At the end of 1983, however, given the divisions among the political opposition, the Thatcher forces had suffered no political reverse as a consequence, the situation having developed in such ways as to favour the right rather than the left. There was at this time no discernible evidence of mass outrage among trade unionists towards Thatcher policies. Among the reasons for this was that competitive sectional bargaining in conditions of relative labour shortage had for some time produced results which were sometimes disagreeable even to trade unionists themselves. In Clegg's words: 'Compared with the period up to 1970, the strike record of the last twelve years has been dominated by large-scale, official, set-piece stoppages, most of them in the public sector, in which . . . it is through hardship inflicted on the consumer that the strikers seek to influence the government.' As workers in the public services developed a new militancy, they took up with great vigour the standard methods of trade unionism – the closed shops, the strikes, the attempts to regulate and restrict labour supply and protect jobs. Attitude surveys assiduously polled the public after experiences of rubbish rotting in the streets, ambulance drivers, firemen, and water workers withholding services, and social security staffs denying applicants whose need was far greater than theirs. They invariably found substantial proportions among trade unionists reacting with some disgust and being prepared to agree that unions have too much power. Such evidence must be handled with caution. When people condemn trade union behaviour it is usually the behaviour of unions other than their own that they have in mind. Nevertheless the evidence was to prove useful to Heath and Thatcher governments claiming popular backing for anti-union legislation. These governments drew support, too, from the fact that many even among traditional Labour supporters were losing faith. Who, after post-war experience, could convincingly claim that the labour movement offered any practical demonstration of a more decent way of arranging things?

Current aspirations and the future

Yet the assertions and confidence of organized labour was, with rare exceptions, being exerted within a comparatively limited range of bargaining aspirations. What stood out was the relative conservatism of the claims being made. They might conceivably have been far more ambitious. They might have sought, for example, to improve employee pay, status, and general treatment relative to those enjoyed by top management and other favoured groups, thereby pressing for a more egalitarian society. They might have sought far more widely and vigorously to weaken the concept of labour as a commodity, by which it is taken for granted that they can be hired or discarded as management interests demand, and insist instead that productive exigencies adjust to *their* needs rather than the other way round. They might have pressed the claim that their work be made more intrinsically satisfying by being invested with greater discretion. They might have shown increasing resentment towards their subordination to hierarchical authority and demanded increased participation through open-ended forms which go far beyond the manipulative 'human relations' containments.

Claims along this dimension could come to include a demand for effective participation at those highest decision-making levels which determine the aims, conduct and destinies of plants, companies, industries, national economies and the relationships between them. Such aspirations would require for their realization major shifts in social values and priorities, the structure of power, authority and influence, the distribution of rewards and privileges, and concomitantly no doubt in the pattern of ownership and class stratification. Is it possible to detect stirrings of pressure in any of these directions?

There are few signs of rank-and-file employees aspiring to narrow the ranges of wealth, income and status. The present very great inequalities serve to sustain social values which put predominant emphasis on an acquisitive and competitive getting and spending, and in the absence of any effective alternative vision of how men might live together these will increasingly influence the aspirations and behaviour of the rank and file just as they do those at the top of the hierarchy. It could well be that a severe narrowing of the ranges would both express and reinforce a shift in social values away from competitive acquisition. But leaders of employee collectives do little to offer their members any such alternative vision. Given that present values continue to hold the field and that the enormous permitted variations of wealth, income and status continue to symbolize the value set on competitive acquisition, employee collectives will be expected by most of their members to behave accordingly.

Is there no likelihood of the collectives ever trying to break the vicious circle by seeking to lead members towards the vision of a more equal society? The point here is that no union or even group of unions could hope to pursue such a purpose within the restricted range of one industry or even one sector of the economy. A drive to promote egalitarian values would have to be society-wide. This means, not an industrial movement, but a political movement, using the institutions and methods which that term currently implies, in a campaign for power to effect the necessary institutional changes. Here much depends on the leadership offered by the political movement, for it is likely that many, if not most, trade unionists see the present range of rewards as an inevitable response to unchangeable laws of human nature, and would need convincing by their political as well as their industrial leaders that an egalitarian programme was viable. Little leadership of this sort has been forthcoming. Equality figures more prominently in political rhetoric than in political programmes. Meanwhile employee collectives, though impelled by values which are nourished and sustained by the existence of very high levels of income and wealth, relate their own aspirations not to these levels but to those more nearly approximating to their own. There seems no present sign of this changing.

About aspirations along other dimensions there is rather more to say. There have been some signs, for example, that resistance to the concept of labour as a commodity is stiffening. Following the example of Upper Clyde Shipbuilders there have been scores of less publicized instances where employee groups have occupied factories scheduled for closure. Such groups are aware only of wanting to protect their own jobs and disclaim any revolutionary or radical political views. Yet their behaviour represents an act of group self-assertion against a principle hitherto considered integral to industrial life in the West – that propertyless wage- and salary-earners must place themselves at the disposal of the changing and fluctuating labour demands of employers and managements – a principle itself highly political, needless to say. Strikes against actual or threatened redundancy in British Telecom, steel, and coalmining, for example, may indicate a growing disposition among sufficiently motivated groups to stand firm against the implications of an intensifying pace of economic change. Only time can show whether these gestures constitute the early signs of a response destined to grow and strengthen, or whether they are no more than symptoms of passing moods.

Some commentators professed, for a while, no such uncertainty with respect to a dimension discussed in Chapter 5 – the degree of active discontent manifested by rank and file towards low-discretion work which affords them little or no intrinsic satisfaction. Confident assertions were made that positive rejection of such work was stiffening throughout the Western world. In Britain, however, the condemnations of fragmented, dehumanized work emanated as much if not more from middle-class observers as from the millions of wage- and lower salary-earners who perform it, and as we noted earlier the unions themselves reveal no leadership initiatives designed to awaken or strengthen aspirations in this field of work experience. Employee consciousness of a poverty of experience in their work tended to be manifested in the form of responses to inquiries by academics or the media, rather than as a spontaneous assertion accompanied by demands for change.

This passivity of employees and their collectives on the subject is an invaluable resource for those anxious to preserve the *status quo* in work organization and job design. It enables them to counter criticism with the assertions that most rank-and-file employees shun discretion and responsibility and that would-be reformers are merely trying to impose on others their own values and preferences. The likely truth is, as we have seen, more complex. Men who have never experienced intrinsically satisfying work can hardly be said to have 'chosen' intrinsically unsatisfying work. They have been constrained to submit to it by such factors as family, education and expectations acquired through social conditioning and job experience. Since, in order to preserve their mental health, they are likely to adapt to this situation (or, to use alternative terms, resign or reconcile themselves to it), it is not surprising that they fail to exhibit attitudes more characteristic of those whose family, education and social conditioning have given them very different expectations and aspirations. Passivity may, in other words, symptomize an adaptation to what is seen as inevitable, rather than a voluntary choice from among known and understood alternatives. The fact that employees and their unions in Britain are at present advancing few active claims for intrinsic involvement in work is fully compatible with the possibility that many find their work profoundly unsatisfying but do not see significant change as a realistic aim. Accordingly they adapt their aspirations to what they have learned by experience is within reach.

There is nothing inevitable about their maintaining this passivity towards job design. The debate about the quality of life, stifled for the time being within the atmosphere created by Thatcherian Conservatism, may some day revive. There seems no logical reason why employee collectives should not respond to a quickening interest among members in the quality of their own working lives by leading campaigns against management on this issue. At present such possibilities seem remote. The avowed intention of the Thatcher administrations to check rising expectations has been effective at least to the extent that several millions of people, now enduring the emptiness and futility of unemployment, would be glad of almost any job, however low in intrinsic satisfaction. It may well be some considerable time before many of the debates of the 1960s and 1970s are resumed, if ever.

Of one thing we may be certain. Rank-and-file employees will receive no encouragement from employers and managers, from banking, commercial, financial and advertising interests, or from leading politicians of any party, to pursue greater intrinsic satisfaction in work *at the expense* of economic efficiency, productivity and growth. Where they can be reconciled there will be no problem. But where the first threatens the second, the demand for intrinsic job satisfaction is likely to get short shrift, or come under efforts at manipulation towards more 'responsible' objectives. The influences bearing upon us to pay almost any price for efficiency and growth are already, of course, very great. As yet we offer little resistance. Even those among us who are consuming abundantly show few signs of satiation, and there are considerable numbers still far short of this happy state. The forces arrayed against any demand for intrinsic work satisfaction at the expense of efficiency and growth are therefore potent.

Speculative and tentative though this discussion of future possibilities has inevitably been, it has at least alerted us to the possibility that trade unions and organized work groups do not have to be supportive of the present *status quo*. Certainly the continuance of collective bargaining, if that remains a central purpose, requires that they abstain from attacking those entrenched prerogatives which management currently sees as essential to its functions (just as it requires the same restraints of management). But, as we have seen, management's definition of these entrenched rights is not fixed and unchanging. Having changed already, they could presumably change further.

The possibility of increasing resistance obviously introduces a crucial consideration bearing on the unions' chances of success in any programme of 'encroaching control'. Nevertheless the point emerges clearly from this as from earlier discussion that employee collectives participating in managerial decision-making can choose either to accept management's current definition of the boundaries of that participation or to seek to extend them. They can choose either to work within the system or to try to change it. Should they seek to press their encroachment on managerial prerogative beyond the furthest extent which management proves ready to accommodate, their strategy would, by definition, threaten the institution of collective bargaining. While this is a conceivable political programme it seems a highly improbable one in the context of modern Britain.

Even when operating within limits acceptable to management, however, collective bargaining can still create chronic difficulties for our society and its institutions. To this type of challenge we turn in the next chapter.

Further reading

Allen, V.L., *Trade Unions and the Government* (Longmans, Green and Co. 1960)

Coates, K. (ed.), *Can the Worker Run Industry?* (Sphere Books 1968)

Flanders, A., 'Trade Unions and Politics' in *Management and Unions* (Faber and Faber 1970)

Harrison, M., *Trade Unions and the Labour Party Since 1945* (Allen and Unwin 1960)

Wedderburn, Lord, Lewis, R., Clark, J., *Labour Law and Industrial Relations* (Clarendon Press 1983)

8 Participation, bargaining and the wider society

Intended and unintended outcomes

The argument to be developed in this concluding chapter requires us to begin by drawing a distinction between a threat to the system that is willed and intended, and a threat that is not willed and intended but develops nevertheless out of people's actions. A simple example will help to clarify the nature of the second type of threat. In the early days of the motor-car, the institution of unrestricted private motoring created no great social problems, for only the tiniest of privileged minorities were able to engage in it. With the increasing equality of access to private motoring, however, have come immense problems such as pollution, congestion, road costs, wholesale destruction of amenity, and, of course, death and mutilation on a large scale. It is safe to assume that few of the participants will these consequences. The motorist wills only his private convenience or pleasure. Yet when large numbers engage in the activity the outcomes include social costs of frightening proportions.

The shortcomings of this example as an analogy to collective bargaining will soon become apparent, yet it offers some points that are illuminating. In the early phases of our competitive and acquisitive industrial society the number of individuals and groups with power enough to enable them (as landowners, manufacturers, merchants and financiers) to use it, in one way or another, in a private quest for wealth and status was relatively small. Although their competitive struggles and the methods they used to wage them could sometimes injure large numbers of those they employed, relatively few of these had sufficient strength themselves either to fight back or to get their difficulties elevated to the status of 'social problem'. Some were able to mobilize a little power for themselves by collective organization and use it to defend, and possibly improve, their position. For a long time the proportion of the working population able to engage in this aggressive defence of their modest interests remained small and, even during the later periods of long-term membership growth, has fluctuated considerably. It remains true today that the coverage in Britain reveals great gaps. Even before the recent losses in membership, large numbers even of male manual wage-earners remained unorganized, and despite considerable strides in unionization among women wage-earners and white-collar employees of both sexes the scope for further recruitment remains considerable. Yet although collective organization is still incomplete, the self-protective power pressures through which groups seek, sometimes to improve their position, often only to defend what they have, already considerably aggravate the inflationary forces now active for so much of the time throughout the industrial world. Added to the inflationary pressures exerted by manufacturers, merchants, financiers, the higher professions and other groups who seek to protect themselves by using their power to raise prices, margins, interest rates, charges and fees, they create or intensify strains on the country's foreign trading position, economic growth, group relations and other aspects of its social fabric. Here, then, we see considerable stresses being created by the ability of organized groups to engage in aggressive power struggles, either for advancement or for defence (which under inflationary conditions also requires predatory aggression). In other words, the gradual extension throughout society of the capacity to practise sectional and group self-assertion through power creates problems which did not exist when this capacity was confined to the relatively few. Even so, these problems began to be remarked on by social critics well over a century ago. Matthew Arnold, in *Culture and Anarchy* (1869), was concerned among other things to argue against English individualism and the cult of self-seeking individual or group assertion which in his view precluded the growth of a truly civilized society and culture. These features of his society he summed up in terms of 'doing as one likes'. The emergence of the wage-earner into the arena through collective action and mass behaviour greatly sharpened such alarms. 'While the aristocratic and middle classes have long been doing as they like with great vigour, he has been too undeveloped and submissive hitherto to join in the game; and now, when he does come, he comes in immense numbers, and is rather raw and rough.' Britain's plebs had never been anything like as 'undeveloped' and 'submissive' as Arnold appeared to think, but the essence of his argument was valid enough. Its more doom-laden implications failed, however, to materialize. Such was the pragmatic shrewdness and skill which predominated among Britain's ruling order that, given the political and social system which they had the good luck to inherit, they were able gradually to construct a settlement with the organizing working class which greatly moderated what Arnold defined as the rawness and the roughness. Yet the basic difficulty not only remained but grew to crisis dimensions after the Second World War when long-term full employment, and the power it conferred upon many sectional groups, combined with a weak and inefficient economy to create severe instabilities.

Such problems were not confined to Britain. All industrial and industrializing countries suffered to varying extents. But among the advanced nations, Britain, with her highly vulnerable economy, open to an aggressive and predatory international manufacturing and financial capitalism, is among those for whom the problems have become politically central. Her ability to maintain a rate of economic growth to satisfy ever-rising private aspirations and ever-expanding public programmes depends on coping adequately with those problems.

Collective bargaining and the British problem

Yet the same political and social heritage, elements of which enabled a pragmatic ruling order to facilitate at least partial and peaceful integration of an organizing working class, is now presenting stubborn obstacles to the kind of institutional change which many consider necessary and desirable. As was noted in Chapter 1, certain features of that heritage manifest themselves in stronger forms than do the corresponding features in other advanced nations. The result has rendered difficult those shifts in national dispositions and direction which governments and men of affairs have argued to be imperative. These include readier acceptance of managerial and state 'leadership', of the overriding importance of technological advance, and of the need for a willing adaptation to change and innovation.

For example, the assumptions and stances of individualism, by which the citizen defines his own interests and demands the freedoms necessary to pursue them (either alone or in concert with others through an instrumental collectivism), are still tightly woven into the texture of our common life. And by comparison with other countries, organized groups, whether of wage-earners or professionals, have tended to pursue their sectional interests in restrictive and demarcative terms – a consequence of Britain having suffered no massive disruption which separated us from our pre-capitalist past. The tradition by which the better-placed wage and salary earning groups protect their interests against unwelcome change by asserting restrictive practices, often through the processes of a direct democracy, is alive and well and seems, even making every allowance for Thatcherite policies, likely to remain so. There is, of course, no inevitability by which traditions survive and flourish. Many perish unmourned. Traditions persist when an adequate number of people have an interest in keeping them alive, and the direct restrictionist democracy of the work group, long the privilege only of apprenticed craftsmen and professionals, has spread far beyond its earlier boundaries simply because people found it a valuable way of defending themselves and their families against economic forces and arbitrary rule. Along with this still goes a certain predominant view of the state which, despite the more generous teachings of late nineteenth-century New Liberalism and later Labourism, is still seen by many at all social levels as a combination of threat and milch-cow. The 'state' carries, in Britain, little emotional significance as a symbol and spokesman for common citizenship, common duties, and common needs. The 'public good' remains today, for most of us, thin and insubstantial, with little power to move. Men in authority have no symbols of a higher entity or higher good with which to reinforce and legitimize their command, unlike their counterparts in Germany and Japan. 'We have not the notion,' wrote Matthew Arnold, 'so familiar on the Continent and to antiquity, of *the State* – the nation in its collective and corporate character, entrusted with stringent powers for the general advantage, and controlling individual wills in the name of an interest wider than that of individuals.' Since such notions strengthen central authority, there are many in Britain who will strongly resist them so long as Britain remains in its present highly unequal shape. This explains why many of those who want radical social change resulting in the reduction of inequalities feel unable to support 'national interest' policies which they would welcome if applied within such a context, but which if applied in the present context would simply reinforce the *status quo*. A practical example is incomes policies of the sort peddled by most post-war British governments.

Three further points can be added to our picture of the political and social heritage. Firstly, there are the effects of a sharply contractual *laissez-faire*, which led to industrial relationships more deeply and widely marked than elsewhere by the win–lose, zero-sum, adversary stance – a gain for one 'side' being automatically defined as a loss for the other. Secondly, there are the effects of a policy which sees it as no part of the state apparatus to attempt long-term analyses and plan appropriate responses, but rather deals in short-term piecemeal adaptations to immediate pressures and exigencies. This was accompanied by a policy of preserving, to an extent compatible with maintenance of the *status quo*, an appearance of even-handedness between the classes; of 'holding the ring' and of encouraging peaceful settlement, through voluntary institutions, of the endless series of workplace disputes to which the adversary stance gave rise. And finally, there are the effects of that aristocratic disdain for direct involvement in trade and industry (though not for their profits), which it is frequently argued was transmitted to the upper middle class via the Victorian public school and Oxbridge traditions. This, it is said, blunted what might have been a more fiercely competitive approach to business and money-making and elevated instead the ideal of public service – an ideal which played its part in easing working-class movements into a contained participation in industrial and political decision-making. To this day, it is considered to have played its part in creating what is in some ways an 'anti-enterprise' culture, with adverse effects upon the quality of industrial management. This should remind us that observers concerned to lift the discussion of Britain's economic weakness above the level of merely 'scapegoating' the unions have long been ready to acknowledge the shortfall in entrepreneurial flair among British employers and managers.

Taken together with other aspects of the strategy of rule which Britain's ruling order had chosen to apply – the non-militaristic state, the gradual refinement of the rule of law, the piecemeal concession of civil and political rights to claimant groups – these created the context for the fashioning of social decencies widely admired abroad and described best, because not uncritically, by George Orwell in *The Lion and the Unicorn*. But it was a formula neither for dynamic and far-seeing economic innovation nor for a state-supported onslaught by employers upon the workplace and professional restrictionism which was among the social forces impeding it. The cultivation of a reputation for even-handedness towards labour organization that began to reveal its tiny beginnings early in the nineteenth century became too important a feature of the regime's legitimation to be jettisoned except under the direst emergency, and by the twentieth century the popular vote also had to be considered.

Here, then, we see British society increasingly bedevilled by the persistence and universalizing of the values it encourages and the attitudes it generates. At the same time, trapped within the limits and conventions of its own political system and heritage, it affords little scope for bold initiatives designed to promote different values and attitudes. The Thatcher administrations have pressed harder against those limits than any other government of recent times, but success is not so far conspicuous except in the reduction of inflation, achieved only at vast human and economic cost.

The Thatcher governments were more unabashed than most predecessors in their partial abandonment of that appearance of even-handedness which 'responsible', 'national' government in Britain is conventionally thought to require. The sections of society and of political thinking most conscious of that abandonment were, of course, those of organized labour and socialism. Yet the same sections felt they had already suffered a measure of the same abandonment at the hands of Labour ministers. After the Second World War, pressures had begun to build up which soon forced all British governments increasingly to override the convention of 'holding the ring' and to become one of the contestants – invariably in support of the employers where pay, strikes, and condemnation of restrictionism were concerned.

The economy had been rendered vulnerable by six years' neglect of capital investment at home and by the massive sale of British-owned capital assets abroad. At the same time demands on it grew rapidly, especially after the mid 1950s. More than ever before, Britain became a society aspiring to a high-consumption way of life, with people being urged by many pervasive influences, including mass advertising which was soon extended to television, to get and to spend. Traditional limitations on working-class expectations were swept away by full employment, workplace power, rising earnings, television, and the break-up of old communities through rehousing. Public spending was no less expansive. The National Health Service, far from stabilizing medical spending through some once-and-for-all achievement of good health, proved a bottomless pit of expenditure. Local government outlays, military spending, education and housing made their own demands.

The economy proved unable to accommodate these combined pressures, especially given the resolve to maintain Britain's openness to intense foreign competition and to permit a massive outflow of British capital seeking more profitable investment abroad. Among the handicaps were the inflationary pressures aggravated by a sectional collective bargaining which accepted only partially and for limited periods, if at all, the exhortations brought to bear by governments and sometimes union leaders. Intermittent efforts to supplement exhortation with statutory enforcement, or with government-imposed restraints on public sector incomes, exerted only temporary effects, usually cancelled out by the uprush of claims which followed relaxation of the policy. With shop-floor pressures often carrying earnings far beyond the rates established through formal top-level negotiation, many wage-earners were lifted by inflation into the tax-paying category. Their attempts to make good both their tax losses and the expected continuing price rise became major aggravations of the process.

Apart from the one limited venture towards the so-called 'social contract' between the Labour government and the TUC in 1974–5, no attempt was made to win the consent of organized labour by negotiating a comprehensive economic and social strategy which achieved compromises on public spending priorities and included the planned movement of wages and salaries. Few had any ideas about what such a settlement might contain or how it might seek the all-important control of innumerable work groups all fighting for their own case up and down the country. Yet in the absence of a comprehensive approach which demonstrably attempted 'fairness' by including, among many other things, the income and wealth of top executives, shareholders, and the higher professionals, no moral credibility could attach to the policy.

Here, in fact, lay a central weakness. Here was a highly unequal society that had long boasted of its individual and group freedoms; that had evolved a state whose senior servants had inherited strong traditions against long-term planning; that had elevated the competitive pursuit of private interests to primary importance; that had intensified that pursuit by dangling before itself the rich cornucopia of modern material wealth; and whose only national symbol was a decorative television monarchy more the vehicle of private fantasy and press vulgarity than of any sentiments of collective citizenship and collective needs. It was not a favourable context within which to propagate, with any moral conviction, the principle of group self-restraint for the sake of the common good. The surprise is that as much restraint was achieved as there was.

Reforming the system

Along with these attempts, both statutory and non-statutory, to secure pay restraint there developed a consciousness that Britain's system of industrial relations, hitherto widely admired for its informality, its flexibility, and its minimal reliance on law for procedural support and substantive content, was failing to respond fast enough to new needs. Regulation was failing most precisely where it was most needed – at the workplace. From some critics came emphasis on the need for rapid technical and organizational change and for efficient and orderly handling of the issues and disputes to which, in a period of rising shop-floor power, such changes gave rise. Far too little creative directorial and managerial attention was being directed, it was said, to matters which were generating forms of disorder that were bad for the economy as well as for the company – chaotic and irrational pay structures, inappropriate methods of payment, excessive overtime, clumsily handled redundancies, 'unfair' dismissals, and non-existent or inadequate procedures for handling grievances on all these and other issues. Others stressed the need for legislation to reduce disorder by guaranteeing a wide range of employee rights hitherto hardly figuring in union claims but giving rise to sporadic discontent. Champions of sexual and racial equality made their own demands. From Conservative directions, especially, came pressures for a more heavily regulative and punitive framework of industrial relations law which it was hoped could contain the unions and, more expressly, workplace behaviour. Senior management and boards of directors, too, must make a far more positive and considered contribution. Many observers noted that too many British boards were inclined to leave the tricky and distasteful arena of labour relations to lower levels of management. Instead of formulating a coherent long-term strategy and philosophy of industrial and personnel relations, they waited on events, leaving managerial subordinates to meet a succession of exigencies with a hand-to-mouth, piecemeal opportunism, and taking an active role only when it was forced upon them by a crisis.

What it all appeared to add up to was the need for a far more structured system at plant and company levels. Representatives of management and employees needed, as it were, to take the present loose and inadequate arrangements by the scruff of the neck and remould them into a pattern of collaborative negotiation and dispute settlement from which both sides, along with the economy, would derive greatly increased benefit. Top as well as middle managers would work with securely based shop stewards within properly constituted formal procedures to handle their problems in the context of a carefully considered long-term company strategy.

If the Royal (Donovan) Commission on Trade Unions and Employers' Associations (1965–8) supplied the precept of this reconstruction it was certain earlier examples of 'productivity bargaining' in the 1960s that appeared to supply the practice. In a few cases, managers, union officers, and shop stewards had worked together in long and taxing negotiations to realize meticulously analysed plans whereby precisely specified comprehensive changes in work organization, making for greater productivity, were rewarded with precisely specified and generous increases in pay. Was this to be the long-sought cure for British disease of workplace disorder and restrictionism? Was British management at last taking in hand that typical workplace situation where 'custom and practice' ruled and inefficiency thrived? Productivity bargaining at its comprehensive best seemed as if it might be an important part of the broader reconstruction.

Certainly by all appearances, and in some respects more than appearances, the British system of industrial relations was transformed during the 1960s and 1970s. At the workplace, both sides greatly increased specialist provision for dealing with industrial relations. There are estimates that the number of full-time shop stewards probably quadrupled during the 1970s, with shop-steward organization itself becoming more sophisticated through the wider emergence of senior-steward structures and convenors. Parallel with this on the managerial side went a considerable increase in specialist employee relations and personnel management staffs, particularly after the mid 1970s. More responsibility was shown towards industrial relations issues by boards of directors themselves.

The outcome was a notable spread of properly constituted formal grievance procedures, which now became part of the normal fabric of workplace industrial relations, at least in manufacturing industry. Union strength lent itself to pressures for increased union security. The (post-entry) closed shop spread rapidly, many managements finding it, at a time when they felt they needed all the regulative devices they could get, a method of increasing the representativeness and stability of collective bargaining. The check-off system by which union dues were deducted from pay by the company grew until by 1978 it covered 73 per cent of union members in manufacturing and 72 per cent in non-manufacturing industry – one of the most important advances in union security in the history of British trade unionism.

Non-manual employees participated fully in these developments. In large manufacturing establishments, especially, the institutions and sanctions of collective bargaining that developed for these categories were increasingly like those of their manual counterparts. Here and in public services, white-collar workers' resentment at their declining position relative to manual workers produced a major qualitative change towards greater militancy and an acceptance of what most of the other unions had long accepted already – that times and circumstances called for access to, and pressure on, governments. Large white-collar unions like the NUT and NALGO began to affiliate to the TUC in order to secure a voice at this level – though not to indicate any mass conversion to the traditional link still existing between the predominantly manual unions and the Labour Party.

Even middle managers became caught up in the unionization boom. Many of them were coming to feel squeezed between increasingly organized pressure from below and a top management that might now be more remote and impersonal than ever before. It could not be assumed that the old slogan 'The Company will always look after *us*', could be relied on in the new conditions. Mergers and take-overs were producing managerial as well as lower-level redundancies, and in other respects, too, managers might find themselves as much the subject of low-trust calculation as those they supervised. Some of them were becoming more conscious of the deep ambiguities in their role and their self-image; they felt themselves to be both agents of capital, concerned with helping to extract a surplus from a workforce, and members of the workforce itself.

Finally, the increase in formalized workplace joint rule-making and managerial involvement in the shaping of workplace relations affected the importance and standing of 'national' or industry-wide bargaining, whose regulative significance had already, in many industries, been weakened by the post-war growth of informal, unsystematic dealings at shop-floor level. Most unions decentralized collective bargaining functions to some extent over the period.

Some of these changes were in directions strongly approved of by those who hoped for more constructive relations between management and the managed. They appeared to provide the necessary joint institutional setting for that considered and coherent company strategy which would not only more successfully maintain order and minimize disruption, but also facilitate the creative, positive-sum negotiation of work systems from which all parties would gain. Fuller recognition and integration of shop stewards by unions; greater security assured them by management; improved co-ordination between the stewards themselves; a rational, consistent company strategy on all manpower issues; the establishment of systematic joint procedures at the workplace – these seemed the necessary pre-conditions for that qualitative change in labour relations so widely seen as one of the required contributions towards a more adaptive and efficient British economy.

Necessary conditions have to be distinguished, however, from sufficient conditions. Whether structural and institutional arrangements produce certain hoped-for results depends upon the will, motivation, and habituated dispositions and perceptions of the participants. Certain kinds of arrangements may be necessary for making possible certain kinds of behaviour, but they do not in themselves guarantee that the behaviour will be forthcoming. The Conservative government's Industrial Relations Act of 1971, for example, attempted to provide a heavily regulative framework of law and practice for the conduct of industrial relations at company and plant level as well as at industry-wide level. It became an embarrassing failure when both sides made it evident that, for their own good reasons, they had no intention of using most of it. Similarly, the indications in preceding pages of marked changes, especially at company and plant level, are susceptible of a different interpretation from that of a widespread will towards reform in the direction of jointly pursued collaboration benefiting both sides.

The increase in specialist employee-relations staffs, for example, has been attributed less to a widening company resolve to apply a rational, consistent, and creative strategy in this field, and more to a felt need simply to grapple with the mass of complex labour legislation appearing on the statute book. Marsh reports, in a survey of manufacturing industry (1982), that companies 'have tended to develop cautiously, empirically, and with no intention of upsetting the traditional function and authority of line management in dealing with employees'.

Although in larger and more complex multi-establishment companies there is now some tendency for boards to give more regular consideration to employee relations, it is hard to detect any major move towards planned forward strategies in this field. And if by 'policy' what is meant is an explicitly formulated system of principles by which all levels of management can decide what to do in any particular set of circumstances, it has to be said that company boards still concern themselves little with policy-making. The traditional British style persists by which boards fall back on *de facto* methods, commonly endorsing decisions taken elsewhere and involving themselves directly only when the situation is judged sufficiently serious to merit their attention.

It is hardly surprising, then, that Marsh (1982) found no more than 'a moderate movement in the "Donovan" direction of "comprehensive and authoritative agreements" at plant and/or company levels'. Informal and unsystematic shop-floor bargaining, unrelated to similar activities elsewhere in the plant or company, clearly continued in many factories. Even the trend towards formalization was producing little codification of rules, practices, and policy in the form of handbooks for managers. Industry-wide or national agreements, though very infrequently in manufacturing forming the sole basis for workplace settlements, were nevertheless found by Marsh to be still exercising 'considerable influence' in that improvements in terms and conditions negotiated nationally continued to be widely applied. On the whole, though, and especially when the non-manufacturing sectors are included, the judgement of Daniel and Willward (1983) is that emphasis has to be on the diversity of systems of pay determination.

If the overall picture of change in board and managerial style is mixed and equivocal, it is even more so on the union side. Undy *et al.* (1981) found it not to be 'developing in any easily discernible direction according to a common pattern or trend. Indeed, if anything the government and structure of British unions appear to be more diverse, contradictory and conflicting at the end of our period of study than they were in 1960.'

In terms of funding, research, strategic planning (even of strikes), and general organization, British unions can hardly be said to offer a dazzling example to the rest of the world. Seventy years ago Sidney Webb wrote of the 'wonderful development of the [German] central trade union offices, with their expert staffs; the skill and wisdom with which they obtain and utilise their own statistical information; their really remarkable efforts for the education of their members; their training schools for trade union officials – all this is in striking contrast with the haphazard methods of British wage-earning democracy.' G.D.H. Cole supported this picture. But another Fabian, W. S. Sanders, doubted 'whether it would ever be possible, or even advantageous, for English trade unions to adopt the strongly bureaucratic form of control which is exercised by the German trade union officials, and on which the highly centralized form of organisation largely depends. A people who have grown up under the iron regime of the German military system are capable of a degree of obedience to officials of voluntary organisations which would in England be considered derogatory to individual dignity and liberty.'

A comparison today would have to repeat some of these points. But it would do so in the context of such facts as that the German trade union movement collapsed without a struggle in the face of Hitler's 1933 attack, whereas the British movement, having survived the inter-war slump in good order, co-operated in a total war to destroy the fascist threat and yet emerged with its independence as strong as ever. There are many dimensions along which to measure trade union movements and the capacity for sheer survival is one of them. Perhaps a flexible pragmatism and a disposition towards short-term expedients contributes to that capacity.

Despite all this, many of the changes in the workplace situation have been in directions urged by reformists and represent a considerable transformation in the face of Britain's industrial relations. Surely these 'necessary' conditions have sometimes been completed by the 'sufficient' conditions? In some cases they undoubtedly have. But a recent verdict by an experienced empirical researcher is that from the reformists' point of view the achievement is small. Batstone's judgement (1982) is that these organizational changes reveal little association with greater efficiency and reduced conflict. The rate of productivity growth declined after the beginnings of reform; the poorest productivity records in the 1970s were to be found in those industries where the reform package had been most fully implemented; and strikes increased most dramatically after the late 1960s precisely in those sectors where grievance procedures and sophisticated shop steward structures had been newly developed. Detailed studies reveal that only a small minority of productivity bargaining agreements led to any substantial productivity improvements; and Clegg has noted that many of the companies which negotiated apparently successful productivity deals in the 1960s were again faced with problems of low performance and substantial overmanning during the 1970s.

These findings suggest that habituated stances and dispositions on both sides, powerfully shaped by, and rooted in, past experience, were determining how the 'reformed' structures were used. On the employees' side, these include the wary zero-sum approach, the adversary posture, and the instinct to preserve and extend as much job-control through 'custom and practice' as can be squeezed out of management – all combined with an intense sectionalism which remains as little moved by wider sympathies or 'national interest' arguments as are multinational companies and City speculators ranging world-wide for the fast buck. Management and ownership exhibit the reciprocal characteristics. Both sides are shaped by the particular nature of Britain's class structure and neither side takes any serious political steps to change it – ownership being constrained within a political system of immense inertia; the working classes being disposed to preserve what they consider a tolerable accommodation and to reject the alternative visions offered them as being insufficiently convincing to be worth risking what they have already.

Industrial relations and the New Right

Meanwhile, in the absence of the British economic miracle, Labour and Conservative governments continued to thresh about with no lasting success within the same limited range of expedients by which it was hoped to bring inflation under control and the economy into a healthy condition. It was left to Labour Chancellor Healey during the administration of 1974–9 to take decisive steps towards a heavier reliance on monetarism. The attack on money and credit supply had its designed effects; the pace of economic activity slackened and unemployment rose above the million mark for the first time since the war. That this symbolic event produced no mass expression of public outrage must be reckoned a fact of major political significance. The oft-repeated belief that there could never be a return to the mass unemployment of the inter-war years – that this must be considered a political constant of British 'public opinion' – was now proved false. The lesson was not lost on those increasingly influential sections among the Conservatives who proclaimed that the broad strategy pursued by the party over the past century, of keeping within hailing distance of the pace set by Liberal or Labour reformism, had produced a steady slide towards the left and increased state involvement and spending; a slide which must now be halted and reversed.

The first Thatcher administration therefore set about greatly intensifying monetarist policies, massively increasing unemployment and bankruptcies, reducing taxation particularly for the better-off, limiting the growth of national and local government expenditure, and encouraging employers to take advantage of reduced union strength at the workplace to eliminate restrictive practices and introduce more efficient working. Reforms conceded to a strong trade union presence had demonstrably failed 'to meet the nation's needs', so the necessary changes must now be imposed by state and management upon unions weakened by mass unemployment.

A sequence of legislation followed which sought not, as in the manner of 1971, to creat overnight a comprehensive new framework for industrial relations, but to pursue a step-by-step movement towards weakening the power, influence, and status of organized labour. This included attempts to strengthen the degree of individualism in the labour market, to weaken the closed shop, and to tighten control of picketing and 'secondary' tactics. Also introduced, as we have seen, were provisions which opened up union funds to legal attack in the case of stoppages deemed not to be in furtherance of a 'trade dispute'.

Among later Conservative innovations in labour law was one which renders trade union immunity from civil actions for damages allegedly suffered by aggrieved parties during official strikes conditional upon the union having first held a secret strike ballot and having secured a majority of the votes cast. Secret ballots are also required for the election of union governing bodies. Unions are to be required, as already noted, to hold regular ballots on whether they maintain a political fund, the hope manifestly being that, especially in the white-collar unions, members will vote against and thus deprive the Labour Party of funds. Other indications of the new style included a confidential Cabinet Office document of 1982 which instructed the Office to exclude trade union notables from membership of Royal Commissions and public bodies at national level. Also under attack were such long-standing features of the industrial relations system as the 1946 Fair Wages Resolution (the latest in a series going back to 1891), which sought to give some protection to the pay received by employees of government contractors, and the structure of statutory Wages Councils, which have tried with little success to protect particularly low-paid workers.

These and other legal changes, too complex to be elaborated on further, may not prove in practice the crushing attack they seem on paper. Some have more symbolic than practical significance. Yet even the symbolism is important because it reinforced a marked change in political tone. Not since the Coalition government of 1919–22, which included such spokesmen as Lloyd George, Churchill, Birkenhead, and Eric Geddes, had there been such open hostility by prominent figures of the administration towards the leaders of organized labour, such open contempt for the values of the welfare state, and such implied disparagement of society's casualties and losers. During 1981, the second full year of the first Thatcher administration, the richest 5 per cent of the population increased their share of the nation's marketable wealth from 43 to 45 per cent; the richest 25 per cent from 81 to 84 per cent. Poverty accelerated dramatically. Figures issued by the Department of Health and Social Security showed 15 million people living on the margins of poverty in 1981 compared with 11.5 million in 1979 when the first Thatcher administration took office.

Some uneasiness was evident among those sections of the Conservative Party which believed that these were not the best long-term methods of maintaining that conservation of the *status quo* which had been pursued so successfully over the past century. There seemed some justification for their concern. Was not Thatcherism a blatant rejection of that One Nation theme which, in the hands of men like Baldwin and Butler, had served Conservative interests so well? And would not significant sections of the electorate accordingly reject it?

Economic decline and the Labour Party

Yet in the short run, Thatcherism was to undermine not the Conservative but the Labour Party. The reason lies in the fissured geology of political Labour and its inability to bear indefinitely the stresses and strains put on it by national economic failure and the methods chosen by Labour governments to cope with that failure. Governments of both colours had felt impelled by economic instabilities since the war to intervene in areas previously treated as sacred to 'voluntarism'. And since even Labour governments, whatever their rhetoric, were in practice concerned only to modify marginally the structure of society as they found it, much government intervention in the economy seemed to the unions and to many socialists to be designed to force the wage-earning and lower salary-earning classes to carry the burden of adjustment, especially in the field of incomes policy. Long before the onset of Thatcherism, that appearance of even-handedness between the classes, that convention that governments merely 'held the ring' within which the contestants fought out their private battles, had already been deeply compromised in ways unprecedented in peacetime. And it had been compromised by Labour as well as by Conservative governments. This increasingly highlighted the fact that the dividing line most threatening to Britain's political system ran not between the Conservative and Labour parties but down the middle of the Labour Party. The Labour right was far nearer to the Conservatives with respect to economic diagnosis and management – and a good many other things – than it was to the Labour left. The structure survived so long as the right was able to contain the left. This became increasingly difficult after the early 1970s, when the left succeeded in getting the party opened up to members of groups and organizations previously proscribed for their 'extremism'. The strengthening left then set out to attempt to control the centre and right through such means as the reselection of MPs and an electoral college for the choosing of party leader. Not even the Labour Party's historic elasticity survived this, and the Social Democratic Party came into being, with the remaining centre and right continuing the struggle within Labour itself.

The polarization of British politics, represented at one end by Thatcherism, and at the other by a strengthened farther left, benefited the former rather than the latter. The 1983 general election produced a fall in the Labour vote of 9.3 per cent on the 1979 result – 'the sharpest fall incurred by a major party at a single election since the war'. Certainly the so-called Thatcher 'landslide' expressed only partly an embracing of the Conservatives and rather more a rebuff to Labour and a flirtation with the Alliance. For Labour this was a mournful continuation of a trend – in 1959, 62 per cent of manual manual workers still voted Labour; in 1983 the figure was 38 per cent. Among trade unionists the Labour vote was only 7 per cent ahead of the Conservatives. Nevertheless these figures expressed not only abstentions or desertions to the Alliance but also some positive switching to the Conservatives. Among Labour deserters as a whole, for every one staying at home and for every three favouring the alliance, one switched to the Consevatives. Labour remained the first, though not necessarily the majority, choice among the slowly dwindling 'traditional' working class on the council estates, of the public sector, of Scotland and of the North. But it appeared, for the time being at least, to have lost the new working class. Among private-sector workers it ran neck and neck with the Conservatives; among manual workers owning their houses or living in the South, the Conservatives had a commanding lead and Labour came third behind the Alliance. 'The transformation of working class partisanship over the past quarter century must rank as the most significant post-war change in the social basis of British politics' (Ivor Crewe,

The Guardian, 13 June 1983). Experience warns us, however, against the kind of power-worship that views present party strengths and weaknesses as embodying not only current contingencies but also future destinies. Nevertheless it has to be acknowledged that on recent and present showing, working class support for the Labour Party is a wasting asset.

Yet although the 1983 Tory landslide majority of 144 seats was a product of Britain's highly distorted political system and not an expression of the popular vote, it is clear that Conservatism continues to retain what it has always enjoyed: the political support of substantial sections of the organized as well as the unorganized working class. There is continued disbelief that Labour is able to offer a more efficient way of organizing things; no mass movement towards Labour being evident even among the 4 million unemployed. In addition there are many populist issues besides economic management on which Labour exerts, to put it mildly, no magnetic pull for many working class voters – home ownership, racial and sexual equality, taxation and rates levels, social security 'scroungers', and a bellicose stance towards other countries on occasion. There are many wage – and lower salary-earners who, while they may or may not be mobilized as Conservative voters on these issues, find no appeal in the Labour stance towards them.

There are reasons, in fact, for believing it to be not entirely fanciful to see the line dividing the Two Nations as increasingly running not between the working class and the rest, but through the working class itself. On the favoured side of that line are those who are relatively secure and comfortably placed; who expect to enjoy ownership of their home and all the other appurtenances of modern living that the middle and upper classes take for granted; who may be wary about generous levels of social spending and their effects on taxation rates; and who may perhaps be suspicious or even punitive in their attitude towards recepients of welfare. Here is the emergence in new forms of what for centuries was a well-recognized gap between the upper and lower strata of a multi-layered working class; a gap which narrowed after 1914 but which now seems to be reopening to create an American type of social pattern. The effects of this trend upon the texture and temper of the trade union movement seem likely to be enhanced by post-war changes in its composition. The weight and influence of the old manual wage-earning sections are being reduced by the growth of white-collar and professional organizations whose members, though they may accept the industrial leadership of left-wing officers, may not share their politics. Pay militancy and socialism, which some socialists convince themselves must, ultimately at least, go together, have in fact no necessary connection. With changes in the composition of the movement now becoming translated into stuctural changes in the composition of the TUC General Council, unity may be harder to maintain than before. There have even been signs on the industrial front, also, some white-collar unions may be ready, given what seems virtually certain to be an indefinite period of mass unemployment and bargaining disadvantage, to adopt a more consistently co-operative stance towards higher management that has been general in the British movement. This, too, could foster a divergence from the older manual-worker tradition, with its adversary industrial stance accompanying the automatic political affiliation to Labour.

'Macho' management and shop-floor 'realism'

Reference to mass unemployment reminds us that not even this was able to stem the haemorrhage of Labour support. Yet on the face of it one might have expected its presumed consequences to stiffen the resolve of organized labour to vote against the party currently in office. The fact that they did not should alert us to the possibility that especially for those still in work the situation was far from being as harsh as sometimes presented.

For a while appearances certainly seemed to point to a dramatic subduing of labour's post-war exuberance. The shift in the balance of power at the workplace was seen as making possible a reassertion of managerial authority, so long felt to be in abeyance. High glee was expressed in some managerial circles at what was presented as a turning of the tables – even as vengeance. 'Management', proclaimed Sir Hector Laing, chairman of United Biscuits, ' are in the saddle' (Turner, *Daily Telegraph*, 13 and 16 February 1981.) Others, more prudent or public-relations conscious, confined themselves to expressing appreciation of a 'new spirit of realism' on the shop floor. One industrial correspondent described managers everywhere as reporting in 1981 that 'during the past two years they have achieved manning levels and shop-floor flexibility of a standard previously thought unobtainable in this country. In many factories we have caught up with German levels of efficiency though not with the Japanese' (Smith, *Daily Telegraph*, 13 June 1981). On a similar impressionistic level, other industrial journalists described how 'all over British manufacturing industry managers are celebrating their return to life and power, like eunuchs miraculously restored to wholeness and potency' (Turner *Daily Telegraph*, 13 and 16 February 1981). Thus at last was being achieved that long-delayed and long-awaited break-through to the full modernization of the British economy. 'Real unit labour costs are falling . . . as productivity is raised by the massive once-for-all slimming operationby British industry', declared a Quarterly Bulletin of the Liverpool University Research Group in Macroeconomics (October 1981). To some it seemed that Thatcher-inspired 'macho management' was achieving the desired result.

But whatever degree of circumspection was forced upon organized wage– and salary-earners by the shift in workplace power, other factors significantly brightened the picture for those in work. For much of the first Thatcher administration a strong oil-supported pound made imports cheap; earnings grew faster than the retail price index; and house values also rose. Except in the highly unlikely event of the unemployed organizing themselves into an effective political force, there seemed no reason, from the government's point of view, why the policy should not continue, provided an adequate level of growth could be resumed.

This seemed most likely to come from labour-intensive service industries and from such developing innovations as microelectronics and the whole field of 'communication' and 'information' techno-logies. The Thatcher government was aware, however, as were other European governments, that the pace of technological change depends partly on the attitudes towards it of workers, managers, consumers, and the wider public, and that in the eyes of innovators these attitudes left much to be desired, particularly, of course, those of employees. Perhaps it was understandable that, given the long-standing reputation of British employees in general towards work-place innovation, the Prime Minister should suggest that, within an international programme of research into new technologies, the UK should take the lead in enquiring into these 'public attitudes'.

The Department of Trade and Industry, commissioning this programme of research in 1983 from the then Social Science Research Council, now the Economic and Social Research Council, declared that the programme should have as 'its principal objective the formulation of generalisable lessons for industry and government on how to secure greater acceptance of new technologies by developing their positive aspects, and minimizing their negative aspects, from an enhanced understanding of the cultural and organisational determinants of public attitudes. Acceptance of new technologies at the workplace would be the main, but not the sole, focus of the work.' In other words, academic researchers were invited to take part in processes of opinion-management of the sort which modern governments feel more and more driven to undertake, and in pursuit of which they invoke the aid of professional communicators and specialists. It would be, the Council secretary Dr Cyril Smith declared, 'an important test' for the social sciences – not hitherto the object of benign approval by leading members of the Thatcher administration. Whether or not this particular programme is successful in moulding responses at the workplace – or anywhere else – the initiative is significant not only in showing how the resources of academic research are being drawn more and more into the service of government purposes, but also in revealing further extensions of governmental intrusion into industrial relations – this time in the form of systematically mounted propaganda designed to change dispositions which have been widely regarded as particularly prominent in British shop-floor attitudes.

Economic failure and an old nightmare

These attempts are all too understandable, for economic growth has now become desperately important for British governments. Continued national failure here will present them with a dilemma both of whose horns threaten acute political pain. They must either take even more measures against public spending, including spending on health, pensions, and welfare, or attempt to maintain public spending by increases in taxation. Given predictably increasing outlays on pensions and mass unemployment, it is future prospects as much as imminent burdens which create the nightmare for the better-off classes. It is the kind of nightmare that was glimpsed by the so-called 'social imperialists' eighty years ago. Doubting Britain's ability to withstand world-wide competition from Germany and America under a system of free trade, they urged governments to secure a monopoly exploitation of empire markets and raw materials and to erect tariff barriers against the rest of the world. This tariff revenue would finance social welfare programmes and thereby meet the growing expectations of the rising democracy of a partly enfranchised working class. Leo Amery explained his dread that a stationary or regressive economy would sharpen class conflict. Without economic growth, increased public spending could only be met by greater encroachments upon the better-off, whose inevitable resistance would drive the working class towards socialism. If the better-off retained their commitment to parliamentary democracy they would lose this struggle to the sheer weight of numbers. The inference was obvious.

There seems, in the Britain of the second Thatcher administration, when the wage-earning and lower salary-earning classes have just rejected the Labour electoral manifesto so resoundingly, small likelihood of Amery's nightmare materializing in quite the form he predicted. Nevertheless, governments rightly fear great political strains of some sort if adequate economic growth is not soon resumed, especially when oil revenues begin their decline.

Mrs Thatcher made several speeches after the Falklands War in which she expressed the hope that the unity, pride, and spirit of common purpose demonstrated in that campaign would be carried over into a wider movement of national regeneration expressed in economic terms. A British economic miracle always seemed unlikely, however, under her administration if it depended on mass sentiments of that sort. She and her colleagues had already spent three years extolling the virtues of individualism, proclaiming the value of competitive self-seeking, urging the need for higher rewards to the talented, the innovators, and the forceful, and conveying disparagement or even contempt not only for the collectivist labour movement but also for society's losers and casualties.

The conditions for a new social partnership?

In so doing they had celebrated, in word and deed, characteristics which have rarely been employed so crudely and overtly as the systematic bases even of Conservative administrations, but which have long enjoyed a good deal of support at all levels of British society. These characteristics have occasionally yielded to sentiments elevating the notions of a common fate and a common effort in the interests of all, but these periods have been confined to the two world wars, and even then did not evoke the degree of self-abnegation demonstrated by the Germans and Japanese. Nevertheless it is instructive to examine the circumstances and policies which made possible the British wartime mood of national unity. Somehow transcending the popular awareness of black markets, of cynical corruption, of jealousies and empire-building in all departments of wartime endeavour, was the consciousness of a sharp shift towards equality both in material distribution and in social relations. Combined with the widespread belief that the war was worth fighting, this mitigated the organized sectionalism of British society.

There may be little likelihood of presenting the struggle against economic decline to a peacetime public in terms comparable with the struggle against a regime exceptionally horrible even by twentieth-century standards. Yet perhaps this is what would have to be achieved before the British could be brought to see their economic plight as a common and personal reality which called for sectional and individual restraint. And even then that reality would probably need strong reinforcement by dramatic shock treatment which, among other things, sharply and conspicuously reduced the privileges enjoyed by the most favoured strata and levelled up the conditions of the most deprived. Few outcomes may seem, at the moment, less likely. Yet the wartime experience suggests that the British people are not totally without the capacity to find satisfaction in a common social endeavour, and their history certainly reveals the slow growth of a disposition to guarantee each other a humane respect and certain expressions of social generosity. No historical trend exists, however, which can ensure that they will continue to build on these foundations a society that seeks to minimize the inequalities and vulgarities of competitive acquisition and sectional self-seeking. But, by the same token, nothing rules it out.

What has to be said is that so far no political party has discovered the language and the institutions which might enable the British people to unlock these potentialities within themselves. The right currently falls back on market forces, greater rewards for 'success', and a widening of class differences. Whatever the effects of this emphasis they seem unlikely, on present showing, to include a unified movement of national regeneration towards a British economic miracle. The left presents a wide diversity of contradictory formulae which include, for example, what comes across to many people as a form of public ownership that offers neither a superior work experience to employees nor a more responsive and humane face to consumers; unrestrained freedom for sectional collective bargaining; restraints on sectional collective bargaining with little or no convincing reference to restraints on higher privileged incomes; attitudes which appear to convey considerable nonchalance towards the liberal freedoms; and only rare attempts to disentangle the several meanings of 'patriotism' with the aim of rejecting the unworthy ones and nourishing the rest. At present these and other policies of the left are failing to mobilize the necessary political support even among those at whose welfare they are directed.

What then of the future? It may not have escaped readers of this book that its author is hardly an unqualified supporter of the *status quo*. But I will have expressed myself obscurely if it has not also emerged that there are aspects of British society and traditions that I deeply respect and wish to retain. Many of them are connected with painfully constructed defences against the arrogances, impertinences, and corruptions of power. I find great appeal in that long radical tradition, adorned by such names as William Morris, R. H. Tawney, George Orwell, and Edward Thompson, which seeks to reduce the abundant inequalities in British society, along with the humbug and flunkeyism, while retaining what is best in a country which still cherishes, though now more precariously, many social decencies. This tradition includes a strong love of country, which it so defines as to exclude bellicose nationalist assertiveness against others, and regards the Conservative bid to appropriate patriotic sentiments as effrontery.

The egalitarianism urged in the first edition of this book was not, however, pressed simply for its own sake. The argument was that the only possible chance of strengthening and making manifest such latent capacities as existed amongst the British people for joint endeavour towards a common aim – in this case that of promoting a relatively inflation-free economic growth to underpin family well-being and civilized public purposes – lay in remodelling the common life towards a shape more easily recognizable as a community in some full and genuine sense. This might just make it possible to draw the trade unions into constructive participation in an economic programme which embodied an agreed strategy on all the major economic and social variables including the movement of incomes.

These arguments were advanced at a time when the unions were approaching the peak of their power within an acquisitive, individualistic society possessing no historical concept of a 'higher good'; a society in which there is a widespread heritage of restrictionism, intense sectionalism, and adversary relations. Given that unionism was spreading more widely in the public and white-collar sectors, among women, and even into managerial ranks, the prospect was of ever fiercer sectional struggles and the continued aggravation of inflation.

The political expedients to which successive party leaders turned had only passing effectiveness, if that. And there were many among the politically interested who felt unable to support any form of pay restraint, however desirable, so long as it was unaccompanied by a serious practical concern with the gross inequities with which Britain, like other societies, abounded.

Could radical social change in egalitarian directions promote the desirable heightened community consciousness? Would the trade unions, within such a context, feel able, along lines recently suggested by Kitching (1983) 'to offer whole-hearted co-operation to capitalism but demand in return . . . concessions which aim quite consciously to change the fundamental nature of capitalism?'. Could they be encouraged eventually to develop a pre-emptive research and planning capacity, taking strategic initiatives and learning through experience what productive, exchange, and planning mechanisms best accommodated the conflicting interests inevitable in a complex society? Or could they be brought at the very least to co-operate in a tripartite economic strategy which planned for growth with minimum inflation, having a genuine voice in a wide diversity of economic and social variables?

The difficulties, of course, spoke for themselves. Historical continuities can be immensely powerful. It is indeed, as a leading historian J. H. Plumb has argued, ' a salutary thought that no stable society has ever yet altered the fundamentals of its social and political structure without revolution or overwhelming disaster in war . . .' Could Britain's political system take the strain of a radical reconstruction? Shortly before the First World War, substantial sections within the ruling order indicated a readiness to defy parliament and the constitution and accept civil war within the United Kingdom rather than acquiesce in Irish Home Rule. In such a situation, what might be lost that is of inestimable value to those very strata who were intended to be the principal beneficiaries of such a reconstruction? Yet Britain's deep-rooted historical continuities include the political system itself, with its strong tradition of respect for constitutionality and law. A great deal would depend on whether the Labour Party could mobilize a convincing and forceful popular base for such a programme.

In the end, Labour governments, persuaded that this was impossible, moved further and further away from any such conception and towards monetary orthodoxies and large-scale unemployment. Organized labour responded predictably with its own orthodoxies. The events of the winter of 1978–9, when the crumbling understandings of the 'social contract' finally collapsed in a wave of bitter and socially damaging strikes, convinced many that this was the collapse too of Labour's pretensions to be offering a more efficient and more decent way of doing things. Edward Heath had earlier referred to the unpleasant and unacceptable face of capitalism; events now seemed to be confirming a growing consciousness, widespread even among trade unionists, that there was an unpleasant and unacceptable face of trade unionism.

This was immensely helpful to the New Conservatism which took office in 1979. Determined to stop inflation, to raise the rate of profit, to redistribute income and wealth towards the better-off, to celebrate the individualistic competitive struggle, and to halt the long-term drift towards high public spending, the Thatcher administrations had to bend their efforts towards subduing the industrial and political strength of Labour. If this meant reversing the styles of the older Toryism and pressing hard against the British political tolerances and conventions, then so be it.

We are not directly concerned here with the full political implications of this changing style, but it is relevant to observe that Britain's governing and party system has long rested on the observance of certain reciprocities of restraint. The Thatcher administrations offered many crude affronts to these conventions. Future governments drawn from the present Opposition parties are likely to experience intense pressure from supporters to be at least as summary and heavy-handed towards Conservative interests. Not for nothing are some leading Tories deeply uneasy about Thatcher methods of handling the suppression of trade unionism at GCHQ Cheltenham, the imposition of rate-capping on local authorities, and the arrangements for abolishing the Greater London Council and metropolitan county councils. Precedents are being set that may strengthen the hand of hard-line reformers in decades to come. Revolutionaries who seem to wish to raze to the ground and start again are, of course, always delighted, for precisely this reason, when the ruling order overrides the conventional reciprocities – and indeed many attempt to goad it into such behaviour in order to build up class tensions and 'raise consciousness'. But even some among those reformers who, though radical, wish to stop far short of revolutionary extremities, may paradoxically not feel wholly displeased that the Thatcher governments have set new post-war standards of un-restrained ideological conventions and behaviour.

Such is the interpenetration nowadays of economics and politics that managers who give thought to company labour relations policy need to consider it in its fullest possible context. What do Thatcher-type policies and style offer modern management? Earlier references to impressionistic evidence showed some commentators and managers in high spirits. Others were more wary. One industrial correspondent of long and wide experience noted 'the new breed of management hawks' who spoke of vengeance and urged the need to 'grab back' authority now while they had the chance. But would they be capable of maintaining their new resolve when circumstances changed again?

'When . . . the government runs out of steam, the unions get their act together, and . . . the economy picks up again, it is a fairly safe, if depressing bet, that the unions will go in for vengeance and grabbing back too. What we are seeing now is a short-term psychological shift in managerial will. Not a fundamental shift to "realism" on the shop floor' (Torode, *The Guardian*, 8 January 1981). The Chairman of the Advisory Conciliation and Arbitration Service declared in his *Annual Report* of 1981 that while 'some commentators feel that more constructive attitudes among the parties can already be discerned', others had found a tendency for managers to take advantage of 'the shift in the balance of power' by disregarding agreed procedures of negotiation and consultation. This, he argued in a lecture to the first ACAS national conference, marked an 'emerging school of "macho management"' which offered little in long-term solutions to industrial relations problems'. He offered a warning that some industrialists were clearly prepared to endorse. 'Industrial relations will certainly not thrive on the basis that "vengeance is mine". . . .' Commenting at a press conference that there had been references to 'the new sense of realism', he warned people not to assume that when the upturn came 'we shall not be returning to the bad habits and practices that have so contributed to our poor economic performance in the past'.

Both warnings were apposite. While it was doubtful whether managerial restraint would 'improve' the long-run basic nature of Britain's industrial relations, it was highly likely that managerial militancy would 'worsen' them in the short-run, following the upturn. And secondly, it was scarcely to be supposed on past experience that one period of workplace weakness would produce a permanent shift of perceptions and policies among organized labour. But perhaps even this one period had permitted management to effect major strategic improvements in the techniques and organization of production? Reliable evidence on this must await comprehensive empirical research. But some clues are already available. There is no reason to doubt that many shop stewards throughout industry have considered it judicious to bend with the wind; show themselves readier to meet management initiatives; and take a more cautious view of their constituents' readiness to adopt industrial action of one form or another. But from the point of view of long-term trends, it is essential to know which of two sets of possibilities produced the much vaunted productivity improvement. Was it an outcome of permanent changes like a rise in the quality of machinery and/or a permanent reduction in shop-floor resistance to new machinery and work practices? Or was it simply the result of a one-off purge, produced by recession, of the less productive plant, labour, and management? Two academic studies appearing in 1983 – using different statistical methods – one by Smith-Gavine and Bennett, the other by Mendis and Muellbauer, offered the conclusion that it was predominantly the latter; that there has been no breakthrough in productivity growth and that the apparent evidence otherwise is mirage rather than miracle (Keegan, *The Guardian*, 23 August 1983).

The chairman of ACAS repeated his warning in the *Annual Report* of 1984. 'It would be misleading to conclude that there has yet been a permanent and radical change in British industrial relations. Some commentators have suggested that the magnitude of industrial and economic change under way in Britain may be leading to a transformation of attitudes and behaviour; also that the downturn in industrial action and decline in resistance to change that has occurred will prove to be permanent. ACAS believes that unless further action is taken by the parties now, union–management relations in many sectors may take on a more combative character as and when the economy picks up.' Employers generally must, for example, agree to greater involvement by employees, since involvement 'is an essential part of building greater trust between management and workforce, and without this we will never get our industrial relations right'.

The CBI's Director of Social Affairs considered (*The Guardian*, 16 May 1984) that mutual trust and a sense of common purpose were in fact 'now developing' out of the increasing employee involvement being introduced by many companies. His discussion of 'involvement' mentions the need for employers to consult and communicate directly with all employees; to train foremen and supervisors in the skills of effective communication; to inculcate employee involvement as an intrinsic part of good management; to consult in both good times and bad, and after consultation to report back on decisions taken.

Those with long memories may experience here a strong sense of *déja vu*. Here are the echoes of the Human Relations manuals of forty years ago; here are the same hopes that they will promote 'greater efficiency, commitment, and trust, leading to shared benefits'; and here, finally, is rejection of that *bête noire* of Human Relations: 'the concept of distinct and conflicting interest groups within a company'. There have always been companies where perspectives like these have served managerial purposes and there is no reason to assume that this will change. As a universal formula, however, it is likely to have no greater chance of making its way than in the 1940s and 1950s. The CBI spokesman finds, however, 'in many firms' an improved employee understanding of business realities and a greater interest in efficient working practices. But even he is concerned not to over-egg the pudding. 'On both sides there are too many cases of employers and employees confronting each other rather than the mutual challenge'. Between this and the ACAS Chairman's judgement that evidence of employers 'properly involving their employees' was as yet 'only patchy', there may be but a very small gap.

What, in the CBI view, could threaten or even destroy this development? First, the pressures emanating from the EEC towards compulsory employee representation on company boards and towards works councils with rights to demand disclosure of information, business forecasts, and company plans. The CBI maintains its vehement hostility towards all such proposals. But another danger will come with the upswing. 'As the economic recovery gains strength, and some of the 'fear' engendered by the recession fades, so the risk of confrontation becomes all the greater.'

Of all these appraisals of post-Thatcher styles and prospects, the sceptical note is probably the more convincing for those with any knowledge of the historical dimension of Britain's industrial relations. Yet predictions of a return to the bad old ways when economic recovery passes a certain threshold beg a crucial question. Will the threshold ever be passed?

This raises one of the most fascinating speculations about the New Conservatism and its abrasive tone and methods. How far ahead have its strategists calculated its consequences? The frustrations and hatreds it has already generated are apparent, not least on miners' picket lines. Although these are hardly as historically unique as many appear to think, there is no doubt but that, coming on top of a five-year sequence of wounds and humiliations visited upon the labour movement, the nightly television spectacle of British police and British strikers engaged in bloody combat will leave deep scars on the social fabric. Books will be written describing how Ian McGregor was selected by the Prime Minister as the front man for finally chopping the National Union of Mineworkers, the heroic shock troops of labour, down to size. Even Conservatives may come to doubt whether these were the best ways of trying to build a resilient, unified, and adaptable Britain. But perhaps this was not, after all, the object?

The release of the frustrations and hatreds now being created, even were unemployment to fall only marginally, would probably be explosive from the point of view of pay movements and inflation unless dramatic steps were taken towards a new political settlement of the sort sketched above. Politically, too, Conservative interests would be lucky to escape some possibly painful *quid pro quo* behaviour. Is there a quiet expectation, therefore, that Marx's 'reserve army of labour' can be kept permanently large enough to keep organized labour sufficiently subdued so that the critical threshold is never passed?

Or is it supposed that even without paying this heavy price there is a future in which the unions become ever weaker and more hog-tied by a network of punitive and restrictive legal bonds? Some of the more exuberant among the New Conservatism's supporters conveyed the impression of having glimpsed such an Eldorado. Mr Walter Goldsmith, shortly before retiring in 1984 as Director-General of the Institute of Directors, questioned the government's continued acquiescence in the ACAS terms of reference, prominent among which is encouragement of the extension of collective bargaining. Should Mrs Thatcher really be underpinning the dogma that collective bargaining is necessarily a good thing?

These are heady dreams indeed. Even Mrs Thatcher is likely to be made aware that by far the greater weight of British management has no wish to dispense with collective bargaining, which will therefore survive with or without her tolerance of ACAS. This means that the unions, too, will survive. Membership losses since 1979 are not yet disastrous. The latest figures available at the time of writing show that at the end of 1982, the total figure for the UK was around 11.5 million, having fallen from the peak figure of around 13.5 million in 1979. This was a faster rate of decline than the fall in employment. In 1981 and 1982, for example, membership fell by 11.6 per cent while employment fell by 5.5 per cent. But the movement has recovered from far greater proportionate falls in membership than this and in any case a closer look at the figures does not yet justify complacency among its enemies. The largest relative falls have occurred in unions covering employees mainly working in manufacturing industries – a result to be expected given the decimation of that sector. The smallest relative falls, *and some increases*, appear in unions with members mainly in service industries, which are expected to grow.

It appears to be the belief, nevertheless, of some employers and managers in the so-called 'sunrise' industries that they will be able to develop free of trade unionism. This belief was also entertained by certain of the 'sunrise' industries of the 1930s. Among them was car assembly, which did not become, however, a conspicuous example of co-operative harmony.

All in all, there is as yet little to suggest that Britain's industrial relations scene, embedded as it is within a society that is probably more organizationally sectionalist than ever before, is undergoing some basic change either towards a permanent creative partnership between capital and labour, or towards a lasting management ascendancy that will enable them to assert their prerogatives unchallenged. British unions are unlikely to languish into ineffectualness; nor are most of them likely, under existing social structures, to turn to 'class collaboration' in the hope of fatter crumbs from rich men's tables. Yet historically they have predominantly demonstrated that though they intend no positive co-operation with capitalism they do not intend either to attempt to replace it with a different system within any finite period of time. Some see this as a determination to have the worst of both worlds.

As already suggested, what is highly likely is that any vigorous upswing would bring back, probably in intensified form, all the standard British features of a tightening labour market. Government attempts to avoid them by maintaining unemployment at present levels might well introduce elements of real desperation into Britain's social and political system, not necessarily among the unemployed themselves. Long-term deprivation of work appears to induce apathy in its victims, except perhaps among the inner-city young. It is already clear, however, that outside the unemployed the Thatcher style has contributed to hatreds and frustrations of a pitch not seen before in post-war Britain. These must surely register themselves in some way and at some time upon the social and political scene.

The probability exists, therefore, of either industrial turbulence, renewed win–lose contests and intensified inflationary pressure, or continued mass unemployment with its vast human and economic cost and its long-term effects upon the social and political fabric. How may these affect the British scene, particularly the industrial relations scene? We have already registered that there is no sign yet of a popular base for a radical political programme designed to help British society to start working its way out of the institutional structures, traditions, and habituated perceptions and behaviours which so limit its economic and social achievement. We must imagine the probable instabilities irrupting into a political scene shaped by Thatcherism and by the Labour failure to create such a base.

The significance of this is that Thatcherism has intensified trends towards government authoritarianism which to some extent are world-wide and which have certainly been at work in Britain for some decades. The symptoms are many and diverse, but some examples may be offered. Privileged members of British governments, Labour as well as Conservative, have taken momentous decisions about the nation's defence system that have not been shared with parliament or even with the whole of the Cabinet. Techniques of opinion-management by public and private bureaucracies, including the ministerial or armed services 'leak' designed to serve governmental, departmental, service, or private career interests, have become greatly strengthened by scientific developments and professional specialization in communication and persuasion. And whereas in some countries the state has been forced to give ground in terms of 'open' government and freedom of information, in Britain the various elements of the Establishment continue the tradition of supporting each other in a perpetual and mostly successful struggle to preserve secrecy. The Official Secrets Act is exploited to this end, and true British humbug was displayed in the six-month prison sentence on a girl clerk for a leak far less politically sensitive than many perpetuated by her masters. In so far as these facts are perceived, by groups with strong feelings about an issue, as a denial of democratic rights, they may be driven by sheer frustration and desperation towards increasingly assertive direct action.

This is the context in which the Thatcher administrations singled out for favour in the public services the police and armed forces, and chose to give the former increased powers. Some chief constables appeared to be disinclined to wait to be given them and simply assumed them. The principle that they are 'servants of their community' has, on occasion, been flatly repudiated. Official vigilance over the danger of overmighty police and security officers has become distinctly blunted since the nineteenth century. Traditional uneasiness even at ruling class level towards the idea of a 'national' police has disappeared. The Association of Chief Police Officers handled an elaborately co-ordinated national strategy towards miners' picket lines in the 1984 strike.

Post-war Labour Home Secretaries have been apparently no less eager than their Conservative counterparts to concede police and security services increased powers and to condone, for example, much fudging of answers to parliamentary questions about telephone-tapping. The growing impotence of parliament in the face of increased state powers, official secrecy, opinion-management and party discipline has become evident in these as in far greater matters. The Thatcher government may have made a clumsy botch of its suppression of trade unionism at GCHQ Cheltenham, but the unions remained suppressed nevertheless, and an ominous precedent for the trade union movement has been securely established.

Even aspects of the rule of law have suffered erosion. In 1977, for example, a Labour ministry enacted legislation which transferred whole categories of offences from the Crown Courts to summary jurisdiction, thereby extinguishing the right of the accused to opt for trial by jury. The Thatcher government, with doubtful constitutional propriety, consulted the Master of the Rolls about industrial relations policy. This has to be seen in the context of constitutional assumptions about the independence of the judiciary from the executive and the convention that the former does not involve itself in giving detailed advice of an overtly political nature to the latter. His recommendation that the courts should play a greater role evoked from the 1984 *Annual Report* of the Advisory Conciliation and Arbitration Service a sharp reminder of the 'strong possibility' that 'the judiciary could become linked in some minds with the interests of one party as opposed to another'.

Finally, the debasement of press standards has probably reached new post-war depths. The 1983 electoral campaign for the Bermondsey parliamentary seat was notable for semi-criminal harassment of one of the candidates, Peter Tatchell, by sections of the national press, using methods that were exceptionally dingy even for Fleet Street and which repay study by those confident that British freedoms are still secure.

All these features of the modern British state have potential relevance as elements in the total social context within which industrial relations are conducted. Of course the justifications offered in the defence of some of them can be made to sound reasonable enough – the need for modern governments to communicate complex problems and policies clearly to the public; the requirements of 'national security' in a world of nuclear tensions, espionage, 'terrorism' and 'subversion'; the high crime rate and the importance of maximizing police efficiency and streamlining the procedures of justice in order to 'protect the freedoms of the ordinary citizen'. The significance of these features of the modern state for industrial relations derives, however, from the use that could be made of them by governments which succeeded in convincing themselves and large sections of the public that industrial stoppages and restrictionism were a threat to 'the nation's' economic security which 'in the interests of all' could no longer be tolerated; that militant industrial leadership must have subversive political intent; and that the 'national interest' requires the inclusion in police computer records of industrial 'troublemakers'.

Persistence in this style could, along with other features of Thatcher policy, result in an industrial and political scene more harsh, vengeful, and embittered than has prevailed in Britain for a long time. The full seriousness of the prospect stems particularly from two of its features. As we have seen, the New Conservatism gives signs of repudiating, to some extent, those political accommodations and tolerances developed by, for example, Baldwin and Butler, building on older Tory traditions. The question that presents itself is whether powerful sections among Britain's middle and upper classes are moving towards bringing to an end the political stance on which her peaceful democratic development has rested. The fact that, as always, they may continue to carry significant sections of the working class with them does not render the prospect less fateful for the future shape of British society. Secondly, the fracturing of the parliamentary opposition and its division by mutual hatreds so strong as probably to preclude electoral co-operation, introduces the possibility that Thatcherism may become perceived as beyond effective attack by normal parliamentary and party methods, thereby putting a premium on extra-parliamentary pressure.

There has probably never been a greater need for the individual citizen – the employer, the manager, and the trade unionist, along with all the rest – to evaluate the conflicting interpretations of how things are going; to decide what sort of Britain he or she wants to see; and to act accordingly. In these pages I have already made clear that in my view current trends will not produce a permanent subduing of the industrial and political strength of organized labour, nor will they promote closer co-operation and consciousness of a community interest among the many strongly organized and mainly self-seeking sectionalisms that comprise British society.

Some Conservatives, feeling their own doubts, have indicated that in their view Thatcherian policies and political style are not the best ways to conserve. They may yet have the opportunity, possibly after severe strains, to apply a long-standing British political instinct to renew social cohesion. But this does not mean there can ever be a return to the system as it operated before the 1970s. The Labour Party is not the same Labour Party and the trade union movement will emerge from the present experience deeply marked, almost certainly in conflicting ways. There is, perhaps, a sense in which a whole political and industrial tradition has been played out. This does not mean that British society is incapable, on some level, of continuing, perhaps for some considerable time, relatively comfortably. It might even be possible, if Thatcherism proved, improbably, to be a temporary deviation, for more conciliatory Conservative governments to promote mutually helpful understandings with the TUC. It may be that a political sufficiency of the British people would be prepared to settle for this kind of pragmatic makeshift, accompanied though it might be by long slow decline. But it is highly doubtful if, given present institutional textures and the present stock of political and social ideas and impulses, British society is capable of the sort of renewal necessary to sustain long-term adaptation at a high level of economic and social welfare and public spending.

A central element in any such renewal would have to be a concept of community needs that had some practical behavioural significance for everyday life. The task of devising the relevant institutions is immense, for we know already that the present stock of Labour Party ideas on the subject has not mobilized the necessary popular base.

What surely can be said with some confidence is that a programme for reconstructing British society would have to be very different from the one assumed by old-style socialism. An ever-growing white-collar sector and a shrinking body of wage-earners, many of whom, besides being tax-payers, reach eagerly for that house-ownership that the middle classes have long taken for granted – these hardly provide fruitful soil for the old-style vision, especially when there is added widespread indifference to nationalization as much of the British public understands it, suspicions about 'socialist' attitudes on 'patriotism' and defence, and a quickening interest in private education and private health care. Although there is some reason for believing that latent impulses towards a more egalitarian reconstruction are more widespread among the British people than these observations suggest, they will certainly not be mobilized by the old formulae.

Perhaps the shortage of practical ideas does not matter too much just at present – though Kitching's suggestion of 'pre-emptive unionism' (1983) raises important possibilities. The immediate need is to bring as many people as possible to recognize that reconstruction is necessary; that the country is moving in some ugly directions; that many social decencies are in danger of being submerged; and that economic renewal cannot be satisfactorily sustained as a continuous process within the present pattern of institutions and traditions – their most divisive and embittering features now intensified by the New Conservatism.

It has to be hoped, for example, that our masters can be brought to grasp that no constructive programme for Britain, whatever its nature, can securely go forward on a basis that excludes, snubs, and attempts legally to hog-tie the organizations that represent half its population at work. This is not to suggest that organized labour can be exempted from the tally of disagreeable developments. The preceding pages have already demonstrated otherwise. Trade unionism offers its own threats to the social decencies. Yet to humiliate and blacken it as the Thatcher administrations have done is not only to arouse profound uneasiness about the long-term intentions of the New Conservatism – if it has any – but also to fail completely to grasp the fuller significance of these organizations to which half their working fellow-citizens commit themselves. As against the really large-scale menaces that threaten social freedoms, their record in Britain is not yet equalled among labour movements elsewhere. A deeply-rooted tradition of collective bargaining and workplace direct democracy cannot co-exist with a totalitarian regime, and British trade unions have predominantly shown themselves powerfully resistant to the political appeal of dictatorships – or indeed of any other nostra that threatened their central functions, which require a considerable measure of economic and political space for their exercise. Given the recent celebration of Orwell's *1984*, we may be inclined to feel that there could be worse verdicts on the major institutions of Britain's industrial relations. An even larger question, however, is whether ways can be found of combining this admirable tradition with pursuit of the economic well-being necessary for achieving worthy social purposes. On this, the most sorely-pressing issue facing the British people, the situation remains open.

On the outcome rests the issue of whether the quality of British life – which for all its inequity, its humbug, and its hypocrisy, is among the better cultures to have been produced by *homo sapiens* – can reverse the unpleasant directions of recent decades. By one of life's more sour ironies, the 1984 coal-strike pictures of blood, hatred, and Thatcherian attempts to break the power and spirit of Britain's most cohesive workforce, coincided with vivid reminders of Britain's final great collective contribution towards the liberation of Western Europe from fascism in 1944–5. The over-fifties may have recalled that during that struggle not only were the social classes closer then they have ever been before or since, but there was also a widespread notion abroad that egalitarian structural changes must ensure that they never drew apart again.

The poignancy of the contrast may have been sharpened, for those with long memories, by recollections of the House of Commons debate in September 1939 which finally nerved the Chamberlain government, after many years' appeasement of German fascism, to take a stand against one of the most evil regimes humanity has ever created. As the Labour spokesman, Arthur Greenwood, rose to put the case for this fateful decision, he was greeted with the famous cry from Leo Amery on the Conservative benches, 'Speak for England, Arthur!' Perhaps, in the not too remote future, a Conservative spokesman may emerge who evokes a similar appeal from the reverse political direction.

Further reading

Atkinson, Tony (ed.) *Socialism in a Cold Climate* (Unwin Paperbacks 1983)

Bain, G.S., (ed.), *Industrial Relations in Britain* (Blackwell 1983)

Batstone, E., Boraston, I., Frenkel, S., *Shop Stewards in Action* (Blackwell 1977)

Batstone, E., *Reform of Industrial Relations in a Changing Society* (Dublin: IPC House 1982)

Brown, W., (ed.), *The Changing Contours of British Industrial Relations* (Blackwell 1981)

Clegg, H.A., *The Changing System of Industrial Relations in Great Britain* (Blackwell 1979)

Crouch, C.J., *Class Conflict and the Industrial Relations Crisis* (Heinemann 1977)

Crouch, C., *The Politics of Industrial Relations* (Fontana/Collins 1979)

Daniel, W.W., Willward, N., *Workplace Industrial Relations* (Heinemann 1983)

Flanders, A., *The Fawley Productivity Agreements* (Faber and Faber 1964)

Flanders, A., *Management and Unions* (Faber and Faber 1970)

Fox, A., *History and Heritage: The Social Origins of the British Industrial Relations System* (Allen and Unwin: 1985)

Hawkins, K., *The Management of Industrial Relations* (Penguin 1978)

Kahn-Freund, O., *Labour Relations: Heritage and Adjustment* (Oxford University Press 1979)

Kitching, G., *Rethinking Socialism* (Methuen 1983)

Marsh, A., *Employee Relations Policy and Decision Making* (Gower 1982)

Moran, M., *The Politics of Industrial Relations* (Macmillan 1977)

Panitch, L., *Social Democracy and Industrial Militancy* (Cambridge University Press 1976)

Undy, R., Ellis, V., McCarthy, W. E. J., Halmos. A. M., *Change in Trade Unions: The Development of UK unions since 1960* (Hutchinson 1981)

Wedderburn, Lord, Lewis, Roy, Clark, Jon, *Labour Law and Industrial Relations* (Clarendon Press 1983)

Wiener, M.J., *English Culture and the Decline of the Industrial Spirit 1850–1980* (Cambridge University Press 1981)

Index

accountability of management, 105
  see also participation
'adversary' perception, 49
Advisory, Conciliation and Arbitration
  Service (ACAS), 199, 208–11, 214
agreements, 142, 144
  and obligation, 27–30, 39–40
'alienation', 60
Amery, L., 202–3, 218
anti-authority strategies, 51
Arnold, M., 183–5
aspirations, current, and future of
  participation, 176–81
Association of Chief Police Officers, 37, 199,
  214
Australia, 128
authoritarianism, 19, 20, 49, 213
authority, decline in respect for, 52–3
'autonomous work group', 130, 140

Baldwin, S., 10, 38, 197, 200, 214
Batstone, E., 194
Bennett, 209
'betterment', see industrial welfare
Blumberg, 140–1
boards, see employee directors
Braverman, H., 136
Bullock, Lord and Report, 124–6
'business' issues in decision-making, 106,
  158–9
Butler, R., 197, 200, 214

Cadbury family, 77
Campaign for Nuclear Disarmament, 167
Chamberlain, N., 218
character, organizational, 101–3
Clegg, H.A., 176, 194
Coalition Government (1919–22), 10, 196
coercion and its limits, 44–65, 66–7
  control through, 55–9
  effective, conditions of, 59–61
  failure of, 61–4

identification with management, lack of,
  48–51
management and search for legitimacy, 51–5
problem-solving and win-lose situations,
  46–7
  see also control, power
Cole, G.D.H., 193
collective bargaining, 22, 35, 143, 157
  agreements, 142, 144
  government and political power, 150–3
  management and, 143–4
  model, standard, 144–6
  model, standard, divergence from, 146–50
  participation through, 111–12
  role and meaning, 139–56
  role in Britain, 153–5
  see also participation, bargaining, etc.,
    trade unions
Committee of Enquiry on Industrial
  Democracy, see Bullock Report
commodity, labour as, resistance to, 178–9
communication failures, 89
Communists, 37, 53
compliance, motives for, 36–43
  see also coercion, control
conditioning, see social conditioning
Confederation of British Industry (CBI), 29,
  31, 125, 209–10
consent
  and control, 66–8
  economic man and significance for
    management, 97–101
  employee perceptions and determinants,
    93–7
  fallacy of 'social man', 90–3
  human relations approach, 87–90
  organizational character, 101–3
  and 'social' and 'economic' man, 86–104
  see also industrialization and strategy of
    consent, participation and consent
Conservative Party and governments, 10, 36,
  63, 179, 213, 216

and economy, 55, 165, 169–70, 187, 195–7, 202–3
and general election (1983), 25, 198
'new', 25, 174–5, 200, 207, 210–11, 217
and security/law and order, 199, 213–14
and trade unions, 21–2, 37, 64, 151, 164–6, 174–6, 189, 192, 207–11, 216
see also Thatcher
contract and master–servant relationship, 74
control, 131
and coercion, 55–9
and consent, 66–8
early industrial, 71–3
pre-industrial, 69–71
see also coercion, power
cultural differences in industrialization, 19
see also Germany, Japan

Daniel, W.W., 193
decision-making, 105–8, 140
see also participation
defence system, 213
democracy
clash between varieties of, 168
control and, 53–4
industrial, 123–3, 125–6,
see also Bullock dependence, 56
see also coercion
Department of Health and Social Security, 197
Department of Trade and Industry, 201
'direct action' debate, 166–9
discretionary aspects of work, 60–3, 84, 92
enlarged, 135
and prescribed aspects, 105–8
and trust, 109–10
Donovan Commission, *see* Royal Commission

'economic' decisions, 106
'economic man', 97–101
Economic and Social Research Council, 201
economy, problems, 55, 165, 169–70, 187–8, 195–203, 206
EEC, *see* European Economic Community
egalitarianism, 205–6
election, general (1983), 25, 198
employee: directors, participation through, 119–28, 210
perceptions and determinants, 93–7
relations experts, 192
see also coercion, collective bargaining, consent, control, participation, trade unions
employer response to strategy of consent, 74–5, 76–85

industrial welfare, 76–81
scientific management, 81–5
employers, *see* management
enriched job discretion, participation through, 128–37
European Economic Community (EEC), 105, 119, 124, 129, 210
expediency, motives for, 36–43
extra-parliamentary action, 166–9

failure of collective bargaining, 146–50 *passim*
Fair Wages Resolution (1946), 196
'fairness', 99–100
France, 128
Freedom of Information legislation, 167
future of participation and current aspirations, 176–81

GCHQ Cheltenham, 199, 207, 214
Germany, 203, 218
competition from, 75
industry, 19, 20, 49, 73, 119, 128–9, 193–4
trade unions, 193–4
Goldsmith, W., 211
government
and collective bargaining, 150–3
ruling strategy, 48–9
see also Conservative, Labour
Greater London Council, 207
Greenwood, A., 218
groups, *see* social man

'harmonization', 105
Healey, D., 195
Heath, E., 176, 207
Hitler, A., 194
Human Relations approach, 85, 86, 91–3, 95, 97, 99–103, 110, 114–16, 210
and participative supervision, 113–15
and social man, 87–90
humanitarianism, 51
'humanization', 128–9

identification with management, lack of, 48–51
ideological control, 53
individualism, 19, 21–3, 52
Industrial Democracy (TUC), 122–3, 125–6
industrial issues, distinct from political, 159–64, 166
Industrial Relations Act (1971), 192, 196
industrial welfare, 51, 76–81, 89
industrialization, impact of, 71–3, 75
industrialization and strategy of consent, 66–85

contract and master–servant relations, 74
control through consent, 66–8
employee response, 74–6
employer response 76–85
industrialization, impact of, 71–3
past, idealization of, 69–71
pre-industrial work relations, 68–9
inflation, 169
  see also economy
Institute of Directors, 31, 211
interest groups, *see* 'direct action'

Japan, industry in, 19, 49, 73, 203
'humanization of work', 128
'quality circles', 136
job design, 107, 129, 131–3, 179
discretion, participation through, 128–37
satisfaction, 98, 133
joint consultation, participation through,
  116–19

Keegan, 209
Kitching, G., 206, 217

Labour Party, 10, 63, 164,
and 'direct action', 166, 168
and economy, 165, 169–70, 195–202, 206
and general election (1983), 25, 198
in government, 24, 36, 152, 195, 199, 206–7,
  213
and security/law and order, 199, 213–14
and Thatcherism, 197–202
and trade unions, 151, 160, 164, 166, 175–6,
  188–9, 207
leaders, 46, 99
trade union, 30, 37, 39, 172–3, 190
legislation, 162–3, 167, 175, 192, 196, 198–9,
  213–14
legitimacy, management search for, 51–5
Liberal Party, 195
Alliance with SDP, 22, 198
liberalism, *see* individualism
Lukes, S., 58

McGregor, I., 211
'macho management', 119, 201
management, *see* coercion, collective
  bargaining, consent, control,
  participation, society and the
  organization
manipulative techniques in participative
  supervision, 114
March, A., 193
Marxism, 21, 136, 211
master–servant relationship, 69–71, 73–4

material technology, 13–18
media, 200, 214
Mendis, 209
Millward, N., 193
model of collective bargaining, 144–6
divergence from, 146–50
monetarism, *see* Thatcher, economy
moral involvement, 112–13, 141–2
and decision-making, 108–11
Morris, W., 205
motivation, 128–9
Muellbauer, 209

NALGO, 191
National Health Service, 167, 187
'national/public interest', 151–2, 174, 185
National Union of Mineworkers, 38, 211
National Union of Teachers, 191
Nazism, 53
'new' Conservatism, 25, 174–5, 200, 207, 210–
  11, 217
NUM, 38, 211
NUT, 191

obligation, 27–30
moral, 141–2
motives for, 36–43
Official Secrets Act, 167, 198, 213
One Nation doctrine, 10, 197
Organization for Economic Co-operation and
  Development (OECD), 129
Orwell, G., 186, 205, 217

participation, bargaining and wider society,
  182–219
collective bargaining and British problem,
  184–8
economic decline and Labour Party,
  197–202
economic failure, 202–3
intended and unintended outcomes, 182–4
and New Right, 195–7
new social partnership, conditions for,
  203–18
reforming system, 188–95
  see also collective bargaining
participation and consent in decision-making,
  105–38
collective bargaining, 111–12
employee directors, 119–28
enriched job discretion, 128–37
joint consultation, 116–19
moral involvement, 108–11
participative supervision, 113–15
prescribed and discretionary work, 105–8

participation and *status quo*, 157–81
  aspirations and future, 176–81
  'direct action' debate, 166–9
  industrial and political issues, 159–64
  managerial prerogative, 157–9
  'politicization' of industrial relations, 169–76
  Thatcher government and Labour politics, 165–6
partnership, new social, 203–18
past, idealization of, 69–71
pay, 97–100, 169, 189, 193
  see also 'economic man', economy
'personnel' decisions, 106, 141
Plumb, J.H., 206
pluralism, 144, perspective on business enterprise, 21, 26–32, 42
police, 37, 199, 210, 213–14
political and industrial issues, distinction between, 160–64, 166
political power structure and collective bargaining, 150–3
'politicization' of industrial relations, 169–76
politics, *see* Conservative, Labour, Liberal
poverty, 197
power
  creation of, 56–7
  political, 150–3
  and promises, 27
  of trade unions, 24, 125, 131, 176, 190, 205
  use of, 57–8
  see also coercion, control
'pre-emptive' unionism, 217
pre-industrial work relations, 68–9
prescribed and discretionary aspects of work, 105–8
press, debased standards, 200, 214
problem-solving relationship, 46–7, 82–3, 86
'productivity bargaining', 190
profit-sharing, 118–19
promises, *see* agreements
public expenditure, 187, 195, *see also* economy
'public interest/good', *see* 'national interest'

'quality circles', 136
'Quality of Life' debate, 128

radical perspective, 205–6
  on business enterprise, 23–4, 32–6, 38, 40, 42
  and collective bargaining, 149–50
reciprocity, *see* trust
reform of system of participation and bargaining, 188–95

revolutionary disruption, 172–4, 207
Right, new, *see* new Conservatism
Rowntree family, 77
Royal (Donovan) Commission on Trade Unions and Employers Associations (1965–68), 29, 30, 39, 122, 190, 193

Sanders, W.S., 193
Scandinavia, 128–9, 132
Scargill, A., 37
Scientific Management, 81–7, 89, 110
SDP/Liberal Alliance, 22, 198
security/law and order, 37, 199, 210, 213–14
Shell, 129, 132
Smith, C., 202
Smith-Gavine, 209
social change, 157–8
  class, 16–17, 121, 183–4, 186
  conditioning, 54, 67, 115, 134, 179, 'contract', 164, 188, 207
  decisions, 106
  'man', 87–91
  and material technology, 13–18
  partnership, conditions for new, 203–18
  'responsibility', 24
Social Democratic Party, 22, 198
Social Science Research Council, 201
society and the organization, 13–44
  material and social technology, 13–18
  motives for compliance, expediency and obligation, 36–43
  pluralist perspective, 26–32
  radical perspective, 32–6
  Western society, nature of, 18–26
  see also participation, bargaining and wider society
Soviet Union, 53
state, concept of, 185–6
  see also government
status and industrial welfare, 79–80
status quo, see participation and *status quo*
strikes, 176, 207, 211
  miners' (1984), 37
  'unconstitutional', 29
structural reform, 188–95
subordination, acceptance of, 54
  see also social conditioning
'sunrise' industries, 212
supervision, participatory, 113–15

Tawney, R.H., 205
Taylor, F., and Taylorism, 81–7, 89, 110
'technical' issues in decision-making, 106, 158–9

technology, material, 13–18
technological change, 201–2
Tatchell, P., 200, 214
Thatcher, M., and government, 23, 119, 179,
    187, 199–201, 215–18
  and economy, 55, 187, 195–7, 202–3
  and general election (1984), 25, 198
  and labour 197–202
  and security/law and order, 199, 213–14
  and trade unions, 37, 64, 165–6, 174–6,
    207–11, 216
  see also Conservative Party
Thompson, E., 205
Torode, 209
trade unions, 22, 38, 211
  communication failures, 89
  development of, 20–1, 52, 75
  dues, 190
  and employee directors, 121–7
  and 'fairness', 99–100
  and 'humanization' of work, 131
  and independence, 121
  lack of resources, 33
  leaders, 30, 37, 39, 172–3, 190
  membership losses, 211
  power of, 24, 125, 131, 176, 190, 205
  structure, 193
  and subordination, 54
  see also collective bargaining, Conservative,
    Labour, participation, Royal
    Commission, Trades Union Congress

Trades Union Congress (TUC), 30, 39, 175,
    191, 216
  divisions in, 165
  and economy, 169
  and employee directors, 125–6
  and industrial democracy, 122–3, 125–6
  and 'social contract', 164, 188
  see also trade unions
trust, 46–7, 69, 74, 83–4, 86, 92, 109–10,
    143
TUC, *see* Trades Union Congress
two-tier system of employee directors, 123–4

Undy, R., 193
unemployment, 63, 179, 211, 212
'unitary' frame of reference, 32, 42
  and collective bargaining, 146–9
United States, 75, 116, 128, 129
Upper Clyde Shipbuilders, 167, 178

Volvo, 129, 132

Wages Councils, 196
Webb, S., 193
welfare approach, *see* industrial welfare
West Germany, *see* Germany
Western society, perspectives on, 18–26
white-collar unions, 191, 205, 216
win–lose situations, 46–7, 86, 118
'workers' control', 105
  see also participation